LECTURES

ON THE

ECCLESIASTICAL HISTORY

OF THE

FIRST AND SECOND CENTURIES.

LECTURES

ON THE

ECCLESIASTICAL HISTORY

OF THE

FIRST AND SECOND CENTURIES.

"If then it appears so hard and so little knowne how to govern a house well, which is thought of so easie discharge and for every man's undertaking, what skill of man, what wisdome, what parts can be sufficient to give lawes and ordinances to the elect household of God? If we could imagine that He had left it at randome without His provident and gracious ordering, who is he so arrogant, so presumptuous, that durst dispose and guide the living arke of the Holy Ghost, though he should finde it wandering in the field of Bethshemesh, without the conscious warrant of some high calling?"—MILTON.

BY

FREDERICK DENISON MAURICE, M.A.

CHAPLAIN OF LINCOLN'S INN.

Wipf & Stock
PUBLISHERS
Eugene, Oregon

Wipf and Stock Publishers
199 W 8th Ave, Suite 3
Eugene, OR 97401

Lectures on the Ecclesiastical History of the First and Second Centuries
By Maurice, Frederick Denison
ISBN: 1-59752-667-3
Publication date 5/3/2006
Previously published by Macmillan and Co., 1854

TO THE

REV. JOHN BREWER, M.A.

My dear Brewer,

I hope that neither you nor any one else will suppose that I wish to make you responsible for the sentiments of this book, because I have claimed the privilege, without asking your leave, of inscribing it to you. Though you know nothing of the contents of it as it now stands, it would never have seen the light but for your encouragement. I do not know whether I ought to number that among the many kind acts for which I owe you my warmest gratitude; but I certainly thank you more for what I have learnt from you, and for your uniform and disinterested friendship, than for tempting me to the publication of one more book. I only hope that it may prove one half as useful now that it has been written with some care, as you dreamed that it might be if it were taken directly from the notes of my former pupils.

Believe me,

Sincerely and affectionately yours,

F. D. MAURICE.

PREFACE.

These Lectures have never been delivered anywhere. When my connexion with King's College ceased, I was asked by a kind friend to authorize the publication of the notes which some of the students had taken down from my lips. He was aware that my Lectures were extempore, and that I had no reports of my own by which I could correct theirs. Nevertheless, he fancied that he should be able to trace my meaning, and to present it in an intelligible form to the reader: he even insisted that I should leave the matter wholly in his hands; an arrangement to which, except for his sake, I willingly consented.

But I soon found that he had imposed upon himself a task which it would be on many accounts painful for him to perform. If he had corrected the Lectures according to his own judgment, he might have made them much more valuable than they ever were; but he was too conscientious and modest to take this course; he was therefore obliged to leave the notes just as he found them, and the very best notes—as those who have taken notes and read them know—convey oftentimes an impression as different as possible from that which the speaker intended to convey. The very preservation of his words and phrases is often fatal to his sense, because the relation of them to each other has, very likely through his fault, not been apprehended.

As I adhered to my promise, I was not aware how far the intention of my kind friend had succeeded till some sheets of the Reports were in the press. My Publisher was dissatisfied with them, and urged me to cancel them. I could then do nothing less, in justice to him, than recast the whole work from the beginning. It would be a falsehood, I saw, to pretend that I was reproducing my old Lectures; I had not the means of doing that. All I could do was, to try to produce Lectures something in the tone and spirit of those I originally delivered, but with the narratives and thoughts expanded or condensed as I judged might be best for the convenience of the reader, and for the elucidation of the subject, after I had reflected on the method which I had followed with my pupils, and the errors and defects of it.

I will only add, that I have not attempted to exchange the familiarity of the lecture-room for the solemnity of an historical style. The latter might be more agreeable and respectful to the reader, but the former is more natural to me. I have been too long in the habit of addressing young men to be able to divest myself of the feeling that I am still speaking to them when I am writing down words for some unknown reader. Nor can I pretend that I wish to lose these associations, or any by which we are bound to those from whom we are separated on earth. The responsibilities which we have incurred by our intercourse with them we cannot cast off; may it not help us, to think that they are still listening to us?

May 18*th*, 1854.

CONTENTS.

LECTURE I.
THE JEWISH CALLING 1

LECTURE II.
THE OTHER NATIONS 13

LECTURE III.
THE SECT AGE OF THE JEWISH COMMONWEALTH 34

LECTURE IV.
THE KINGDOM OF HEAVEN 46

LECTURE V.
THE NEW SOCIETY IN JERUSALEM 55

LECTURE VI.
SAMARIA AND SYRIA 69

LECTURE VII.
THE CHURCHES IN GENTILE CITIES 80

LECTURE VIII.
ST. JAMES, ST. PETER, AND ST. PAUL 95

LECTURE IX.
ST. JOHN 115

LECTURE X.
THE APOCALYPSE 136

Lectures on the Second Century.

LECTURE I.
THE DIFFERENT CHURCHES IN THE SECOND CENTURY: JUDÆA, SAMARIA, SYRIA 163

LECTURE II.
(THE SAME SUBJECT CONTINUED.)
CHURCHES IN ASIA MINOR 184

LECTURE III.
(THE SAME SUBJECT CONTINUED.)
CHURCHES IN GREECE AND EGYPT 205

LECTURE IV.
(THE SAME SUBJECT CONTINUED.)
CHURCHES IN ITALY AND GAUL 240

LECTURE V.
(THE SAME SUBJECT CONTINUED.)
THE AFRICAN CHURCH 269

LECTURE VI.
THE CHURCH AND THE GODS 289

LECTURE VII.
(THE SAME SUBJECT CONTINUED.)
THE FAILURES OF THE CHURCH IN THE BATTLE WITH THE GODS . 313

LECTURE VIII.
THE CHURCH AND THE EMPERORS 342

LECTURE IX.
THE CHURCH AND THE PHILOSOPHERS 363

LECTURE X.
THE CHURCH AND THE SECTS 385

LECTURE I.

THE JEWISH CALLING.

I AM going to give you lectures upon Ecclesiastical History. I would rather say 'Church' History than Ecclesiastical, because the word is a shorter one; but I am not sure about the origin of the word Church, and I could not explain it as well from the Bible. The word Ecclesia is a New Testament word. Its derivation is obvious. The whole history, both of the Old and New Testament, is a commentary upon it.

[margin: LECT. I. Church and Ecclesia. [The ordinary derivation of Church from Κύριος is disputed.]]

As the New Testament is written in Greek, we, of course, wish to know what the Greeks generally meant by this word. The question is easily answered. An Ecclesia was an assembly called together by a herald. But when you are interpreting New Testament words, you must not think only or chiefly of Greek usages. You must remember that the New Testament writers were Jews. Even when they used classical words, they used them in a Jewish sense. It often happens that their Jewish feeling led them to give a Greek word a meaning more exactly answering to its etymology than the ordinary one did. So it is in this instance. Ecclesia, if you strictly adhered to the verb and the preposition from which it comes, would suggest

[margin: Classical meaning of Ecclesia. Etymological meaning more important for the New Testament.]

the thought of calling *out*, rather than of calling *together*. Well, and that thought explains, I believe, the use of the word by the Apostles in the New Testament, because it is one which possessed the Prophets in the Old Testament.

Characteristic of the Bible.

I hope you will never forget that the Bible is the history of God's acts to men, not of men's thoughts about God. It begins from Him. He is acting and speaking in it throughout. The first chapters of Genesis speak of His creating the order of the world, and of His creating man in His own image; of His breathing into a man the breath of life; of His giving him a helpmeet; of His putting him under a law; of His teaching him to give names to the creatures. This itself is the history of a *calling*. God is calling all creatures into distinct existence, and calling out Man to rule them, and to be like Him.

Prominence given to God's calling of men.

The first man did not believe in this calling. He distrusted his Maker, and tried to be independent of Him; so he made himself dependent on his wife, and on the creatures he was to govern. But God's order, the Scripture teaches us, was not lost because men fell into disorder. That which He had established must remain, however many or however few knew His purpose or entered into it. The whole Bible after this is the history of a calling out. It is not, mind you, that God calls any men into a state different from that which He has made for men. He calls them into that very state; and they show their rebellion and their fallen nature, by not liking that state, but preferring some other to it.

If you run over the history of the Old Testament in your minds, you will see that I am not talking at random, when I say that it is all a commentary on this word 'Ecclesia.' First you have God calling out a man, Abram; sending him forth into another country; promising him that his descendants should possess it; establishing a covenant with him; causing him to wait for a son; making that son the heir of the covenant. This calling is grounded upon a *Revelation.* God reveals or unveils Himself to Abraham. Now and then we hear of visions that were presented to the bodily eye of Abraham. But even where these were granted, they were for the sake of raising him above what he saw with his eyes. The real revelation was to Abraham's heart. God made him feel that he had a righteous Ruler over him. He believed Him, and trusted Him, and so became a righteous and true man. He was called out to witness of this Lord of his spirit, this righteous Being whom he could trust.

Lect. I.
Calling implies Revelation.

So was his son Isaac, and his grandson Jacob, and the twelve Patriarchs. All these had the sign of the covenant, the sign that they were separated to an unseen Being. Circumcision witnessed that they were not to follow their flesh, but to serve the God who was drawing them away from it. Those Patriarchs did, as you know, follow their own inclinations; they were most of them self-willed bad men. They were not the less, men called out. Their sin was that they did not believe in their calling. The covenant was nothing to them. Joseph, who did believe

The Covenant.

ON CHURCH HISTORY.

LECT. I. it, who acted as a called man, claimed the calling for his brethren as well as for himself.

The Nation. So far, we have had the calling out of a man and the calling out of a family. Not of a family that was better and purer than all other families, but of one which could bear witness to all others, that God is the Author of families,—that He has established the order of husband and wife, of father and child, of brother and sister; and that these ordinances would go to wrack and ruin if men were left to themselves, and He did not watch over His own handiwork. Now, if you recollect what you have read in the book of Exodus, you will see how a Nation was called out, just as a man had been, just as a Family had been. Do not fancy that you know what that word 'Nation' means. It is often on your lips. You yourselves, thank God, belong to a nation. But it takes a long while to learn what that privilege is; still longer, to know how we may use it rightly. I believe the book of Exodus is a great help in discovering the secret. No book teaches us what a nation is like that book. It says that God spoke to Moses in the bush, and told him that He remembered His covenant with Abraham, and Isaac, and Jacob, and that His Name was the I AM, and that He cared for the poor slaves who were bondsmen in Egypt, and that Moses was to command the king of Egypt, in His name, to let His people go. That Name, the I *The Law;* AM, was the ground of the existence of the Jewish *Idolatry.* nation. In that Name the law was proclaimed from Sinai. In that Name all the ordinances of the people stood. They were a nation because He was their God. And they were called out, to testify to all the nations of the earth, that this Lord is *the* God; that the God of Abraham, and Isaac, and Jacob, whom they trusted, and in whom their children might trust, was He, from whom all the commandments came. He had called them out and chosen them; therefore they were not to fancy Him in the likeness of any thing in heaven above, or in the earth beneath, or in the waters under the earth. They were not to have gods whom they made, or whom they could see, but a God who had created them, whom they could believe, and in whom they could put their trust.

The Passover, which was to remind all their descendants of their deliverance from Pharaoh, was to remind them also, that they were called by God; that they were the witnesses of Him as a Deliverer, whilst the greater part of men,—the Egyptians as much as any, — thought their gods were tyrants, like the Pharaohs. This Passover was a feast for the whole people. Each family was to partake of it. Each family was to understand that it was called out by God, dedicated to Him. The blood on the doorposts was a sign that their Deliverer had marked them out for His. When they ate the lamb, they were taught that they were united to Him, and that this was the secret of their union to each other.

You will recollect, again, that it was not only the nation, as a body, that was called out and consecrated to God. Every officer in the nation was also a called man. Aaron was called out to be

Lect. I.

The Passover.

The Officers of the Nation called men.

the high priest; his sons were called to be priests; Bezaleel and Aholiab were called out to make the curtains of the tabernacle. All these people are said to be set apart to God for a special work. Then they are endued by Him with powers for that work. You will observe that order which the Bible points out to us. I shall often have occasion to recal it to your minds, in my future lectures.

The Priest. My great object at present, is to bring this fact of a calling before your minds, and so to make you understand the word *Ecclesia*. I am not therefore so careful to dwell at this time upon the particular offices to which either Aaron or other men were called. Still I must say a word to you on that point too; otherwise you will not know what the called nation meant, or what its business was. The Priests, you will recollect, were first of all to offer Sacrifices. That was the office of a priest everywhere, among the Egyptians as much as among the Israelites. All people everywhere, or almost all, felt that there were powers over them, which might do them good or do them harm. They felt that they had offended these powers. They felt that they must do something to make peace with them. The wisest men among them were those who must tell them *what* they were to do. They must tell them what *sacrifices* they

Heathen Priests. ought to offer. When a people became governed and civilized, as the Egyptians were, these priests, or wise men, became an organized body; the sacrifices and worship which they prescribed, became, in a measure, sacrifices and worship for the whole people.

I use the words " in a measure," because you must not suppose that the worship of all Egypt was the same. There was a difference between the worship of Upper Egypt and Lower Egypt, for there was a difference in the condition of the two regions; and so the powers that seemed to make them fertile or barren were thought to be different, and the ways of conciliating them different. Moreover, there were differences between the classes of the people, which also affected their services. The worship of the priests themselves was more refined than the worship of the kings whom they advised, and of the people whom they kept down.

You will see how much the Bible doctrine of priests and sacrifices must differ from this. The living God, it says, Himself called out the nation to be His nation. He chose the priests to be His ministers, and the ministers of the people. He appointed the sacrifices. He was not a power which the people were to make friendly by offering Him something, or giving up something to Him. He *was* their Friend. He had revealed Himself to Abraham as his Friend; He was revealing Himself to them as their Deliverer. He was revealing Himself by His law, and by all His acts, as a Righteous Being, whose mind and purposes are the same always; not as a capricious power, who may purpose one thing to-day, and be persuaded to do another to-morrow. His priests, therefore, could never be merely clever men, who were to find out the things which would please Him or pacify Him. He declared His will; He appointed

The two compared.

Duties of the Priest.

the Priests to be witnesses of it. They were to bless the people in His Name. They were to set forth His righteousness, His holiness, to them. They were to watch over the bodies of the people as well as their spirits, to show that He cared for their health, and was the healer of their sicknesses. But the more they testified of God's righteousness, and of God's desire that the people should be righteous, the more they made the people feel that there was something wrong in them, something which needed to be taken away. The more they said, 'God is your Ruler and you are His people,' the more they felt that they had been rebellious, and were not acting as if they were a people, but were quarrelling with each other. The more they heard that He cared for their health, the more they felt that the sicknesses and diseases which were among them proved that there was something in them and in the world which was at strife with His will. They wanted to be at peace with Him then, not less, but more than other people did. They needed to give up something, that they might be at peace with Him, as much as any other people did. But what they had to give up in order to be reconciled to a righteous Being, was their wrong, their disobedience. He bade them confess the acts which they knew had been contrary to His law. He appointed the sacrifice,—not something specially precious, but a sheep or an ox,—which signified that they were submitting to His will. He Himself called it a peace-offering, a trespass-offering, or a sin-offering. He promised them forgiveness and remission.

THE JEWISH CALLING.

You will see by-and-by why I have said so much on this point. We shall find how much it has to do with ecclesiastical history. What I would have you take notice of now is, that the priest was not only called himself, but that his family was called also. It was an hereditary office. The same duties, the same sacrifices, which were appointed for one generation, were also for the next, and the next, and the next. Observe too, that the priest, though he had such high functions in the Jewish commonwealth, was not the highest person in it. Moses was before Aaron. The guide and the lawgiver of the people was called to his office in as distinct and marked a manner as he who offered the sacrifices. Joshua was called to lead the people into the promised land. Every judge was called out in some special emergency to deliver the people from oppressors, and to pronounce what was right and wrong between man and man. These offices, you know, were not hereditary. But there came a time when the people desired a king and obtained one: first, a king who was self-willed, and ruled them after his own pleasure; next, one who was said to be after God's own heart, and who ruled them prudently with all his power. The difference between them was, that one felt he had a power which belonged to him, the other, that he was called to his office, and was to be a witness of God's righteous dominion. With him, we are told, God made a covenant that his seed should reign after him. All were to reign as called men, to bear witness of a kingdom which was over them and over their subjects.

Lect. I.

The Priestly Family.

The Lawgiver and Judge.

The King.

LECT. I.

Loss of the sense of a calling the sin of Kings, Priests and People.

You will recollect that neither the nation at large, nor most of the priests, nor most of the kings did righteous acts, or exhibited a righteous character. You will recollect also what we are told was the cause of their sin. They forgot the covenant of their God; they did not believe that they were a people, or priests, or kings, called out by an invisible God. The people murmured in the wilderness; for they did not trust God. They set up idols when they came into the promised land; for they did not trust God. Their priests became sottish, selfish, ministers of idolatry; for they did not trust God. Their kings became arbitrary, unrighteous, imitators of foreign habits and worship; for they did not trust God. This is the Bible account of the matter, and we shall not be able to find or make a better. I am anxious that you should not try, and that when we advance further in our history, we should be ready to adopt the Scripture explanation of the facts which present themselves to us, not one of our own.

The Prophet.

I have spoken to you of the calling out of the priests and the kings; I must now allude to the calling out of the prophet. You will understand what it was, by the remarks I have just made. The kings, and the priests, and the people, forgot their calling; *he* was called out to remind them of it, and to tell them what doings of theirs were inconsistent with it. Since that was his function, he had need to be sure that God was actually speaking to men, actually speaking to him. That was the ground of his work.

The Word of the Lord.

The Word of the Lord, it is said, came to him. The

Word of the Lord spake to him, and made him enter into the meaning and truth of things. The Word of the Lord made him see that there was a right order which God had established for his countrymen, and that there was a wrong order which they were creating for themselves. The Word of the Lord made him perceive how all events that were happening in his nation, plagues, pestilences, wars, were witnesses for God's true order, and for their departure from it. The Word of the Lord made the prophet see that every transgression of this order must bring its own punishment upon the priests, the kings, and the people, and that it would prevail and assert itself whether men fought against it or not. The Word of the Lord made him see that this order of God was not only over the chosen people who were the witnesses of it, but that the God of Abraham was the God of the whole earth, that His righteousness was the law for the armies of heaven and the dwellers among men. The Word of the Lord made him see that there was One who was higher than all kings and priests and prophets, an elect One in whom God's soul delighted, who was one with Him, in whom He could behold the nation amidst all its errors and wanderings, who would some day be revealed to it as the Lord of it, and of all the nations.

There were lying prophets as there were false kings and idolatrous priests. The sin of all was the same. The false prophets did not believe in the righteous God who had called them and their nation. They did not tremble at His Name. They spoke a lie out of their own hearts, and said, The Lord hath said it. They

False Prophets.

fancied He was a God of power and not a God of truth and righteousness. They conspired with the kings to draw the people into the worship of false gods, the works of their own hands; they puffed them up with vain hopes; they helped to hasten on that captivity which the true prophets told them would be the effect of their transgressions.

Reasons for these allusions to the Old Testament.

You know all these things that I have been telling you perfectly well. You will hear them in other lecture-rooms, illustrated and enforced in connexion with the Old Testament history. It is not my business to speak directly of that; but I could not fulfil my own proper task without bringing these facts rapidly before you. I want you to know what the word 'Ecclesia' signifies in the New Testament, and I could not help you to that knowledge without this preparation. In the next lecture I shall have to speak to you about the other Nations of the old world, and to inquire what they had to do with the called, or chosen Nation.

LECTURE II.

THE OTHER NATIONS.

You remember the promise to Abraham was, "In thee and in thy seed shall all the families of the earth be blessed." That, then, was the end of the separation of Abraham, and of the separation of his family. If we believe the Bible, we shall not put in any other reason, in place of this; least of all shall we imagine one that is contrary to this.

Promise to Abraham.

The history of the Bible explains the words of it. Joseph was a blessing to Egypt. He taught its king of God's government, and how he was to act in conformity with it in his treatment of his people. Joseph's seed would have been a blessing to the Egyptians, if they had not forgotten their covenant, and if the Pharaohs had not forgotten the lessons of Joseph. The words of Moses were lessons of wisdom and truth to the Egyptians as well as to the Israelites. When he acted as God's deliverer of His people, he was a witness of that which God wishes for all people. Tyranny is worse for the tyrants than for the slaves. Moses proclaimed the true God of the Egyptians as well as of the Jews. He showed what was the true power which the magicians and enchanters who deceived them were mimicking and turning to mis-

How performed.

chief. He declared the commandments which were good for the Israelites because they were good for all human beings.

Separation of the Israelites; whether inconsistent with the promise.

Perhaps it will strike you that the Israelites were told not to make marriages with the other nations, but to keep aloof from them, and that this is inconsistent with what I was saying. Not the least. The history shows us how consistent it is. When they became like the nations round about, they could not be a blessing to them. Those nations became a curse to the Jews,—hindered them from bearing witness of the true and living and righteous God, the God of the whole earth. They sunk into low, brutal, grovelling idolaters; they ceased to care for anybody but themselves. Their own vile appetites were their masters; they were helpless slaves, not kings and teachers of the world.

David and Solomon.

When David reigned as the man after God's own heart, he began to set an example,—a very imperfect one indeed, as the Scriptures tell us, one mixed with many failures and sins,—but still an example of right and true government, to the nations around him. He did not decline intercourse and fellowship with them. He glorified the Lord God of Israel; but you will recollect how often he says in the Psalms, that He was the God in whom the Gentiles might trust. His son Solomon, the wise king, felt that it was a part of his calling to be the friend and teacher of other lands. Nor did this turn to his mischief, till he became proud of his wisdom and a tyrant over his own people. While he sought the friendship of the nations that he might be a blessing to them, he fulfilled the hopes and prophecies of his father. When he sought them to gratify his own vanity and lust, they turned him into an idolater and a fool.

The Prophets; how they speak of the Nations.

The prophets who arose after the division of the two kingdoms, speak to both Israel and Judah of the danger they were in of following Syrian or Phœnician fancies, and of going down to Egypt for help. But they cared much more for Syria and Phœnicia than Ahab or Ahaz did, who borrowed from them. They cared much more for all that went on in Egypt, than the cowardly counsellors of Hezekiah, who wished him to depend upon it. You will find, all through these prophets, continual allusions to the history of the surrounding nations. It is assumed, that God is interested in their doings, as He is in those of the chosen people; that His judgments for one are judgments for the other; that the same everlasting laws belong to both; that the sins of both are of the same kind; that Gentiles have consciences which could be spoken to, as much as Jews; that God called them to repentance, and that they could obey the call.

Jewish Nation, a witness against Babylonian tyranny.

When the Jews were taken into Babylon, we are told that God was using His servant Nebuchadnezzar for the punishment of an hypocritical people, and that He was permitting him to establish a great despotism over the peoples of the earth. At the same time we are taught that the Jewish nation was called out to be the witness against such despotisms as these; to testify of a King who ruled in righteousness, not by power and self-will; to testify that a kingdom would be established on the earth, in which One would reign who did not set Himself up above the stars of heaven to be like God, but who, though His name was Wonderful, Counsellor, the mighty God, would not cry or make His voice to be heard in the streets,—would not break the bruised reed, or quench the smoking flax, —would be a refuge to the poor and needy,—and would assuredly bring forth judgment unto victory. The Jews in the captivity appear to have understood, by what they saw of the tyranny and of the idolatry of Babylon, that this was their calling. Their misery in the land of idols had made them perceive the sinfulness and madness of the idolatry which their fathers had practised, and how it had destroyed their very existence as a people. They longed for the home of their fathers, to be again among their sepulchres, to see the Temple rise out of its ruins. When this great gift was granted them, they were most careful to preserve their national distinctions, to separate themselves from people of mixed blood, to abstain from marriages with the surrounding race. They gathered together the books of their law and the inspired words of their prophets. They brought out in their harmony the divine annals of their kings; they made the people understand that these treasures of divine wisdom and human experience were for them and for their children. This was especially the work of the age of Ezra and Nehemiah. After that, we begin to lose sight of the Old Testament records. We leave the people subjects of the great Medo-Persic monarchy, yet with all the old signs of being a distinct nation,

Jews under Ezra.

except that they had no longer a visible king reigning over them.

Now as there are 500 years between the time of Cyrus, who gave the decree for the return of the people to their own land, and the birth of our Lord—about 400, so far as we can tell, between the last of those whom we call prophets and the appearance of John the Baptist—we must inquire how these years were filled up, and how that which happened in them is related to the Old Testament records or the New. This is the busiest and most important time of all in what we call profane history, the time of the great deeds of Persians and Greeks, of Romans and Carthaginians. Do you think we have a right to call this profane history? Do you think what is written in it has to do with man and not with God? Do you think that we can read the wonderful events that are recorded in it and say, This is very well, but this concerns us as secular beings, not as religious beings,—the world, and not the Church? I am sure we cannot say this if we read the Jewish records with faith. I am sure we cannot say it, unless we shut our eyes to the plainest statements in the Acts and Letters of our Lord's Apostles.

As the Lord is said in Scripture to have given a dominion to Nebuchadnezzar, so he is said in like manner to have given a dominion to Cyrus the Persian. A Jew, of course, was bound to believe this. But the Scripture intimates, and all facts would lead us to believe, that Nebuchadnezzar and Cyrus themselves in a manner owned it too. The Babylonian

What is called Profane History.

Nebuchadnezzar and Cyrus.

LECT. II. had very false notions concerning God; notions that converted Him into an arbitrary being, that divided Him into different forms, represented by the fierce lion or the swift eagle. But under these confusions he acknowledged a Lord of the earth; he felt that he was His minister; he had a sense of righteousness, to which we are told in the Book of Daniel that the Hebrew seer was able to appeal; nay, we are told in the same book that after he had suffered severe discipline he bowed himself to the Righteous Lord, and confessed that He was the true Ruler of all. Everything seems to show that Cyrus the Persian, who became the great Asiatic monarch after the Chaldæan empire was put down for its pride and its crimes, held this faith in a righteous Being still more strongly. He ruled over two races. His own, the Persian, was an agricultural people, with great reverence for their kings, and the acknowledgment of an invisible King or Judge, to whom they owed homage. The other, the Median, was a more cultivated race, but a less brave and honest one, in which the Priest or the soothsayer was powerful above all other men. With them there was a belief which springs up very naturally in all human beings, a belief in two Creators, one good and one evil, and that the evil being has most to do with this world. Hence they were led to offer worship and sacrifice to the evil power as well as to the good, and gradually more to the evil than to the good. It is not certain what faith Cambyses, the son of Cyrus, had about this matter. He was a wild frantic man, who had

Cyrus, B.C. 559—529.

Medes and Persians.

Ormuzd and Ahriman.

Cambyses, B.C. 529—521.

a vehement hatred of the priests, and who, when he invaded Egypt, treated the priests he found there without mercy. After him the Median or priestly power got the upper hand for a short time. But it was put down by Darius Hystaspes, who, as we know from inscriptions lately decyphered by Major Rawlinson, proclaimed himself the worshipper of Ormuzd, or the good Being, and in his name went forth to his battles. You must attend to these facts, and remember them; they have much to do with Ecclesiastical history.

Lect. II.
Darius, B. C. 521.

These Persian kings, however, though they had this faith, aspired to be, like the Chaldæans, despots over the world, and to put out the life of all particular nations. That is what the Scripture teaches us to contemplate as such a wicked and godless experiment, though God permits it for a while for higher ends, and that He may stir up men's hearts against it. Therefore, the next step in the world's history is full of interest for those who read it by the light of God's word. The Persian king finds a number of cities in his empire on the borders of the Ægæan Sea, in which men are dwelling of a different race from his. They are trading with wonderful success; though they are few in numbers, they are more than a match for the Persians, because they are wiser. Their cities are governed by clever sagacious men, who have raised themselves to power. They are very restless, sometimes they are treacherous. But they have one great good in them,—love for their ancestors, attachment to the soil from whence they have sprung.

Persian tyranny.

The Greek colonists in Asia.

This binds them together in fellowship with each other, in spite of their partial interests and tendencies to disagreement. They have the sense of a God of light and wisdom who presides over them, who keeps them together, who directs their counsels. They are full of strange thoughts and questionings about the world around them, and themselves, and God. There are in them all kinds of evil tendencies; but there is a struggle after what is true and what is good, which can have come to them from no one but the good and true God.

Greeks in Europe.

B. C. 491, Darius sends to Greece to demand earth and water.

Marathon, B. C. 490. Invasion of Xerxes, B. C. 480.

The Greeks witnesses for God.

These Greek colonists the Persian king tries to put down. He finds that they are connected with two cities in Europe, Athens, and Sparta, to which they look up, and from which they hope for succour. He determines in the pride of his heart that he will put these cities down, he will make Europe his slave as well as Asia. You have read the stories of Marathon and Thermopylæ as boys at school. Read them again now that you are men, now you are called to be citizens of England, and ministers of God's Church, with ten times as much interest as you did then. It was a battle for right, and truth, and God, that was fought in those places. God was preserving Europe from a hateful self-willed tyranny. He was teaching the Spartans and Athenians to care for their homes and hearths, and the sepulchres of their fathers. It was not by false gods, but by the true God, however much they might be mistaken about His nature, that they were stirred to do brave acts which all brave men like to think of.

THE OTHER NATIONS. 21

And God gave them the victory. The great hosts of the world did not prevail over the handful of weak men, as He has promised that they shall not when men refuse to bow down to force, which is not their Lord. It was the belief that there is something stronger than force,—that the spirit in man is stronger than all mere brute power,—which made these Greeks what you have always been told they were, some of the greatest thinkers and the greatest artists the world has had. The same truth which enabled them to conquer the Persians, helped them to conquer the sea in ships, and to put beautiful forms into stone and marble. But this truth might be turned into a lie. Men may become proud of the powers of their own spirits, till they pass first into cunning plotters and traders, then into tyrants, then into mere restless fighters, then at last, into slaves of the very things they were meant to rule. All this happened to the Greeks. All this shows, not that they were wrong in their belief about man's spirit, and the victory it is to have over that which is earthly and fleshly, but that they could not maintain their own faith, because they were worshipping themselves more than God, and because that worship of themselves led them to worship the very wood and stone which God had given them power to mould and to make beautiful.

The truth which is brought out in God's word respecting the Jews, proves itself over again in the history of the Greeks, in their courage, in their wisdom, in their sensuality, in their fall. But after the

LECT. II.

Meaning of their victory.

Macedonian Empire.

fall of the greatest city in Greece from its high estate, there rose up a young Macedonian who felt that a wise people was still meant to subdue mere numbers and armies, and that he might revenge upon the Asiatics the wrongs which they had tried to do in former centuries to Europe. Alexander went forth and subdued the Persian Empire. At thirty-two years of age, after laying the foundations, as he supposed, of one of those empires which the Scripture call Babylonian, he died at Babylon. But his empire was not to be like those which went before him. His generals quarrelled for it: it fell to pieces in their hands. Two kingdoms grew out of it in which we have a special interest. One is the kingdom of the Ptolemies, in Egypt; the other, that of the Seleucidæ, in Syria. The city of Alexandria, of which you will hear a great deal in Church history, became the capital of one; the city of Antioch, which is so nearly connected with the name of Christian, of the other. You remember how Palestine is situated with reference to Egypt and Syria; you will not wonder that it should often have been a battle-field between them. The Ptolemies were clever and accomplished Greek monarchs; they encouraged settlements of the Jews among them, they were interested in the curious customs of a people so unlike themselves. They wished to know what was written in their sacred books. The Septuagint translation of the Old Testament into Greek, was made, according to Josephus, at the instance of Ptolemy Philadelphus, and was added to the library of Alexandria. In that same city, Jews also heard Greek teachers lecturing on the Greek philosophy, and began to compare what they heard with their own divine oracles.

A different kind of relation existed between the Jews and some of the monarchs of Antioch. They too were Greeks. But they were bent, not upon acquainting themselves with the worship of other people, but on establishing their own. Antiochus Epiphanes did not merely care to enslave the Jews; he was determined to make them idolators, and to establish idol-worship in their temple. There were traitors in the camp, priests who were willing to work with him, to help him in setting up the abomination of desolation in the holy place, and in defacing the holy books. But God put it into the heart of one noble family to stand up for the covenant and the law, and to resist the tyrant to the death. There are few finer histories in the world than that in the Book of Maccabees. It belongs to what is called profane history, as much as the history of the Greek Republics does. That is to say, the record of it is not contained in a canonical book. But if you believe the canonical books, and understand what is written in them, you must regard that as well as the Greek narrative, as containing a history of God's doings, of the way in which He awakens the hearts of men and puts into them invincible might to defy the proud of the earth and the oppressor. And though these Jews lived after what is termed the prophetical period of Jewish history, they as much believed that they were called by God, and were in covenant with God as David and Hezekiah did. In

The Syrian Persecution.

Antiochus pillages the Temple, B.C. 170.

The Maccabees.

Their strength lay in the belief of their calling.

24 ON CHURCH HISTORY.

LECT. II.

From Judas Maccabæus to Herod, B.C. 167—35.

that belief lay all their strength. By that, they were able to establish a native government in Palestine; a kind of priestly government; for the Maccabæan family did not become kings till the better part of them had died out, and till a very degenerate and corrupt race had succeeded.

The Jews hearing of the Romans.

I said that the strength of the Maccabees lay in their faith in the strength of God's covenant. They did also many weak and evil acts, which may all be traced to their forgetfulness of it. I think it was this which led Judas Maccabæus to desire the alliance of a great people, whose fame first reached him when he was fighting the battles of his country. What he heard of them, we are told in a curious and interesting passage in the Book of Maccabees, which I will read to you:—

Their character and deeds as reported to Judas Maccabæus.

" Now Judas had heard of the fame of the Romans, that they were mighty and valiant men, and such as would lovingly accept all that joined themselves unto them, and make a league of amity with all that came unto them; and that they were men of great valour. It was told him also of their wars and noble acts which they had done among the Galatians, and how they had conquered them, and brought them under tribute; and what they had done in the country of Spain, for the winning of the mines of the silver and gold which is there; and that by their policy and patience they had conquered all the place, though it were very far from them; and the kings also that came against them from the uttermost part of the earth, till they had discomfited them, and given them a great overthrow, so that the rest did give them tribute every year: beside this, how they had discomfited in battle Philip, and Perseus, king of the Citims, with others that lifted up themselves against them, and had overcome them: how also Antiochus the great king of Asia, that came against them in battle, having an hundred and twenty elephants, with horsemen, and chariots, and a very great army, was discomfited by them; and how they took him alive, and covenanted that he and such as reigned after him should pay a great tribute, and give hostages, and that which was agreed upon, and the country of India, and Media, and Lydia, and of the goodliest countries, which they took of him, and gave to king Eumenes: moreover how the Grecians had determined to come and destroy them; and that they, having knowledge thereof, sent against them a certain captain, and fighting with them slew many of them, and carried away captives their wives and their children, and spoiled them, and took possession of their lands, and pulled down their strongholds, and brought them to be their servants unto this day: it was told him besides, how they destroyed and brought under their dominion all other kingdoms and isles that at any time resisted them; but with their friends and such as relied upon them they kept amity; and that they had conquered kingdoms both far and nigh, insomuch as all that heard of their name were afraid of them: also that, whom they would help to a kingdom, those reign; and whom again they would, they displace: finally, that they were greatly exalted: yet for all this none of them wore a crown, or was clothed in purple, to be magnified thereby: moreover how they had made for themselves a senate house, wherein three hundred and twenty men sat in council daily, consulting alway for the people, to the end they might be well ordered: and that they committed their government to one man every year, who ruled over all their country, and that all were obedient to that one, and that there was neither envy nor emulation among them. In consideration of these things, Judas chose Eupolemus the son of John, the son of Accos, and Jason the son of Eleazar, and sent them to Rome, to make a league of amity and confederacy with them, and to intreat them that they would take the yoke from them; for they saw that the kingdom of the Grecians did oppress Israel with servitude. They went therefore to Rome, which was a very great journey, and came into the senate, where they spake and said, Judas Maccabeus with his brethren, and the people of the Jews, have sent us unto you, to make a confederacy and peace with you, and that we might be registered your confederates and friends. So that matter pleased the Romans well. And this is the copy of the epistle which the senate wrote back again in tables of brass, and sent to Jerusalem, that there they might have by them a memorial of peace and confederacy: Good success be to the Romans, and to the people of the Jews, by sea and by land for ever: the sword also and enemy be far from them. If there come first any war upon the Romans, or any of their confederates throughout all their dominion, the people of the Jews shall help them, as the time shall be appointed, with all their heart: neither shall they give any thing unto them that make war upon them, or aid them with victuals, weapons, money, or ships, as it hath seemed good unto the Romans; but they shall keep their covenants without taking any thing therefore. In the same manner also, if war come first upon the nation of the Jews, the Romans shall help them with all their heart, according as the time shall be appointed them: neither shall victuals be given to them that take

LECT. II.

Pyrrhus invades Italy,
B.C. 281.

Defeat of Philip in the Battle of Cynoscephalæ,
B.C. 197.

War with Antiochus,
B.C. 191.

War with Perseus,
B.C. 171—167.

part against them, or weapons, or money, or ships, as it hath seemed good to the Romans; but they shall keep their covenants, and that without deceit. According to these articles did the Romans make a covenant with the people of the Jews. Howbeit if hereafter the one party or the other shall think meet to add or diminish any thing, they may do it at their pleasures, and whatsoever they shall add or take away shall be ratified. And as touching the evils that Demetrius doeth to the Jews, we have written unto him saying, Wherefore hast thou made thy yoke heavy upon our friends and confederates the Jews? If therefore they complain any more against thee, we will do them justice, and fight with thee by sea and by land."

I have given you the whole of this chapter, because I know no better way of introducing you to a people of whom our history hereafter will be full, and because there is something very ominous and prophetical in this first league between them and the Jews. You will easily suppose that there were some mistakes in the information which a hard-working Jewish soldier got, of a people who were living in Italy. By the Galatians, he means the Gauls in Europe; though he perhaps was not sure whether he was not speaking of the people of the same kindred in Asia Minor. He had heard something of the conquests of the Romans in Spain; but he seems only to have received an imperfect story about their triumph over their old rival in Carthage. He knew more of the conquests which they had begun to make in Asia, and was, of course, more interested in them. In what he says about the Grecians, he brings together the invasion of Italy by King Pyrrhus, and the victory of the Romans in Greece; though these events were separated by a long interval. He is not right in saying that Rome was ruled by one man. These mistakes were very natural ones, and, on the whole,

Judas had a very clear impression of a vigorous, energetic, triumphant people, who were gradually forcing other people to accept their government, because they had first learnt to be governed themselves. That was the secret of the Roman success, God gave them their power, as He gives all men their power. But He gave them what is much better than power, and is the beginning of it,—a sense of right, and order, and obedience, of the reverence which the child owes to the father, and of the authority which the father has over the child. These principles which lay at the root of their minds, had brought forth the discipline of their armies. At home there had been many fights between the different classes of which the state was composed; but through these their society had been made stronger, and they had learnt more how one class of men in a nation must depend upon another. They had committed a great many wicked and tyrannical acts in winning their dominion, every one of which was to have its due recompense of reward afterwards. Their evil acts had mingled with the false notions which they had of the powers above them, and had made them falser; but they did confess a God of righteousness and order, who kept men in order, and required men to be righteous, though they might very often set this faith at naught in their practice. Be sure you remember these things. I cannot tell you how much they will help you in understanding God's government of the world in the later times as well as in those I am speaking of.

Their righteousness.

Their faith.

LECT. II.

Extent of their conquests.

Asia.

Africa.

Well, this Roman empire, then, was destined to swallow up much of those which preceded it, and to have a dominion which did not belong to them. It did not conquer all the old Persian empire. There its power was disputed by the Parthians, a mountain tribe, which subdued some of the fairest provinces of Asia, and which adopted many of the Greek customs and the Greek worship. The Romans conquered the countries in which Alexander's successors had been established, and set up Roman laws and Roman magistrates in the midst of them. But they did not drive out the Greek language, or establish the Latin in them. In many places they themselves learnt the older language; and the ablest men of Rome came to the Greek cities and learnt under Greek teachers. You must not think, then, of the Eastern world or of the Greek, as Roman, though they were under the Romans.

In Africa the case was different. Egypt, in its chief city, had been made thoroughly Greek by the Ptolemies, and there the Roman language scarcely penetrated at all: in the country districts the old tongue of the people was still spoken. But, in the part of Africa of which Carthage had been the centre, after that city was destroyed and a new Carthage built, the Latin language, the Latin institutions, and all the Latin modes of thinking, spread most rapidly. The city which bore the name of Rome's great rival, was thoroughly Romanised: only in the rural districts the Punic, or Carthaginian language, still for a long time lingered. These are points which you will have need to recollect; they have much to do with our subject.

Western Europe.

But there is another part of the world which is more interesting to us than these. It was called into existence, I might almost say, by the Roman conquests, the Roman government, and the Roman language. Judas Maccabæus has told us of the Roman triumphs in Spain and Gaul. Those countries were to become, by degrees, almost Latin nations. We shall hear, by-and-by, of great changes which they underwent—of different tribes which subdued them. But, amidst all these, they have never lost the effect of their Roman discipline. Rome found them mere tribes, and organized them and civilized them. She made them cultivated provinces of her great empire. Another power was needed to make them nations in the true sense of the word. What that was, we shall hear by-and-by. But this was the appointed preparation for it.

Britain.

What was the case with Britain? I cannot give you the whole answer to that question at once. The history must give it you by degrees. But I must tell you here, that Britain was, in one sense, more indebted to Rome than even Spain and Gaul. The Phœnicians came to our island to look for tin;—the Greeks had a dream of such a place. In after times, when Britain had undergone many changes, our ancestors had wild fancies about Trojan colonies which had settled here, and races of kings that dwelt here. These legends are worth actually nothing. Julius Cæsar really discovered our island, and brought it into the history of the world, fifty-five years before the birth of Christ. He found, indeed, a people with many strange practices,—with sacrifices and a priesthood, of the same tribe with the majority of the inhabitants of Gaul, connected with them by their worship. These priests must have had a higher knowledge once. They had the relics of it. But they had not imparted it to the people. They kept them low and brutal. And so their own worship became more and more savage and brutal;—it became the worship of evil powers and not of good. That is a necessary law. It goes on in all countries where the priests do not feel that they have a calling of God to raise and educate the people. Julius Cæsar was the appointed deliverer of Britain from this condition. He was the ablest Roman of this time. He understood, better than any man, what Rome could do to civilize and organize people. He scorned the vulgar ambition of his rival, Pompey, to enrich himself by conquering the old, worn-out monarchies of the East. He aspired to call a new world into existence in the West, and God used him to do that work. He did not know what all the strange thoughts meant that were working in the minds of the British priests, or of other priests. He had no good news for the people about an unseen world. But he could put them in the way of subduing the outward world, as God meant them to subdue it; instead of crouching to it, as their priests taught them to do. He could teach them to make roads, and punish crimes, and submit to laws. That was a great lesson, for which

Lect. II.

Priesthood relics of a higher wisdom.

Benefits of Roman Government.

we have to be grateful to him. And the reason I have stopped to tell you this, is not merely out of love to my own land, but because Britain is as good a specimen as one can find, of what Rome did for the world, and of what it could not do; and because Britain, more than any country in Europe, comes into existence just at the very time when the New Testament history begins.

There was one country in western Europe which the Romans knew of, but which they could not conquer. That country is Germany. I shall not say anything of it to you now, but I shall have a great deal to say hereafter of its influence upon Gaul and Britain, as well as upon the whole of Christendom. I wish you only to recollect that when one speaks of the Roman or Latin world, you are not to think of that country as included in it. It was not an undiscovered region, as Norway, and Sweden, and the greater part of Russia was. Roman armies fought in it, and sometimes perished in it. But it was a collection of tribes, out of which a kind of power quite different from that which Rome exercised was in due time to come forth. Nations were to be formed out of those tribes; and Rome, as I have said, could not form nations,—it was itself ceasing to be one. *Germany.*

That is the last point I shall speak of in this lecture. I have told you that Judæa was a distinct and separate *nation*, and that it was a witness against those great *empires* which tried to be universal and to swallow up all nations in themselves. Rome, as it is described to us by Judas Maccabæus, was a nation, *Nations and Empires.*

standing upon an acknowledgment of a righteous Being, though it was continually confounding Him with the works of His hands; confessing a law by which individuals and nations are bound, though it was very frequently violating that law in its own acts; reverencing the bonds of the family, though those bonds were always liable to become loose. But the false worship, the violations of right, the breaches of domestic discipline, were now becoming stronger than all which restrained them. The factions of leaders, the divisions of classes, made mockery of the law to which they all appealed. Money was mighty over the order of the State, and the consciences of men. The ablest citizens might, in such a time, become the subverters of the commonwealth. After a wretched civil war, Julius Cæsar, the beloved of the people, became Dictator. Men who dreamed that they could restore the old Roman Republic conspired against him and slew him. That act hastened its fall, and threw it into the hands of a much worse chief. Octavius Cæsar became the ruler of the world which Rome had subdued, and was hailed as a deliverer from its anarchy. He was called the Imperator or General of the Republic. All its civil offices and institutions gathered round him who bore this military name. The most civilized part of the universe did homage to one whose title and whose glory was that he was the chief of the army. But he was not only called a general: he was also called a God. The union of names expresses the inmost feeling of the people of that age. Mere power, the power which comes forth in hosts, was their god. He who governed them was really in their minds the King of kings and Lord of lords. They might worship a multitude of powers, as they had done before; they might have abundance of religion, and be full of fears about the future and the unseen world. But this was the person to whom they looked up; this Man-god was, he to whom priests and peoples bowed down.

The Man-God.

LECTURE III.

THE SECT AGE OF THE JEWISH COMMONWEALTH.

Lect. III.
Character of the Jewish witness.

THE Jewish nation, we have seen, was especially called out to bear witness against that kind of society which I described at the end of my last Lecture. I do not mean that it was to declare war upon any great empire of the world; I do not mean, even, that it was always to resist any great tyrant of the earth who made war upon it. Hezekiah fought against Sennacherib, and was delivered out of his hands. But Jeremiah told the inhabitants of Jerusalem, in the days of Nebuchadnezzar, that their duty was to yield. In fact, Nebuchadnezzar was an instrument of God for delivering them from their miserable and godless native rulers, from the corruption, brutality, anarchy, into which they had fallen. Nevertheless, in the one case as much as in the other, every true Jew who understood the calling of his country was a witness against these governments of mere power, these governments which destroyed old land-marks, a witness for a King who reigned in righteousness, and who ordered the bounds of men's habitations. He was a witness against kings who set themselves up like Lucifer, and called themselves gods. He was a witness for One who was ruling over men in meekness and equity, who was stooping to men, who was caring for the poor and the needy. This witness was borne by the true Jew in his lowest estate, as well as in his most prosperous. Perhaps it was never borne more faithfully or with greater effect than by those who were captives in Babylon.

We may ask, then, what sort of witness was the Jewish people bearing in the days of Augustus Cæsar, concerning the sort of dominion which he had set up, one which was so like the tyrannies of the Asiatic monarchs, only that it had grown out of a better state of things, not yet altogether subverted. I will endeavour to give you the answer. There had been, as I said, a series of native princes in Judæa, the Asmonæan princes they were called, who owed their power to the great Maccabæan struggle, but who had none of the spirit of their ancestors, being low, plotting, bad men. It was clear that there was not more of morality or godliness among the Jews than there was among the other people who submitted to the Roman yoke. They fell under it just as naturally as any others did. As far as the body of the people were concerned, it made little difference; they were probably, on the whole, subject to a juster rule than they had been. There was more order in their exactions, though they were imposed by a foreigner. Cneius Pompey had entered their temple; but it was not the manner of the Romans to interfere with the religious rites of the people they conquered. The priests continued as they had been before; sacrifices

Jews in the age of Augustus.

Decay of National life.

were offered according to the rules of the law; the Heathen governors were less likely to interfere with such matters than the native.

The Idumæan king reigning under Rome.

According to the custom of the Romans in many countries, a king was set over their Jewish subjects, who of course was answerable to the ruling state, and might be removed at its pleasure; though it was quite as likely that his son would be permitted to reign after him. The man they appointed was not a Jew but an Idumæan, Herod, who, though he was first promoted by Mark Antony, was clever and supple enough to keep his kingdom under Mark Antony's rival and conqueror, Octavius Cæsar. So when Octavius became Augustus and the emperor of the Roman world, Herod reigned over Judæa, and contrived to get himself called "Great," either while he ruled, or after his death. He was great according to the notions of greatness which men had in that little age. He knew how to get power, and to keep it when he had got it. He was as bad a husband, and father, and prince as there well could be. But the men he governed were worse than himself; they were the kind of men whose motives a man like him could see through, and whose tricks and plots he could overreach by his own.

Wherein the state of the Jews was like and unlike that described in the Old Testament.

It is no new thing for us to hear of the chosen people being stiff-necked and corrupt. Moses and the prophets are telling us that of them, in every page of the Old Testament. They were essentially now what their fathers had been; but there were many outside differences which are of very great importance in themselves, and which led them to think that they would never have done the evils which were charged on former generations. There was no worship of Roman gods now, as there had been of Phœnician or Egyptian gods, in the days gone by. The people hated idolaters, and believed that they hated idols. There was no indifference about the books of the law; they were copied out with the greatest diligence, and commented upon with great learning. The Scribes, the copiers and teachers of the law, were as much venerated as any men in the community. Not only the law itself was honoured, but all the sayings of wise men that had been handed down about it, were honoured also. The services which had been so often neglected by their forefathers were acknowledged as divine, and scrupulously observed. Besides the Temple at Jerusalem, synagogues had been established in the different towns of the land, where the divine books were read and expounded.

Scribes, Elders, Synagogues.

During the Maccabæan period there had risen up a class of men who felt the importance of adhering strictly to the commands and ordinances of the law themselves, and who were careful in enforcing the observance of them upon others, fearing, no doubt, lest the same bad consequences should come from the indifference to them which the prophets told of. These men, called Pharisees, were now the prevailing and popular teachers of the land. They were more numerous than any other sect, and had far more influence. They were looked upon as *the* reli-

Pharisees.

gious men of the age, the standard of religion to all others, though very few might hope to reach their standard. Besides their reputation, many of them derived influence from their wealth. The people thought that God had given them money, as He gave Abraham flocks and herds; that it was a sign of His approbation, a pledge of better things which He would give them hereafter. The Pharisees exhorted them earnestly to strive for those things, that were to come to them in a future world. They said there would be a resurrection of the just and of the unjust; rewards for the one, punishments for the other. They pointed out what was the likeliest way of obtaining the first and avoiding the second. But they did not neglect that which was going on in the world around them. Josephus, the Jewish historian, shows us that they were busy in all the intrigues of Herod's court, sometimes plotting against him with members of his own family, sometimes ready to work with him when he was willing to promote their objects.

Of course he did not trust these Pharisees. He tried to make their religious views and their secular views serve his ends. He had about him friends who were devoted to his interests. In the days of his descendants, and probably in his own, these were called Herodians. Their main object was, to watch over the interests of the Idumæan family, to prevent the Romans from setting it aside, and to prevent the Jews from favouring any native prince who should be a rival to it. For they had reason to dread this danger. It seemed a very strange and monstrous thing to Jews, that they should be under a foreign yoke at all; that they should have to pay taxes to the Romans; that the faces of men who were collecting customs and tributes should be meeting them at the turn of every street. That sight was most painful to the richer people;—*they* probably cared more about throwing off the yoke of the Roman Cæsars. The poor and the ignorant, I suppose, felt the nearer tyranny most. They would have liked, above all things, to get rid of Herod and his family. They knew enough of the words of the prophets, either by common fame or by the teaching of the scribes, to be aware how much they spoke of a Son of David, who should one day set up His throne in their land, and who should be a Helper and Friend of the poor. No wonder that such words stirred their heart's blood, and that they were ready to listen to agitators and brigands who told them that they were sent from God, to deliver His people from their chains, and make them greater than all the people of the earth. Such men arose, it would seem, especially in Galilee, where the people were most ignorant and most trampled upon as an inferior race. They drew their followers into the wilderness, committed many crimes, and made their condition worse than it was before. *Cries for a native king. Insurrections.*

There was another body, different in their objects from both the Pharisees and the Herodians—certainly with far fewer disciples than the former. These were the Sadducees. Almost from the time the Pharisees began to exist, these had been their *Sadducees.*

opposers. They thought their strict observances and regard for traditions unnecessary and mischievous. "The law," they said, "enjoined plain duties;—sound morality was more important than religious ceremonies. These might be of use to keep vulgar men in order,—the higher and wiser did not want them. Nor were they better for thinking about a future state, or dreaming of communications from invisible powers;— they could keep themselves just and merciful without such helps: and was not that what God required?" The people did not heed these teachers;—their doctrine did not speak to them in the least. They found it very hard to be just and merciful; and the Sadducees did not tell them how they were to become so, and how others might become so to them. The Pharisees spoke to fears that were in them; now and then to hopes that were in them also. The Sadducees treated them as if they had neither.

Essenes. Another class I may just mention to you, for the Jewish historian speaks of them, though the Scripture does not. Those whom he calls Essenes were men of earnest minds, who were disgusted with the quarrelling of these sects, and with the corruption in the Jewish cities, and who thought that they might establish a more healthy and pure community, something more like the kingdom the prophets spoke of, in the rural districts of Judæa. One cannot tell how many of these communities were formed, and how much of good or evil there was in them. They pointed out a want that was in the hearts of the people, a want which was nourished in the best of them as they prayed and read the Old Scriptures. A number of such men there were, who might, or might not, join the Essenes. They are described in the Gospels as men and women who were waiting for the kingdom of God.

The sense of calling lost.

You will see, then, that there was very little sense indeed in the minds of the Jews, that they were a people called out by God, to do a work for men. In truth, they did not feel themselves a people at all. Some of them thought it was a great honour to be Pharisees; some, to be Sadducees; some, to be Herodians. But what was the honour of being Israelites? The great men did not like to be confounded with the vulgar, irreligious, or ignorant herd who bore that name. They therefore rejoiced in it only in as far as it separated them from the Heathens, as it denoted them not to be a portion of the world which God had cursed. For that was their view of the promise to Abraham,—all the families of the earth were *cursed* for their sakes. What followed from this notion?

Religion is substituted for God.

They no longer looked upon God as the righteous God. They did not glory in *this*, that they were to know Him who executed righteousness in the earth. He was the God of the Jews, just as Apollo was the god of the Greeks. They regarded Him as more selfish, more partial, than the gods of the Heathen were. The only meaning which they put upon the words, that He was not made in the likeness of any thing in heaven or on earth, was, that He was removed from all sympathy with men; that He made decrees for them, but that He did not care for them. This was the belief of men who pretended to worship

LECT. III.

Inward idolatry and slavery of the chosen people.

the God of Abraham—the God who had said to Moses, "I called you out of the land of Egypt, out of the house of bondage,"—the God whose Word came to the prophets, that they might testify to Israelites, and to all nations, against injustice and falsehood. He had revealed Himself to their fathers. They read, studied, almost worshipped the books that contained the revelation. But, instead of accepting it or believing it, they made up another being out of their own conceits, —a being who was like their own cruel, covetous selves;—they made him the object of their prayers and their sacrifices. The sin which the prophets had charged upon their fathers, was their sin. They were given up to covetousness,—that is, to self-seeking.

Mammon worship.

They worshipped themselves, and God only as the image of themselves. In a very little time they were incapable of thinking of any thing as really worthy of pursuit or admiration, except money, and what money could buy.

Relation to Roman despotism.

Do you think that these men could testify against the Man-god who reigned over the Roman world? Do you think they could say, "This is not the King of all the earth; there is another altogether different King, who has kept the universe together, and will show Himself in it, and will compel the rulers of it to feel His might?" Could they bear any such message as this to mankind?—They, who had the very heart of all the Roman idolatries and corruptions in them,—they who were just as much setting up idols as the Romans were,—they who had not half so much sense of righteousness and justice as was still left in their masters,—they whom Isaiah and Jeremiah would have denounced as infinitely more Godless and heartless than the worshippers of Jupiter? And yet, if there was no one to bring this message, the promise to Abraham meant nothing; the Jewish calling meant nothing; the whole of the Old Testament history was a cunningly devised fable.

A voice was heard crying in the wilderness, "Repent, for the kingdom of heaven is at hand." The last words responded to many dreams which all classes of the Jews, at times, were visited by. They hoped for a Jewish king; they believed that such a king must be sent to them from Heaven; they believed that, in some way or other, a true Israelitish kingdom must be a kingdom of God, or a kingdom of Heaven. He who spoke the words was in the deserts of Israel, whither many leaders of insurrections had gone before. But he had none of the tokens of a leader of insurrection, or of a leader at all. Every thing about him was rough, stern, terrible. The word with which he began his preaching was altogether unlike the usual summons to the people to assert their rights, and break loose from the yoke of their oppressors. It seemed to tell them that they were wrong,—that a change must take place in themselves, before they could look for any in the world about them. And presently the preacher spoke to the most religious men in Judæa, the most admired religious leaders of the people, calling them a generation of vipers; asking them who had bidden them flee from the wrath to come; telling them not to say within themselves that they had Abraham to their

John the Baptist.

The Kingdom. Repentance.

father, for that God was able of the stones to raise up children to Abraham.

Effect of the proclamation.

This message, harsh as it sounded, nevertheless drew all Jerusalem and Judæa and the country about Jordan to listen to it. That summons to repent was felt by the hearts and consciences of thousands as a call to them from God Himself, the God of their spirits, the God who had made a covenant with their fathers. From whatever lips the message to their outward ear came, this word to their inward ear must come from Him who knew what was within them, to awaken them to the recollection of bad deeds that they had done and bad thoughts that they had thought. It told them that there was something in themselves that had need to be sent away, that they might be true men, true Israelites. For the first time the meaning of God's covenant, the end and intention of circumcision, became manifest to them. They felt that there were fleshly lusts and desires in them which had degraded them, and were degrading the Nation, and which only God could deliver them from.

Remission of sins.

The Baptism for the remission of sins was accepted as a pledge, that He gave them this emancipation. The words which said that the axe was laid to the roots of the trees, that whatever did not bear good fruit would be hewn down and cast into the fire, told them that a sifting judgment was preparing for their own land, and that each one of them must pass through that judgment, and must seek to have his dross burnt up, if he would not be consumed with it. They said at the same time that the reformation must be a re-formation indeed; that there must be another and better root for their lives than that upon which they had grown hitherto, if any good was to spring out of them. But John said further, "There is One standing among you whom you know not; He shall baptize you with the Holy Ghost and with fire." That was the message to men craving to find out this new root of their lives, craving to be planted upon it; that the real King and Lord of their hearts was at hand and was about to be revealed; that He was coming to work that change in them and in their nation, perhaps also in those stones out of which God could make children, which they could not work for themselves.

Lect. III.

Baptism with the Spirit.

And presently One came to John to be baptized, to whom he said: "I have need to be baptized of Thee, and comest Thou to me?" and when Jesus, who had gone down into the water, was rising up from it, the Spirit was seen to descend in a bodily shape and to light upon Him, and a voice from Heaven said, "This is my beloved Son, in whom I am well pleased."

The Son of God.

LECTURE IV.

THE KINGDOM OF HEAVEN.

LECT. IV.
The sorrows of the Prophet.

WE have seen that the Jews had been taught to regard themselves as a called nation; that the kings, the priests, the prophets, were taught to believe that they were called out to be servants of the nation. The true prophet had to perceive and mourn that the great majority of the nation thought nothing of their calling, that they were not witnesses for God but against Him. Nevertheless, he did not suppose for a moment, when he was in his right mind, when he was under divine teaching, that he was taken out of his nation to have blessings which did not belong to it. He felt that his greatest blessing was to be a member of it, that he must suffer as an Israelite and rejoice as an Israelite; that he could not separate himself from any sorrows that came upon his people; that he could not have any joys which they were not, one and all, entitled to share with him. How could he keep these thoughts in his mind, when he saw his people torn asunder by strifes and hatreds; when each one had a different object from the other; when they were setting up idols each for himself to worship? It was the hardest thing possible to do this. The struggles which the prophets tell us of, in their own minds, show us how hard it was. And yet, unless they could do this, they could not really believe in one God and worship Him. The belief in His unity was not a hard dogma that there are not a great many Gods; it was a belief in a Person who was their God, the God of their fathers, the God of the whole earth. If they did not understand that they were one nation, one Israel, they could not hold this faith practically, they could not live by it and act upon it.

But God enabled them to keep it in spite of all that they saw and heard and felt, which was threatening to destroy it. For as I showed you in my first Lecture, He gradually revealed to them an Elect One, in whom His soul delighted; a King, who was seated on the holy hill of Sion, however the visible kings who were reigning in Jerusalem might be forgetting their calling and their covenant; a Priest who was really uniting men to God, however little the visible priests might understand what was meant by the sacrifices they were offering, the words that were inscribed upon their foreheads, the blessing that they were to pronounce upon the people; a true Prophet, a Divine Word who understood and uttered the full mind of God, however partially true prophets might understand it, however shamefully false prophets might misrepresent it; that there was in one word a Son of God who stood in the most wonderful relation to Men, who was the Ruler of their thoughts, the Light of their consciences, the Awakener of their impulses, the Object of their hopes, who made some aware of

His consolation.

His presence that they might testify of Him as the Lord of all.

The same Person seen under different aspects.

The vision of this Person came out in different forms and measures, to different inspired men. One side of His character and nature presented itself to this man, another to that. It came to them in hours of oppression and sorrow, when their hearts were overwhelmed, and they felt themselves sinking in deep mire where no ground was. The troubles, desolation, captivity of their nation, which mixed with all their individual sorrows, and could not be separated from them, taught them to feel the necessity of such a Person, and to perceive that in Him which answered to their wants. As they compared what they had been taught with thoughts of quite a different kind, sometimes almost of an opposite kind, which had come to other men in other circumstances, they understood that all were pointing to the same Person, that they could only be brought together and fulfilled in Him.

As Priest, King, the Divine Word, the Divine Son.

By degrees it became more and more clear to them that this King, this Prophet, this Priest, this Word of God, this Son of God would one day be fully declared and manifested to men, that by some means or other it would be shown how it was that He was so closely and intimately related to Him whom the Heaven of Heavens could not contain, and yet was also so nearly related to the sufferers and sinners of earth.

The seed of Abraham and David.

Whenever such a Person appeared, they felt that he must be in some manner that Seed of Abraham, in whom all the families of the earth were to be blessed, that Son of David who was to rule over the nations. How this could be they could not tell. Somehow it must be. For as they became more acquainted with the other people of the earth, as they understood the strange thoughts that had been stirring in them, they saw that they too wanted a Friend and Deliverer, that they too needed a Man who should unite them to God. The dreams of such a deliverer had taken various forms. The needs of men's bodies and of men's spirits in different places had created different objects who were to satisfy them. All of these were imperfect, as those who conceived them were imperfect; they were full of evil, for they were made in the likeness of men who had evil in themselves, and who wished to think that the gods could sympathise in their evil. But they all implied a feeling after One who was above man, a standard and judge of men's acts, and yet who felt with them and cared for them. They implied that there was One who was not tied down by local circumstances, as they were, and yet who could feel with those who dwelt on particular spots, who could care for a country and for the individual men who dwelt upon it; who could be, in one word, a Brother of man as well as a Lord of man, the Brother of each and the Lord of each, as well as the Brother and Lord of the whole race. This was the desire of Nations. Unless this desire could be satisfied, all the deepest feelings in men's hearts pointed to nothing.

Now you will not understand what the records mean which are contained in the four Gospels, unless

LECT. IV.

The King of the Jews must be more.

The King and Brother.

This belief

Lect. IV.

the explanation of the Evangelists.

you suppose that those who wrote them believed that Jesus Christ, of whom they speak, was the Person in whom all these anticipations of Jews and of human beings were fulfilled. You will not understand why they record with such emphasis His baptism and the Voice which declared Him to be the Son of God. You will not understand why we are told that He was anointed with the Spirit, with which He was afterwards to baptize those who believed on Him. You will not understand why we are told that He was tempted by the evil spirit, and overcame him. You

The Conqueror of the Evil Spirit.

will not understand why He is said, in the power of the Spirit, to have preached the good news of deliverance to captives, and the opening of sight to the blind; why, in the power of the same Spirit, He is said to

Signs and wonders.

have delivered men from evil spirits, from the diseases which afflicted their bodies, and the madness or uncleanness which possessed their hearts. You will not understand why we are told, that He claimed dominion over the winds and waves, and fed the multitudes with the loaves and fishes. You will not understand why we are told of His raising the dead. You will not understand why He is speaking continually of a kingdom of Heaven or of God. You will not under-

The Parables of the Kingdom.

stand why, in all His parables, He is bringing out the mysteries of His kingdom over the hearts and minds of men, in connexion with the planting and growth of seeds and all the mysteries of the kingdom of nature, in connexion with husbandmen and servants, with kings and subjects, with fathers and children, with all the common life of men. You will not understand why He was transfigured, and His face did shine as the sun. You will understand still less, why He began straightway to tell His disciples that He should suffer many things, and be rejected of the priests and the elders, and be crucified. You will not understand the indignation of the Pharisees against Him, or why it was that the different sects that had never agreed before, felt Him to be their common enemy. You will not understand why He told the Pharisees to render to Cæsar that which bore his image, and to God that which had His; or why He told the Sadducees, who denied the Resurrection, that God was not the God of the dead, but of the living. You will not understand why He called out twelve Apostles to be heralds of His kingdom while He was upon earth; why He told them that they would be able to be heralds of it in a more wonderful sense after He had left the earth; why He said that if they would be chief of all, they must be servants of all. You will not understand, why He should have entered into Jerusalem, and the crowd should have hailed Him as the King, the Son of David. You will not understand why He should have desired to eat the Passover with His disciples before He suffered, or why, at that Passover, He should have taken bread and blessed it, and said, "Take, eat, this is my body; drink, this is my blood." You will not understand why He should have cried, "Father, if this cup may not pass from Me except I drink it, Thy will be done." You will not understand why the Sanhedrim should have condemned Him as a blasphemer, for making Himself

LECT. IV.

The Transfiguration.

War with the Sects.

The Ministers of His Kingdom.

The Bread and Wine.

The Agony.

the Son of God; or why they should have presented Him to Pilate as a rebel, for making Himself a King. You will not be able to enter into the mystery of the Cross and Passion; into the cry, "Father, forgive them;" or into the cry, "My God, why hast Thou forsaken me?" You will not understand the hour of darkness after the crucifixion. You will not understand the calmness and assurance, and yet the wonder, with which the Evangelists recal the words, "He is not here, He is risen." You will not understand why they record so carefully, and yet so briefly, His appearances after the Resurrection. You will not understand why He stood among them on the mountain in Galilee, and said, "All power is given unto Me in heaven and earth. Go ye, therefore, and teach all nations, baptizing them in the name of the Father, and of the Son, and of the Holy Ghost. And, lo, I am with you always, even unto the end of the world." You will not understand why the Evangelists seem to think it a natural thing, that He should ascend up on high, out of the sight of His disciples. You will not understand how all these events are connected with that feast of Pentecost at which the Apostles were met, when the sound of the rushing mighty wind was heard, and the Spirit descended in the likeness of cloven tongues, and sat upon each of them. You will not understand, what was signified by their speaking with other tongues, as the Spirit gave them utterance; or how the great message which they had to deliver to the whole body of the Jews was, "This Jesus, whom ye crucified, is both Lord and Christ;" how they could bid them repent and be baptized; how they could say to them, "The promise of this Spirit is to you and to your children, and to as many as the Lord our God shall call."

LECT. IV.

All this history, which sounds to us at once so familiar and so marvellous, is told, as you know, with exceeding simplicity, in no fine language, with no starts of astonishment. It is all consistent, if we suppose this to be the manifestation of the Person of whom the Jewish nation had been called out to bear witness, of that Root and Centre of human society from whom all its life and order comes, of Him who binds men together, of Him who is the Mediator between God and man. No record is equally reasonable, if such a Person was to be revealed to men, and if a society of men was to be called out for the purpose of revealing Him. All His acts of power, all His words of righteousness, are then so many testimonies that the Lord of man is the Deliverer of man from all the plagues that have come to him for the punishment of his evil, and from the evil itself. All the signs that He gave that He was a Son, and that He came to do His Father's will, are then witnesses what that will is, and what is striving against it, and how that is to be overcome. The Spirit which descended on Him is then felt to be that which unites Him to the Father; the Spirit which He bestowed upon those who were baptized into His name is then perceived to be that which brings men into a fatherly kingdom, and makes them sons of God, and brethren of each other. I do not pretend to explain the history if it does not mean

The ground of the Gospel also the ground of Ecclesiastical History.

this. If this is not the sense of it, I cannot find any connexion in its parts. I do not see how, as a whole, we can call it God's revelation of Himself, or receive it as a Gospel to the world. Finally, if this is not the sense of it, I cannot lecture to you on Church history, for I do not know what the Church is.

LECTURE V.

THE NEW SOCIETY IN JERUSALEM.

THOSE three thousand who were baptized on the day of Pentecost, are often said to be the beginning of the Christian Church, or Ecclesia. In a very important sense, this assertion is true; I shall hope to show you, presently, in what sense. But I do not use this mode of speech, because I believe it might mislead you. The society which appeared in the world, on the day of Pentecost, was not one which had dropped from the clouds. It belonged to the Jewish nation; you can only understand what it was, by understanding what that nation was. And though its appearance was a great event in the history of that nation and of the world—as great an event as one can think of—the Scriptures do not speak of it as marking the beginning of a period, but the end of one. St. Peter told his countrymen that the mighty powers which were bestowed on him and his fellow apostles, were to prepare them and their countrymen for a great day of the Lord. John the Baptist had spoken of that day; of a wrath that was coming; of Christ as having a fan in His hand, with which He would throughly purge His floor. Our Lord Himself

LECT. V.

Strictly Jewish character of the Baptized Community in Jerusalem.

The day of Pentecost a preparation for the end of the Age.

had spoken of that day as one which would come in that generation. The minds of the Apostles, you will find, were filled with the thoughts of it. They were sure that the end of an age or dispensation of the world was at hand. But the end had not arrived. The book of the Acts of the Apostles tells us of the gradual unfolding of a Universal Society, out of the Jewish Society. The principles of it are laid open to us in the narrative of the day of Pentecost. As these principles worked themselves out more and more, the new Ecclesia began to make itself apparent; the shell that had contained it began to drop off. When that shell was quite broken, our History properly commences. But if we are not to make the greatest mistakes respecting the world that was to come, we must carefully attend to the divine narrative of the process by which it was brought out of the world that had been.

The subject of the Acts of the Apostles.

Observe, then, that the people who were gathered at the feast of Pentecost, though they came from a number of different countries, were all either Jews by birth, or men who had joined themselves to the Jews, and acknowledged the God of Abraham to be their God. They were come to a festival which had been appointed in the wilderness. It was not indeed, like the Passover or the Tabernacles, a feast that commemorated some blessing which had been bestowed specially on the Israelites. It gave thanks for the blessing of corn and the fruits of the earth; it reminded them that the living power which caused the seeds in the ground to bring forth, was from God.

Who were met at the Feast.

Character of the Feast.

THE NEW SOCIETY IN JERUSALEM. 57

But it was Jewish still. Jerusalem was the place for holding it. All who came to it, testified that that was their capital and their home.

Lect. V.

It was an old national meeting, then, a testimony to the Jews that they were a people called out and made one, by the unseen God, the God of their fathers. Thither came all the members of the tribes; it was not a gathering of Pharisees, or Sadducees, or Herodians, but of Israelites. When St. Peter explained to them the meaning of the sign which they had witnessed, this is the tone in which he spoke. He told them that the God of their fathers had exalted Jesus, whom they crucified, to be both Lord and Christ; therefore He had shed forth that Spirit upon them. He spoke of David and of David's sepulchre, of Christ as the heir of David's throne, of His resurrection as the witness that He was indeed their King. It was such a sign of kingship as they might not have looked for; but no other would have been sufficient. Only a Conqueror of death could be the complete Conqueror of whom prophets had spoken. Only One who could bestow a Spirit upon men, to quicken their thoughts, to inspire their words, could exercise the powers which prophets had said He would exercise. Whatever more there might be in this sign, of the Apostles speaking to men in their own tongues the wonderful works of God, there was certainly *this* in it. It testified that all Jews, however dispersed, had still a bond of real inward union. The God of their fathers was announcing to them the living Head of their nation, was bidding them be

A National Meeting.

St. Peter's Sermon.

Meaning of the gift of Tongues.

one people in Him. The Spirit who enabled St. Peter to testify of Him could bind them together in Him; if they did not confess Him, they would find an ever-increasing separation of heart and mind from each other, till they utterly ceased to be a Nation.

The Conversion of the three thousand; what was implied in it.

You see then what it was that pricked the hearts of those Jews who said, "Men and brethren, what shall we do?" They felt that the voice which spoke to them was not inviting them to take up a new faith, a new religion, but to believe in the God of Abraham whom they had disbelieved, whose calling they had utterly misunderstood; who, they supposed, was gone far away from them, and whose favour was to be won by services and offerings of theirs. At once the truth burst upon them, that He was caring for them, and seeking for them, and that they had revolted from Him; that He must reveal to them their King and Deliverer; that He must make them right and true within. The words of the old books started to life in their minds. Here was the explanation of them. They had never yet claimed the privilege of their Covenant. They had never yet known what it was to be children of Israel. If God was indeed claiming them to be His children; if He would give them and their sons and daughters His Spirit, the Covenant was fulfilled to them; they might be Israelites indeed.

The Fellowship of Disciples.

If you read the history of the baptized community at Jerusalem, in the chapters from the second to the eighth of the Acts of the Apostles, you will see how this belief was carried out and expressed. We are told that the baptized continued in the Apostles'

doctrine and fellowship, that they ate their bread LECT. V.
with joy and singleness of heart, that no one said that
which he had was his own, but that they had all
things common, that they praised God, and were
daily with one accord in the temple. We have here *Community of goods.*
the picture of a united family in the midst of a city
of sects, a family which pays a quiet, dutiful, free
homage to its visible heads and fathers, but which
owns a higher relationship to the Father who has
chosen them to be His witnesses. The sense of His
free undeserved love makes them simple and glad in
receiving all common daily blessings. These blessings
they do not claim as separate possessions; their
privilege is to share them with their brethren. Their
spiritual treasures are common, they would make
their earthly treasures common too. But all this is *The Temple dearer to them than ever.*
connected in their minds with the Temple. That is
the witness of their sonship to God, and their brotherhood with each other. When they praise God there,
they feel that they are citizens of a kingdom of
Heaven, and that they have strength for their work
upon earth. It is not therefore that they do not
cease to be Jews because they have believed that
Jesus is the Christ. It is that faith which *makes*
them Jews. They cannot see any higher blessedness
than that of being so, in the fullest sense of the
words.

It was at the Beautiful gate of the Temple that the *The Apostolical Powers of Healing.*
Apostles Peter and John, who had no silver or gold
for a lame beggar that was lying there, gave him
instead, the power to rise up and walk. So they

Lect. V.
What these powers denoted.

declared to the people that the healing power which Jesus had exercised upon earth had not passed away, that He was really living and an actual King then; that He was the Prince of Life; that the God of Abraham, and of Isaac, and of Jacob, had owned Him and glorified Him as His Son. As children of the prophets and of the covenant which God made with their fathers, they bade their countrymen confess Him whom God had raised up to bless them, and turn them away every one of them from their iniquities.

Persecutions, chiefly Sadducean.

The Sadducean sect was now uppermost in the Sanhedrim; the high-priest apparently belonged to it. To that sect, the proclamation of invisible powers and of a resurrection was more galling than to the Pharisees. The notion of ignorant Galileans claiming a right to speak on such matters, was intolerable. They must be put down. The new strength of those cowards who had fled from their Master, when He was taken before this same Sanhedrim, of the Apostle who had denied Him to a maid-servant, is manifested. The private and unlettered men can look the scribes and rulers in the face, before whose very names they had trembled. They are sure that they have been called out by One who is higher than all these wise men, to testify that Jesus Christ of Nazareth is the stone that was set at nought by the builders, and is become the head of the corner. Therefore they could say, "Whether it be right in the sight of God to hearken unto you more than unto God, judge ye." The confidence which they felt before the chief priests

Confidence of the Disciples in the King of David's House.

THE NEW SOCIETY IN JERUSALEM. 61

and elders, was the same which they had when they returned to their own company. In public they had spoken of the Stone upon which Isaiah said the Jewish nation stood. In private they lifted up their voice to God with one accord, and said, "Lord, Thou art God, which hast made heaven, and earth, and the sea, and all that in them is: who by the mouth of Thy servant David hast said, Why did the heathen rage, and the people imagine vain things? The kings of the earth stood up, and the rulers were gathered together against the Lord, and against His Christ. For of a truth against Thy holy child Jesus, whom Thou hast anointed, both Herod, and Pontius Pilate, with the Gentiles, and the people of Israel, were gathered together, for to do whatsoever Thy hand and Thy counsel determined before to be done. And now, Lord, behold their threatenings: and grant unto Thy servants, that with all boldness they may speak Thy word, by stretching forth Thine hand to heal; and that signs and wonders may be done by the name of Thy holy child Jesus. And when they had prayed, the place was shaken where they were assembled together; and they were all filled with the Holy Ghost, and they spake the word of God with boldness." You see how the belief that Jesus was the actual King of the Jews, is involved in all their acts, their prayers, their unity.

<small>LECT. V.</small>

<small>Their Prayer.</small>

But was this only a faith or belief of theirs? Did they *think* they were called by God, or *were* they called? This is a very important question indeed for us to ask ourselves. I must answer once for all,—If

<small>TheCalling, how shown not to rest on human faith or feelings.</small>

LECT. V. I did not think they *were* called, if I supposed their calling depended upon their faith, and not their faith upon their calling, I should not be here to lecture to you at all; I do not know what I should have to lecture about. But this is St. Luke's answer, which is a better one than mine. Ananias and Sapphira were members of the community which ate their bread with joy and singleness of heart. They may have had these feelings as much as the rest. We are not told that they had not. We *are* told that the Holy Spirit was as much given to them as to their brethren, for St. Peter says they lied to that Holy Spirit. They pretended to have done a thing which they had not done. When that lie was brought home to their consciences, we are told that they fell dead at St. Peter's feet. This lying is the first crime we hear of after the descent of the Spirit. It is of this we shall have to hear at every step, as we proceed in the history. If you expect that I am going to describe a set of men who were eminently truthful, you will be grievously disappointed. I shall have to tell you of lies uttered by bad men and by good men, lies which have brought more terrible consequences upon those who spoke them, and upon the Church, and upon the world, than the punishment which befel Ananias and Sapphira. You will have to learn the meaning of these mighty and terrible, and yet most consolatory words, "God is true, though every man be a liar;" you will have to see that the called body after the Incarnation and Ascension of Christ proves its identity with the Israelitish nation, by

The Lie to the Holy Ghost.

Its Punishment.

Often repeated in Church History.

testifying of God as much through its falsehoods and its sins, as through its truth and its virtues.

LEC T. V.

Nor must you suppose that this was only the extraordinary crime of two individuals, and that the body of the disciples retained all the unity and gladness which are attributed to them at the outset. The chapter which follows the one respecting Ananias and Sapphira, speaks to us of murmurings of the Greeks against the Hebrews, because their widows were neglected in the daily ministration. Do not imagine from the use of the word 'Greeks' that there was any infusion of a new element, which the Jews would have rejected, into the baptized community of Jerusalem. These Hellenists had already been made proselytes, and had been admitted to the temple worship. Nevertheless, it is needful to notice this strife between people whose origin and whose education were unlike, at this early time, because we shall hear so much of it afterwards. The gift of the Spirit was the sign of a union between those whom customs and language had made different. But men may fight with the Spirit, who seeks to make them one, as Ananias fought with the Spirit, who sought to make him true. The story is important, secondly, as marking out one of the most familiar occasions of strife which call forth these animosities of tribe and race. The Hellenists thought their poor people were not as much regarded as the people of pure and native blood. And, thirdly, as the case of Ananias made necessary the first instance of *discipline* in the baptized community of Jerusalem, so this strife was the means of improving its *organiza-*

The Murmurs of the Hellenists.

Organization.

LECT. V.

Order of Deacons. Natural account of its origin.

The Deacons probably Hellenists.

tion. The Apostles were the only officers of this family hitherto. They had that kind of domestic paternal character which I have spoken of, which was not defined, and was not disputed. Now they bade the community to choose a set of men to whom part of their work might be given, that part of it about which the dispute had been. "Set over you," they said, "men full of faith and the Holy Ghost, who may see to this business. We will give ourselves to the word of God and to prayer." You remember, in how natural a manner, we are told, in the book of Exodus, the institution of Elders in the Jewish commonwealth began. Jethro, the father-in-law of Moses, who had lately come to the camp, saw that he was over-worked. He told him that he was doing what was not wise, and that he should choose men to help him. Moses accepted his counsel. He showed that he was a divine legislator by doing so. He recognised God's voice in circumstances, and events, and human advisers. So did the Apostles and the community at Jerusalem, in the appointment of Deacons.

I cannot say positively, but it seems most likely, that these Deacons were chosen from among that body which had complained; I mean that all, or the greater part of them, were Hellenists, and not pure Jews. Therefore it has appeared to many writers, and I think they are right, that this is a step forward in the history, one which we shall presently understand better. The Hellenists, who were men of heathen descent, if they were not actually born heathens, are a link between the Jews and the other people of the earth.

One might expect *them* to see, sooner than the native Jews, that the Gospel, if it had begun in Judæa, could not be confined to Judæa,—that it was meant for all the families of the earth. The sign at Pentecost of the Apostles speaking with different tongues, would put thoughts into their minds which the regular Israelites would hardly venture to dwell upon. Above all, the words of our Lord respecting the destruction of the Temple, and a redemption that was to come from that destruction, would impress themselves deeply on them; they would perhaps venture to utter them with a boldness, from which the Apostles, to whom the Temple had become now more than ever dear and venerable, would have shrunk.

The consequence.

However that may be, we find that Stephen the Deacon was the first teacher in the Jerusalem community, who was directly accused of speaking blasphemous words against the holy place and the law,—of saying that Jesus of Nazareth would destroy that place, and change the customs which Moses had delivered. Different synagogues are mentioned, as bringing this charge against him before the high-priest. One of them is the synagogue of the Alexandrians. It is not unlikely that these Alexandrians had been suspected by the Pharisees, of being themselves not as strict Jews as they ought to be. The Jews in Alexandria, as I told you, mixed much with Greek philosophers, and had learnt something from them as well as imparted something to them. They might be desirous to divert these charges from themselves, by showing their zeal against Stephen. And besides, no men

The accusation against Stephen.

The Synagogues of Alexandria

F

LECT. V. would have more disliked his teaching than they; for no men were more averse from the thought, that the King of the world and the Lord of men's hearts, could have taken flesh and dwelt among the peasants of Galilee.

Historical character of Stephen's defence.

It is said by St. Luke, that the witnesses against Stephen were *false* witnesses. And certainly, if they charged him with undervaluing the law of Moses, or the temple of Solomon, they must have been. The defence which he made before the high-priest thoroughly clears him of that accusation. It is altogether drawn from Jewish history. No one had studied it more, or had felt the whole purpose and connexion of it more. But then he saw that it was not a history merely of a Covenant, or a Law, or a Temple, but the history of the revelations of the God who made a covenant with their fathers, who gave the law, who dwelt in the temple. It was the promise of a more complete revelation of Him,—of a revelation in that righteous One of whom they had been the betrayers and murderers. And it was the history of the resistance of the chosen people in all ages, to the divine power which had been speaking and working in lawgivers and prophets,— a resistance which had now reached the highest point that it could reach. "Ye do always resist the Holy Ghost. As your fathers did, so do ye."

Ground of his condemnation for blasphemy.

These words sounded in Jewish ears as undoubted proofs of Stephen's guilt. He did believe that the reeds on which they were leaning were broken reeds; he did believe that they were trusting in the law and the temple, and were Atheists all the while. Their own consciences told them the same truth. They were cut to the heart, and gnashed upon him with their teeth. He declared that he saw the heavens opened and the Son of Man standing on the right hand of God. He was not fighting for an opinion; nor was he upheld by an opinion. He believed in an actual Person, in whom men were united to God. That was the blasphemy for which the high-priest had condemned Christ. And now "they cried out with a loud voice, and stopped their ears, and ran upon Stephen with one accord, and cast him out of the city, and stoned him. And the witnesses laid down their clothes at a young man's feet whose name was Saul." "Stephen cried with a loud voice, Lord, lay not this sin to their charge; and when he had so said, he fell asleep."

LECT. V.

His support.

With the account of his death, the history of the Jerusalem community may be said to end. We shall hear of it again, from time to time, in connexion with other topics. In a future Lecture, I shall have to speak of the man who, either at this time, or shortly after, presided over it. But here the narrative begins to expand. My object has been to show you how thoroughly Jewish this first baptized community was; how expressly it was a witness to the Jew, of the intent, and sacredness, and glory of his own calling. It was a witness to him, just as strongly, that he had utterly misunderstood his calling; that he did not know the object and worth of his own institutions. Those who had realized their worth

His death, a critical event in the History.

would be able, in due time, to fulfil the purpose of the original calling much more effectually than they had yet done. They would be able to show that He who was the glory of His people Israel, must, *therefore*, be a light to lighten the Gentiles.

LECTURE VI.

SAMARIA AND SYRIA.

THE death of Stephen may have been the effect of mere mob violence. But, if it was, the Sanhedrim was so well inclined to favour that violence, that they commenced a general persecution against those whom they called the Nazarenes. The Apostles remained in Jerusalem, the other disciples dispersed themselves abroad. Perhaps it is in favour of the opinion to which I alluded in my last Lecture, respecting the class from which the Deacons were chosen, that Philip the Deacon went down to Samaria and preached Christ there. If he was a Hellenist, he may have had less prejudice against a race with which the pure Jews had no dealings. It is true, that the people of Judæa despised also the Galileans, among whom so many of the Apostles were reckoned. But they looked upon the Galileans as uncouth, inferior men;—upon the Samaritans, as deserters from the true faith.

LECT. VI.
Philip the Deacon; in what sense a successor of Stephen.

You remember what we hear of the Samaritans in the Gospels. All our Lord's allusions to them would lead us to suppose, that their minds were more open than those of the Jews to sympathy and kindness;— that, if they knew less, they were more trustful and

Samaritans; their character as deduced from the Gospels.

LECT. VI. grateful. They were feeling their want of a teacher, as the woman showed who met our Lord at the well. They were more liable to be deluded by false teachers than a more hard and suspicious people; but they were also more prepared to welcome a true one. There were many sects among them; but they were not exactly like those we have read of in Judæa. They were craving for some power to come from the unseen world and act upon them. How it should come—how it should act—was the question which led to *their* controversies.

Philip's Message.

We are told that Philip caused great joy in the city, to which he preached of Christ. He told them the thing they were wanting to hear; that there was a mighty King over them; that He had subdued the powers of evil; that He had overcome death; that He baptized men with His Spirit. These words, which sounded so ridiculous and monstrous to the Sadducees, found their way to the hearts of the Samaritans. But Philip had a rival. The Roman empire at that time was teeming with magicians and enchanters. Adapting themselves to the different tendencies of the people among whom they came, they were all alike in this, that they spoke of wonderful agencies in the earth and air, to which men were subject; that they exhibited portents and miracles;

The Enchanter.

that they turned their exhibitions to profit. Simon, probably, mixed many Heathen notions with his teaching, for the Samaritans had much Heathenism in their own creed. Still he must have been a believer in the Hebrew Scriptures—most likely a circumcised man. The message which Philip brought, mingled with his previous dreams and notions. Christ seemed to him, not One who had come to make men righteous, but only a great Power out of the unseen world. In *that* character he believed in Him and was baptized.

<small>LECT. VI.</small>

The people of Samaria had received a message which had done them good: but they were not yet a community. The Apostles Peter and John came down from Jerusalem. Then that gift was bestowed upon them, which had bound the disciples at Jerusalem into a body. The Apostles were the instruments of conferring the gift. They may have wondered themselves, in spite of all the preparation their Lord had given them, that the Spirit should descend upon Samaritans. As might have been expected, the signs and powers which accompanied this gift, not the gift itself, seemed wonderful to Simon. He had been always a trader in spiritual charms. This was a higher kind of charm, which might, he thought, be purchased with money. St. Peter said, "Thy money perish with thee. Thou art in the gall of bitterness and the bond of iniquity." The traditions of the early Church represent Simon as the first of a class of men who looked upon Christ as an emanation from God, or one of the Powers which had descended from a mysterious world into this. On that ground they call him the first of Christian *heretics*. With these traditions are mixed others, which represent him as continuing to put forth *himself* as another great power and emanation from God, and as working

<small>A Society formed by the Spirit.</small>

<small>Simon's notion of spiritual powers.</small>

<small>The different falsehoods connected with the name of Simon.</small>

enchantments along with a woman who was his mistress. Later ages connect his name with the crime of treating spiritual powers and functions as subjects for bargain and sale. The reports respecting him are uncertain; some of them are evidently fabulous. The story in the Acts of the Apostles contains the substance and the meaning of them. If you meditate well upon that, you will have a key to many dark passages in the records of after times.

Ethiopia. Before we part with Philip the Deacon, we have a glimpse of the way in which the news that had cheered the Samaritans and bewildered Simon, may have found its way into another country. The minister of Candace, the Queen of the Ethiopians, a Jewish proselyte, and a reader of the prophets, is taught by the Deacon, of a Son of God who fulfilled the vision of Isaiah. He is baptized into the Name of that Son of God, and goes away rejoicing. But we hear no more of him, or of his country, or of his teacher. The story passes to the life of a young man who was to be the means of breaking down barriers between that country and all countries, which Philip had only begun to shake.

Saul the Greek, the Roman Citizen, the Hebrew of the Hebrews. Saul of Tarsus had had a Greek education in Asia Minor. His father, for some cause or other, had been made a Roman citizen. But he was a Hebrew of the Hebrews. Every other honour that belonged to him looked contemptible in his eyes, in comparison with that. To perfect himself in the law of his fathers and the traditions of the elders, he came up to Jerusalem and studied under Gamaliel, the most learned of the doctors there, the most profound and sagacious of the Pharisaical school. Whether he had heard the preaching of any of the Apostles, does not appear. At all events, he had heard Stephen, and believed the charge against him. The sect to which he belonged, he thought, was certainly bent upon destroying the customs which Moses had delivered, and the sacredness of the Temple. It must be put down. Saul was not at ease in his own mind. The law told him that he ought to be a righteous man. He tried to be righteous, and found that he was sinful. That struggle in himself made him fiercer against those who, he supposed, were despising the law. If he fought against them, he might win the peace for himself which he had not been worthy to receive yet. He was not mistaken. He did obtain it in that way.

<small>LECT. VI.

Grounds of his indignation against the disciples.</small>

The history of him brings us acquainted with a country which we have met with already in the Jewish records, and of which we shall hear much more. The sect which he wished to exterminate had reached Syria. The synagogues of Damascus were infected with the new doctrine. The power of the high-priest, which had been tried in Jerusalem, and had at last succeeded in bringing about the death of Stephen, might crush the evil seed there. Those who called on the name of Jesus might be stoned for blasphemy, in compliance with the Jewish law. If they fled for help to the tribunals of the city, they might be accused of sedition. A man who is thoroughly in earnest, may do much to put down men and women

<small>*Syria.*

Saul's journey to Damascus.</small>

LECT. VI.
Christ revealed in him that he might preach Him among the Gentiles.

who hold a truth, if he cannot put down the truth itself. You will find plentiful proofs of that hereafter. But then there is a danger in the case of *such* a man, that the truth will put him down. It was so with Saul. You have read the story of his conversion often and often; no account of it can be so good as that which St. Luke gives us, and that which he himself gave to the Jews and to Agrippa. He describes Jesus Christ as revealing Himself to him,—as saying, "I am He whom thou persecutest,"—as telling him that it was hard to kick against the pricks. There was a blaze of outward glory around him,—a brightness which blinded his eyes, and made him know that it was no phantom he was fighting with, but a Person, a King, One who had taken a human body and had glorified it. Still it was the revelation which was made of Christ to his conscience—the witness which was borne to him, that a righteous Being was striving with him there, and that he had been fighting with Him there, which subdued him then, and held him captive afterwards. It was this, he says, which fitted him to preach Christ among the Gentiles.

A Preacher first to the Jews.

He was not called to that work at present. When he was baptized, and the scales fell from his eyes, he preached in the synagogues and convinced *the Jews*, and that publicly, that Jesus was the Christ. Like the Apostles at Jerusalem, his message was, that the Son of David had come; though he had learnt that that Son of David must be the Son of God,—that His highest throne must be over the spirits and hearts of men,—that other chains must be broken from his

Nation than any with which Rome could bind it. These thoughts were apparently deepened in his mind, not only by his disputations in the synagogues, but by a period of solitude in Arabia; perhaps, also, by the humiliation of discovering that the disciples of Jesus in Jerusalem were very slow to recognise him as a brother.

<small>LECT. VI.</small>

Meantime, the man in that Jerusalem society who had first proclaimed to his countrymen at Pentecost, that He whom they had crucified was Lord and Christ, had to learn, by a humiliating process also, that he had reckoned men unclean whom God had cleansed. You will not wonder, after what I have told you, that St. Peter had become even a stricter Jew since the descent of the Spirit, than he was before, because he learnt then first to understand what his Jewish calling meant. Therefore it was most natural for him, when he had a vision of a number of unclean animals, which he was bidden to eat, to say, "Not so, Lord; for I have never eaten any thing that is common or unclean." All the precepts and exclusions of the law were sacred in his eyes. And yet everything had been leading him to think more and more of Christ, as the Friend of man, and the Deliverer of man. It would have been horrible to doubt that He had taken the nature of man, and died the death of man; horrible to think of Him as *merely* one of the Jewish race. A man—you will find this out by-and-by for yourselves—may have two thoughts in his mind which he does not the least know how to reconcile; though he

<small>St. Peter at Joppa.</small>

<small>His vision.</small>

LECT. VI. cannot part with either, and though they often distract his practice. If he is a faithful man, God will reconcile them for him, in some way or other. When the doubts are thickening in him, and some light has been let in upon them, there will be an *event* which calls upon him to act. When he does the thing which he has to do, the knots in his mind become disentangled. Three men came to Peter, asking him to go to a Centurion of the Italian band. He went, as he says, without gainsaying, understanding it to be the import of his vision that he was to go. He explained very simply, that God had shown him what he never knew before,—that in every nation he that served Him and worked righteousness was accepted of Him. He perceived that the Deliverer and the King, whom he had proclaimed to his own countrymen, was He of whom Cornelius and his friends had need to hear. They did hear his message concerning Him. The same sign which had testified that the Spirit was with the Apostles, testified that He was with these Roman soldiers. St. Peter said, " Who can forbid water, that these should not be baptized who have received the Holy Ghost as well as we ?"

The vision fulfilled.

New discovery.

The baptism of the Spirit and of water.

Antioch; its place in the New Testament History.

We are told that the community in Jerusalem was startled, as we may well suppose it would be, by what St. Peter had done. He justified himself. And they began to perceive that repentance might be granted to the uncircumcised also. Still there was no thought, that Gentiles could be added to *their* society. A band of disciples in Jerusalem must still testify of the glory of the Temple worship, of the Covenant, of the

Sacrifice. There was, however, another city in which the Jews had a powerful colony, and which was closely connected with all their past history; but which had no temple and no holy associations. The city to which Paul was travelling, when he was stopped by the vision was not, you will remember, the capital city of Syria. That, I have told you, was Antioch. There dwelt a rich, luxurious, rather clever, particularly frivolous, Gentile population. It was a great commercial city of the empire, as corrupt, perhaps, as any I could name. For many centuries, we shall be hearing of it. We are glad, therefore, to be introduced to it, by the divine historian. It holds a very memorable place indeed in his narrative; for there first we see a community growing up, in which there are both Jews and Gentiles, and not merely or exclusively Gentiles that had been already Jewish proselytes. The Heathen inhabitants appear to have perceived, that it was not one of those Societies to which they had been used. If it was a new Jewish sect, it was a sect entirely different from any that had been among them before. For there was a readiness to meet and embrace Gentiles, to associate with them, even to eat with them, which was at variance with all they had known of Jews hitherto. One cannot tell how many Gentiles there may have been in this Antioch society. Most likely, they were few in comparison with the Jews. But they must have been admitted without being circumcised, and the distinction between them and the Jewish believers in Jesus must have been *gradually* wearing away. Perhaps very gradually, for it must have taken a long time to convince any Jew that he could safely break through precepts that were so venerable and divine. A vision from heaven had made Peter see, that there was another law higher than these, to which they must give way. And when he came to Antioch, it would appear that he was ready for awhile to act upon this revelation,—to mix freely with those who had not been circumcised. Afterwards, we learn from the Epistle to the Galatians,—for I believe we ought to refer the narrative in the 2d chapter of that epistle, to this period,—certain came down from James at Jerusalem, who tempted Peter to stand aloof and to "dissemble." There was another good and brave man, a Jew of Cyprus, Barnabas, the son of consolation, who had seen with exceeding delight the growth of the mixed community at Antioch and the accession of Greeks to the faith of Christ. Yet he could not resist the authority of Peter; he was carried away for a while, by the same dissimulation. But he had brought with him out of Arabia a man who had been learning a different lesson. The pupil of Gamaliel, the young Jew of Tarsus, the Hebrew of the Hebrews, who had persecuted the disciples to the death expressly as levellers, now resisted Peter to the face because he was to be blamed. Every thing in the Gospel of Christ which he was to preach, depended upon the question whether He was the Lord of man or only the Lord of the Jews; whether He had redeemed and reconciled men or only a certain class of men. Here then is another great epoch in the Apostolical history. The disciples, we are told, were called Christians first at Antioch. It was not a name, which they chose for themselves. The Heathen population of the city, who were celebrated for their nicknames, probably bestowed it upon them. But it expressed the memorable fact that a community consisting primarily of Jews, and directed exclusively by them, could not be denoted by that name or by the name of any sect among them. New sects might indeed spring up in this community. This name, Christian, might itself be made the symbol of one. But to the disciples it signified that they were witnesses for a King, and a King whom all nations would in due time be brought to acknowledge.

Another critical event.

LECTURE VII.

THE CHURCHES IN GENTILE CITIES.

Lect. VII.
St. Peter's error rose out of the profoundest truth.

You may have wondered sometimes at that passage in the history of St. Peter, to which I alluded at the end of my last Lecture. What I said then may diminish your wonder. It was not only the most natural thing in the world, that St. Peter should cling earnestly and passionately, to his Jewish habits. It was the effect of his divine teaching that he clung to them; if he had not prized them, he would have denied Christ. It was true that he had no right to refuse to eat with the Gentiles at Antioch. That, as St. Paul told him, and as his own vision had told him before, was, in another way, to deny Christ. But he was tempted into this error by the conviction which was the strongest and deepest one in his heart. St. Paul would not have wished him to part with *that*. If he had, St. Paul's own witness would have been an ineffectual witness. He would not have been able to tell the Gentiles that God was calling them, that they were to form parts of an Ecclesia.

The Mission of Paul and Barnabas.

I want you to understand this, because I am now coming to St. Paul's interpretation of this word. It could not be learnt in Jerusalem. It was only beginning to be learnt at Antioch. Its force was to come out when the Holy Ghost said to the disciples, who were gathered together in that city, "Separate me Saul and Barnabas for the work whereunto I have called them."

Lect. VII.

You see how strictly the language respecting a calling, which we have traced through the Scriptures, is preserved here, and how surely Paul and Barnabas felt, and those from whom they went forth felt, that they were not sent on their errand by men, though men might be the instruments and agents in sending them, but by the Spirit of God Himself. You remember in St. Paul's Epistles how vehemently he asserts his title to be an Apostle,—when many wished to deny him the name, because he was not one of the twelve whom our Lord first chose; how certain he is that his designation is as true as theirs, that he was as much selected by Christ Himself for his office as they were. And this he maintained, not for his own sake or his own glory, but because if he had not maintained it, he would have admitted that his Lord's work was bounded by the years in which He was visibly walking on earth; he would have denied that He had ascended up to reign and to fill all things; he would have destroyed the foundation upon which the Church in all ages afterwards was to stand. Never fancy then that St. Paul, because he would not limit God's calling to the Jewish nation, made light of that calling. His whole business on earth was to magnify it, to prove the reality of it;

Idea of a calling never lost sight of.

Paul's right to the name Apostle.

G

LECT. VII. first of all to show what it behoved a Hebrew of the Hebrews to do in order to carry it out; then to show that there can be no true society established upon earth which has not God's calling for its groundwork,—that no society can subsist upon earth, each member of which is not called into it by Him.

Paul and Barnabas in the Synagogues.

You have often heard that the journey which Paul and Barnabas now took, was a missionary journey to different Gentile countries. That statement is true; nevertheless, I would beg you to notice that into whatsoever place St. Paul went, he first sought out the Jewish synagogue. He never thought of delivering a message to other men, till he had first delivered it to those who worshipped there. So it was when they went to Cyprus. "At Salamis," it is said, " they preached the word of God in the synagogue of the Jews." In that island the first conspicuous Gentile convert joined them,—Sergius Paulus, the deputy or governor of the country. He is a specimen of the kind of influence which Heathens were often receiving from Jews who turned their knowledge of the spiritual world into a trade. Elymas the sorcerer, we are told, was a Jew,—one who abused his own light to make other men's minds dark, and who was smitten with bodily blindness as a retribution for that greatest of all crimes. It was a time, as I told you before, when the belief in spiritual *powers* was prevailing more than it had ever prevailed before, though the belief in *righteousness* had never been so weak. It was the calling of St. Paul, as it had been the calling

Sergius Paulus and Elymas.

of Moses, to show everywhere that power is from the righteous God, and that when it is dedicated to the service of evil, it will be confounded.

Again we find the two Apostles at Antioch in Pisidia, going into the synagogue. If you read St. Paul's speech there you will see how entirely it is addressed to the men of Israel; how the glad tidings which he declared to them were, that "the promise which was made unto their fathers, God had fulfilled the same unto them, their children, in that he had raised up Jesus again; as it is also written in the second Psalm, Thou art my Son, this day have I begotten thee." But then he added, "By Him all that believe are justified from all things, from which ye could not be justified by the law of Moses." And he warned them who heard him to beware lest that should come upon them which was spoken by the prophet: "Behold, ye despisers, wonder and perish; for I will work a work in your days which ye will not believe, though a man declare it unto you." Just because St. Paul prized the covenant and law which had been given to his countrymen, he was sure that they wanted something which the covenant and the law could not do for them,—that they needed a *Person* to justify them and make them righteous men. But when he spoke of Christ having justified them by His resurrection, it was clear that his words could not be confined to those to whom they were addressed. The Gentiles asked that these words might be spoken to them, and the next sabbath-day nearly all the city came together to hear Paul. The barrier had been

Antioch in Pisidia.

St. Paul the Jew and the witness against Judaism.

The Gentiles discover the message to be for them.

broken down. A Gospel was proclaimed to mankind. This is marked by St. Luke as a critical moment in the work of the two Apostles. Not only the worst part of the Jews, but devout and honourable men and women, were offended at the boldness with which they declared that it was necessary first to give their message to the Jews, but that since they judged themselves unworthy of eternal life, lo! they turned to the Gentiles. A persecution was raised against the Apostles, of which the Jews were the instigators, but in which they could easily persuade Heathens to take part. They fled from that city, and presently we find them in a purely Heathen population, among the rude men of Lycaonia, who hailed them as gods come down in the likeness of men, and who wished to offer them sacrifices. To them they speak of the God who had made the world and all things in it, and who had not left Himself without witness, giving them rain from heaven and fruitful seasons, filling their hearts with food and gladness, and who was now bidding them turn from their vanities to serve the living God.

You see how thoroughly St. Paul was fulfilling the function of a Jew, while he was bearing this protest against idolatry. But mark how the protest differed from that which the other Jews were bearing. The words contained a message of glad tidings to all the people of the earth. The living God was calling them out of idolatry, was claiming them to be His people. Wherever the sun had been shining, wherever the rain had been falling, there were tokens of His loving-kindness. And the men who had received these blessings were those whom He was now claiming in His Son as members of His own family. It is in this way that the word *Gospel*, or glad tidings, which is one of the favourite words in St. Paul's epistles, is connected with the word *Revelation*, or unveiling, which is another, and with the word *Ecclesia*, which is a third. The good news is, that God has revealed Himself to mankind in His Son, and that He is calling them out by His Spirit to be no longer worshippers of a multitude of things, to be no longer creatures of sense, to be no longer separated from each other, by the different objects which they pursued, and the different impulses which governed them.

Relation of the words Gospel, Revelation, Ecclesia, to each other.

It is just at this point of the history, then, that we hear of an Ecclesia rising up in each of the cities in which Paul had preached, and of his ordaining Elders over it. That was the name which each of these societies took. Any other would have been inconsistent with the lessons which St. Paul had been learning all his life, and with the message which he was now delivering. He was not preaching to them a new religion, he was not forming a sect. He was bidding them cast away religions and sects, that they might own the Father who was binding them all in one, the Lord who had been speaking to them in their consciences, and from whom all the light had come which had shown them what was right and what was wrong, and the Spirit who was working in them to make them choose the right and reject the wrong.

St. Paul, a preacher of God, not the propagator of a Religion.

But we cannot be surprised that the sight of such bodies rising up in the cities where synagogues were,

Offence given by the name Ecclesia.

already established, and including those whom the synagogue looked upon as unclean, should have greatly startled the Jews. Little as they had understood their calling, much as they had sunk into mere religious sects or mere traders, they still gloried in the name of the called and chosen nation. How dared any one take that from them and bestow it upon people coming out of any tribe or kindred of the earth? And this feeling could not be confined to the Jews who rejected our Lord. Those who acknowledged Him, as we have seen, had been awakened to a new feeling of the dignity of their Jewish calling. Was not this a very rude assault upon that feeling? Teachers told the Gentiles in these churches that except they were circumcised and kept the law of Moses, they could not be saved. Their baptism no doubt brought them a certain way, as of old it had brought Heathens to the outer court of the Temple; but unless, over and above this, they received the sign of the old covenant, they never could have the truest and the highest privileges of the chosen people. Such words were heard elsewhere; of course they would soon reach Jerusalem, and be especially listened to there. The Apostles and Elders came together to consider of this matter. We have seen how strong the inclination of Peter was to magnify circumcision, how hard it was for him to mix with Gentiles. The feeling must have been stronger still in James. Yet when they were thus met together, and the whole question came before them, both perceived that they should be giving up their faith in Jesus Christ, even their faith in Him as the Son of David, if they enforced the practices of the law and the sign of the Jewish covenant upon the Gentile people. They acknowledged the genuineness of the work in which Paul and Barnabas had been engaged.

Lect. VII.

James proposed the decision to which they should come. He asserted the worth of the synagogues, in which Moses of old times had been preached in the Gentile cities. He felt how important it was for the Gentiles to abstain from those acts which would give serious offence to their Jewish brethren, and what danger there was, if they fancied themselves free from all legal obligations, of their falling into the practices which had been so much connected with idolatrous feasts and worship. He would therefore write to the Gentiles that they should abstain from pollutions of idols, and from fornication, and from things strangled, and from blood; the union of the more serious precepts with the other two being justified by the fact, which St. Paul afterwards asserted most strongly in his letter to the Corinthians, that it is a sin in the member of a Church to offend and injure the conscience of his brother, in things which are themselves indifferent.

Ground taken by St. James and St. Peter.

The Letter; its meaning.

These precepts, with the positive denunciation of all attempts to put any other yoke upon them, were addressed in letters to "the brethren which are of the Gentiles in Antioch, and Syria, and Cilicia." The letters assume an authority; "It has seemed good to the Holy Ghost and to us." This authority is not said to be based upon any privileges peculiar to that age. The Apostles and Elders had met in the faith

Its authority.

88   ON CHURCH HISTORY.

LECT. VII. of Christ's assurance, that where two or three were gathered together, He was in the midst of them. They were seeking to bind together men in His Name, to remove the obstacles to brotherhood. They were sure that the Holy Ghost was with them in this work; they had no doubt that He was guiding them to what was the best decision for that emergency, though after circumstances, ordained by God, might *The rules adapted to an exigency.* make those rules inapplicable. Why should not they think so, seeing that their decree went upon the ground that the rules which they believed that God Himself had laid down for the chosen body in other generations, were not intended for that generation, and ought to be dispensed with, because they interfered with principles which were unchangeable? You will have occasion to remember what I have said on this point hereafter.[1]

I shall now go rapidly through the remaining chapters of the Acts of the Apostles, chiefly for the purpose of pointing out to you the Churches of which I shall have most to speak in future lectures. In the 6th *Phrygia and Galatia; Bithynia.* verse of the 16th chapter, it is said, "When they had gone throughout Phrygia and the region of Galatia, and were forbidden by the Holy Ghost to preach the word in Asia, after they had come to Mysia, they

---

[1] The two events, of John Mark's return to Jerusalem, in the course of the Apostolic tour, and of St. Paul's dispute with Barnabas respecting him, have both reference to this crisis in the history. They probably denote great suspicion in the first, some in the second, respecting the intentions of St. Paul,—whether he might not be possessed with a zeal for Gentile conversion, which would make him forget the covenant of his fathers. The circumcision of Timothy, mentioned in the beginning of the sixteenth chapter, was probably designed to correct these impressions.

essayed to go into Bithynia, but the Spirit suffered them not." These words bring before us a number of countries in Asia Minor, some of which you meet with also in the superscription to St. Peter's Epistle, one of which is connected with a most memorable Epistle of St. Paul. When it is said that the Apostle was not allowed to preach the Gospel in Asia, the meaning is, that he could not then go to Ephesus, or visit the Greek colonies on the coast of the Archipelago. He was summoned to another work, one which brought him, probably for the first time in his life, into Europe. *LECT. VII.*

Macedonia was a field into which St. Paul had perhaps not thought of entering when he left Antioch. He goes first to Philippi, thence to Amphipolis and Apollonia, thence to Thessalonica, thence to Berœa. The condition of the Churches in this country is brought very livingly before us in the Epistle to the Philippians, and in the two to the Thessalonians. You will remark, if you read them carefully, how very different their circumstances were from those of the Galatians, and of the Churches in Asia generally, though they were exposed to a number of the same influences—especially from Jews. In Philippi there is no mention made of a synagogue; but there were Jews who went out of the city by a river-side to offer prayers. A woman seems to have been the first European convert of St. Paul. Another woman was the cause of his imprisonment. That was not owing to any dread which the Roman authorities had of the disciples of Jesus. They did not distinguish them *Macedonia.*

Philippi.

Lydia.

The Enchantress.

from other Jews. But the traders in enchantments, whose gains were disturbed by the Apostle, had influence with the magistrates to procure the punishment of him and of Silas. The opening of the prison doors was a witness that a God of Righteousness—a Deliverer—was mightier than the powers before which the Philippians were trembling. The jailer, when, in his fear and terror, he asked what he might do to save himself from the power he dreaded, was told of a Saviour in whom he might trust. In His name the seller of purple, the enchantress, the keeper of the prison, were bidden to rejoice together. A Church grew up, of which these were some of the elements. The Apostle of this European Church bore out his witness for the true King, by asserting the sanctity of civil order. He maintained his own dignity and position as a Roman citizen; he would not leave the prison till the magistrates came and fetched him out. In Thessalonica and Berœa, the influence of the Jews was much stronger than in Philippi, though they could not injure the Apostle except by appealing to the fears and prejudices of the Heathen population. "The men who have turned the world upside down proclaim another King, one Jesus," was the argument by which they stirred up the people.

Such an argument would have been quite ineffectual at Athens, the city to which Paul was conveyed from Berœa. He found Jews living in that city—trading in it—probably as little affected by any of its beauties, as they were moved by its idolatries. The spirit of the true Hebrew of the Hebrews was completely overwhelmed by these. Yet no one entered more thoroughly into all that was best and truest in the minds of the idolaters—no one perceived so thoroughly what a witness there was in their poetry, their philosophy, their very worship, against the corruptions to which they had yielded. Their poets had said, "We also are His offspring;" their philosophers had believed that there was a God near them and about them, whom they were seeking to grasp. Amidst all their worship of demons and idols, there was an "unknown God" to whom they were bowing down. He came to declare to them that unknown God; to make known Him in whom they were living, and moving, and having their being; to tell them *how* they were His offspring;—thus to recal them from the worship of things made by art and man's device; thus to bring them into that spiritual world of which they had dreamed. These words were wonderfully adapted to all that had been deepest in the hearts of their fathers. But Paul spoke of a living Judge, and of One who had risen from the dead. This was a demand upon *actual* faith. He called upon them to be right, and not merely to talk of right—to hate wrong, and not merely to speculate about it. The Athenians had passed into frivolous gossips and debaters. A disputation was dear to them, a gospel was lost upon them.

St. Paul's appeal to Greek Faith.

In Corinth, many of the same habits of mind were found which had resisted the Apostle's preaching at Athens. But there St. Paul found the Jewish element more strong; for Corinth was a great trading city.

Corinth.

LECT. VII. He reasoned in the synagogue. Then, as at Antioch, when the Jews rejected him, he turned to the Gentiles. He was not, however, without Jewish converts. The ruler of the synagogue was baptized. The Jews sought in vain to move the Proconsul against him. Gallio was a philosopher—a friend of Seneca: the disputes of Jews about their law were nothing to him. In the Church which grew up in this city were prejudiced Jews, Gentiles who scorned Hebrew formalities, and a third class, who had received an influence from Alexandria. I shall have to say more to you of these parties hereafter. I mention them here, that you may see how various were the spirits with which the Apostle had to deal, and how remarkably the Churches received the character of the countries to which they belonged.

Character of the Church there.

Ephesus.

There is one more which I shall speak of. In some respects it is the most important of all, after Jerusalem. This is Ephesus, a city which had almost as Greek a character as Corinth, and yet which belonged to Asia. It was one of the great commercial emporiums of the world; strangers came to it from all quarters. There was the temple of the great goddess Diana, in whom men had once believed, and whom they still worshipped. Thither resorted the magicians and diviners, in whom they believed still—so far as they believed in anything. There St. Paul encountered the greatest opposition he had ever yet encountered from idolaters—that is to say, from the men who profited by idolatry—the craftsmen who made silver shrines to Diana. It is in the Epistle which he

Character of the city.

wrote to this Church, that he brings out more fully, I think, than any where else, the meaning of his work as an Apostle to the Gentiles—the revelation which had been made to him of all being fellow-heirs in Christ—the truth that there was an older calling than that of the Jew, "because," as the Apostle says, "God hath chosen us out in Christ before the worlds were, to be holy, and without blame before Him in love."

The Epistle to the Ephesians.

The parting with the elders of this Church, which is recorded in the 20th chapter of the Acts of the Apostles, is not only solemn for its own sake, and solemn for all people and ministers who read it in this day; it also marks the conclusion of a stage in the Apostle's labours and in his life. He was then on his way to Jerusalem, to keep the feast of Pentecost. When he came there, James and the elders exhorted him to do an act which would prove his reverence for the law of Moses, and confute the charges which they had heard against him, that he did not live as an Israelite. He followed their advice. But while he was purifying himself in the Temple, a tumult was raised against him. The chief Roman officer in the city came down to quell it. St. Paul was permitted to address the people. They listened to him till he spoke of being sent to the Gentiles; then a new tumult was raised, and his life was in danger. The chief captain again interfered. He called together the priests and the Sanhedrim. St. Paul was brought before them. The Jewish sects were now becoming more violently divided than ever

St. Paul going to Jerusalem.

The Jewish mob.

against each other. The Pharisees were inclined to favour Paul, through opposition to the Sadducees, who were more bent upon destroying him when they understood that he had been bred up by their opponents. A body of zealots conspired to murder him privately. He was saved from them and sent to the governor of the province, who now dwelt at Cæsarea. There he lay in prison for two years, waiting the judgment of two successive governors. Finally he appealed to the Emperor, from the provincial ruler. After he had been heard before King Agrippa, and had desired that his judges might be both almost and altogether such as he was, except his bonds, he set out for Rome. He was saved from shipwreck at Melita. St. Luke's narrative closes when he enters as a prisoner into the capital of the world. You will see hereafter why there could not have been a fitter termination to a book which sets forth the beginnings of the Church upon earth.

LECTURE VIII.

ST. JAMES, ST. PETER, AND ST. PAUL.

You will remember that St. James, St. Peter, and St. John are called Apostles of the Circumcision, and, as such, are distinguished from St. Paul, who is called the Apostle of the Gentiles. You will remember also that their Epistles are called Catholic, and, as such, are distinguished from those of St. Paul, which are addressed to the Church of Rome, the Church of Corinth, the Churches of Galatia, &c. To understand what one of these differences has to do with the other,—why the Jewish Apostles should have this name *Catholic* or *Universal*, which one would have thought was not applicable to them,—you must turn to their letters. It is not my business to explain them to you; but I must glance at them, that I may enable you to appreciate the positions which the writers occupied in the first age, and that you may judge better of what I shall have to tell you respecting the effect of their teachings in subsequent ages.

1. If you open the Epistle of St. James you will see that it is addressed to the Twelve Tribes. I dare say this superscription has sometimes puzzled you. You have said, Did not St. James then write to the

Church—to Christians? Have we not been told that he was the first Overseer or Bishop of the Church in Jerusalem, the mother Church of the world? I think if you read what I said to you about the Society which arose in Jerusalem after the day of Pentecost, you will find the answer to these questions. That Society existed, we have seen, to testify that God had called out the Jewish nation to declare His Righteousness and Unity and Government. You can only do this, it said, if you acknowledge your King; Him in whom God's Righteousness has been manifested, in whom we are a united people, who is the Lord over our hearts and spirits. This Society failed in its witness, if it led the Jews to suppose it was a new sect. Of course they would call it so; but the disciples were, by all their acts and words, to refute the charge. No one, I apprehend, understood this calling of the Jerusalem fellowship better than St. James. When the other Apostles had gone forth in different ways to execute the commands of the Master, he probably remained in the capital. If he was, as there is good reason to suppose he was, the man who is called in the Gospel the brother of our Lord, he had another claim on the affections of baptized Jews besides his divine calling; another claim upon the respect of all the Jews, for he would be of the house of David. The reverence which would be paid to him by the disciples of Jesus would be that which children pay to a father; he would preside over the Christian community by no express election, but by a right which no one would think of disputing, because it would be seen that he was only chief of all by being servant of all. He appears to have succeeded wonderfully in convincing the citizens of Jerusalem, that he had a righteousness which exceeded that of the Scribes and Pharisees. He showed more respect for the ordinances which they worshipped than they did; yet the testimony of his life and of his letter was that the true service and undefiled before God and the Father was to visit the fatherless and the widows in their affliction, and to keep oneself unspotted from the world. You have wondered sometimes, perhaps, that he does not introduce the name of Christ oftener into his Epistle. I think the more you study it, the more you will see that he preaches Christ by that very silence. He sets forth a kingdom over the heart and tongue; he tells his disciples that God had begotten them by the word of truth to be a kind of first-fruits of his creatures; he tells them of one who binds rich and poor together; he shows them that they might believe there was one God, and yet only tremble like devils, whereas the true God was one in whom they were to trust, the Father of Lights, in whom was no variableness, neither shadow of a turning. He was thus leading his countrymen to perceive that One had come who fulfilled the promises made to their fathers, by revealing the God who had spoken to them, and whom they longed to know better. In proportion as the Jerusalem believers in Jesus entered into the meaning of their teacher, they really represented the

His reputation in the city.

His rare allusions to the name of Christ, how explained.

Twelve Tribes. They showed that the called body was still doing its work on the earth.

The great work of St. James then, I conceive, was to preserve this all-important truth, that the divine Society would still go on living, that it was immortal as the Prophets had declared it must be. No one saw more clearly than St. James that a tremendous convulsion was coming on his city and his land. But he can preach patience because he is certain that the great Husbandman is patient; that He watches over the seed which He has put into the ground; and that whatever changes it may undergo, whatever death it may pass through, it will spring up at last, and bring forth its intended fruit. St. James's Epistle teaches us that the called body, the Church, was one nation originally, though it consisted of twelve tribes, and that it must be one always, of however many tribes it may consist. And this is a testimony which gives his Epistle the best right possible to the name of Catholic.

2. If you turn next to the First Epistle of St. Peter you will perceive that it also is not addressed to a Church. The name *Ecclesia* does not once occur in it. But the dispersed in Pontus, Galatia, Cappadocia, Asia, and Bithynia, are described as elect, according to the foreknowledge of God the Father, through sanctification of the Spirit, unto obedience and sprinkling of the blood of Jesus Christ. That name which occurs so rarely in the Epistle of St. James comes before us at every moment, in the letter

of this Apostle. And Christ is presented to us especially as the Corner Stone of a Spiritual Temple, the Head of a Royal Priesthood, the Shepherd of Souls. This language, drawn from the records of the chosen people, was wonderfully suitable to tell the Jews, who were scattered through all countries of the world, and were suffering hardships and contempt from all around them, that they were still one people, when they owned the one Lord, who had always been the true and only bond of their union, and who had now been revealed, that they might feel and claim their fellowship in Him.

I do not mean at all to say that this language is restricted to circumcised men. The position of St. Peter was very different from that of St. James. He was not tied to Jerusalem; he was a Missionary to the outcasts of Israel. He had been taught that the Gentiles, among whom they dwelt, were Christ's subjects, and that he was to claim them for Him. But he, as much as St. James, looked upon the Israelites as still the called and chosen body, to which converts from the Gentiles were to be added. When they were added, they formed one body, or family, scattered throughout the nations; bound together in one invisible Head. The distinctions of tribes and races were lost for him in this great Unity. By no one writer of the New Testament are we so continually reminded that the Unity can subsist only in Christ; that on the rock of His divine humanity the Church must stand, if the gates of Hell are not to prevail against it. No one has borne so strong a protest, by

Language not limited to Jews.

But assumes the Jewish race as the nucleus of any divine fellowship.

LECT. VIII.

Unity in Christ, but no recognition of nations.

anticipation, against any attempt to put him or any man in place of the Son of God; but it is not to him we must look to tell how in this one Fellowship there may be a Church of Italy, a Church of France, a Church of England.

St. Peter's expectation of a new world.

At the same time, St. Peter proclaims even more distinctly than St. James that a tremendous crash and overthrow was coming in his own day upon all society, and especially upon that divine Society, which he believed would, in some wonderful manner, be brought through the fires. He had listened to his Master's words, when he stood by the Temple, and the disciples marked the goodly stones of it. How could he doubt that those words would be fulfilled, as He who could not lie had declared they would, in that generation? I cannot read the words in his second Epistle, without being sure that he believed events were now at hand which could be described as nothing less than the extinction and conflagration of an old world and the birth of a new. And I cannot help feeling that this expectation, though it may also point to something still to come, had its accomplishment then; and that if it had not, Modern History would be a maze without a plan.

St. Paul.

3. You will now perceive, I think, in what especial sense St. Paul was an Apostle of the Gentiles, and why, being such, he was obliged to give his letters a form altogether different from that which St. James and St. Peter gave to theirs. I have shown you that he did not prize his Jewish birth and covenant less than they did; that he addressed the Gospel first to

his own countrymen; to the Gentiles, as he says in the Epistle to the Romans, that he might provoke them to jealousy. He who would have been accursed from Christ for the sake of his kinsmen after the flesh, cannot have been estranged from them by any persecutions which he suffered at their hands. But he was led to perceive that the Jewish calling, though a most true and holy one, was not a foundation deep enough for a Jew himself to stand upon. He was called to testify of the Deliverer of man; he was to say to Greeks and Romans, "You too have a calling in Christ. You do not acquire it when you become one with us. We must become one with you in order that we may realize the blessing which God intends for us." The consequence was that St. Paul had to speak to men just as he found them, to become, as he expresses it, all things to all men. "God," this was the principle which he asserted in his speech at Athens, " hath ordered the times before appointed, and the bounds of their habitation, that they should seek the Lord, if haply they might feel after Him and find Him, though He be not far from any one of us." The history then, the languages, the geographical position, the peculiar temperament and character of every people on the earth, had for him the most divine meaning. They were indications of the method which God was pursuing with them, signs, however they might be disregarded, of the steps by which he had been revealing Himself to them, and had been and was drawing them to Himself.

Lect. VIII.

His love for his nation.

Becomes the assertor of the sacredness of all national distinctions.

102   ON CHURCH HISTORY.

Lect. VIII.
His Epistles to the Romans and Corinthians.

Thus the Epistle to the Romans is marvellously adapted to the mind of a people which had grown great by reverence for Law and for Righteousness, and which had now set up mere Power and Will against both. The Epistle to the Corinthians is addressed to the peculiar habits of the Greek character, to the Greek passion for wisdom, and to all the evils that had grown up beside that noble passion; to the Greek skill in detecting subtle distinctions, and to the party spirit which was the abuse of it. Christ, as manifesting God's righteousness to all who believe, and as justifying men's consciences which the Law accused, is presented to the one. Christ, as revealing the wisdom of God in the weakness of man, as the Head of a body consisting of many members, to the other. If the Roman Church and the Greek Church received his lessons, they would be the means of raising their countrymen out of their corruptions, and of enabling them to exercise the good and glorious gifts which God had bestowed upon them; if not, they might exhibit a worse example than the Heathens had done of their evil tendencies, and of the abuse of God's treasures.

Epistle to the Hebrews.

Some people have said, Since St. Paul was the Apostle of the Gentiles, he cannot have written the Epistle to the Hebrews. Others have said, That Epistle is utterly unlike the rest of his Epistles in style and manner. I cannot admit the force of either argument. I believe his office of Apostle to the Gentiles made him more, not less, able to understand

THE THREE APOSTLES, AND THE LATTER DAYS. 103

the peculiarities of his own nation; more, not less, interested in explaining to his baptized countrymen what *their* calling was, and how they must fulfil it. If he did this work effectually he must make his letter to them entirely different in its whole tone and form, from every other which he wrote. And certainly the writer of this Epistle, whoever he was, has done his work most effectually.

Lect. VIII.
Form of it.

If you want to understand the real meaning of the existence of that people, what was involved in all its institutions, and what was to come out of them when they perished, you should read that Epistle continually. What I was saying to you in my first Lecture, about the kings, and prophets, and priests, and sacrifices, which God appointed for the children of Abraham, finds its interpretation there. All these are shown to involve the existence of One, who is the Brightness of the Father's glory, the express Image of His Person; in whom He had constituted all spiritual powers, ages, worlds; who upheld all things by the word of His power; who in the fulness of time had taken flesh, and humbled Himself to death, that He might overcome him who had the power of death; who is the Mediator of a new covenant, the filial King and Priest; who had offered up the perfect sacrifice which could alone take away sins; who had entered into the holy place, the presence of God, for us. The words, "He hath gone up on high, having obtained eternal redemption for us," and the words, "By which Will we are sanctified through the offering of the body of Christ once for all," seem as if they were meant to

Object of it.

LECT. VIII. sum up the dispensation of the old world, and to introduce the new.

Importance of it to Ecclesiastical History.

I have spoken of this book, not for its exceeding worth,—for you will learn that better from others,—but because there is no book in the New Testament which so much explains the hints that we have derived from various parts of it, respecting the great crisis, which ever since the days of John the Baptist had been said to be at hand. You must not forget, that considerably less than forty years had elapsed since he began to preach. Take away the conception and birth of our Lord, and all the events in the four Gospels, the Acts of the Apostles, the Epistles of St. James, St. Peter, and St. Paul, are included within no greater term of years than that which elapsed between the Duke of Wellington's return from the Peninsula, and the day of his death. During that

The Roman Empire under the first Cæsars.

period, the evil principle of the Roman Empire was more rapidly exhibiting itself, than it ever did in after centuries, even under the worst princes. The restraints on mere will and the reverence for old law which Augustus permitted,—the refinement and literature which he encouraged,—softened, almost glorified his despotism. Under Tiberius it became hateful. A

Tiberius, A.D. 14—37.

man of ability, and at one time of courage, sank more and more into the miserable slave of his own suspicions and his own lusts; first raised up a minister to be the oppressor of his people, then cast him down, to become their worse and more malignant oppressor in his own person. The world sung triumphant pæans at his death, and hailed his successor, the son of a beloved general, as its champion and deliverer.¹ He became the most ridiculous of rulers, yet not the less the plague of his subjects, because he was the object of their contempt. The most wretched female domination appeared in the palace, and was fostered by the weakness of, Claudius. Bright days were promised by the accession of Nero, who had been bred under a philosopher. Before the earth was rid of him, his name had grown into a by-word, a word of terror and disgust to all ages. Anarchy soon followed; Galba was too honest to please the legions, too feeble to rule them. The effeminate Otho prevailed against him so far as to win the purple for a moment; Vitellius gathered up in his own person the wickedness and brutality of all his predecessors. In his days Rome was set on fire; the Capitol was destroyed; after a period of frightful revolution, law and government were restored by Vespasian.² It was believed by the Roman world, that prophecies had pointed him out as the inaugurator of a new order of things.

LECT. VIII.
Caligula, A.D. 37—41.
Claudius, A.D. 41—54.
Nero, A.D. 54—68.
Galba, June A.D. 68 to Jan. A.D. 69.
Otho, Jan. to April A.D. 69.
Vitellius, Jan. to Dec. A.D. 69
Vespasian, A.D. 70.

The picture which the Roman historians have drawn of the crimes of the Roman world generally, and of the capital particularly, during this period, is sufficiently appalling; yet it is far less dark than that which the Jewish historian offers us of his own countrymen. Their plots, seditions, brigandism, murders, were all

Jewish History much darker than Roman.

---

¹ See the opening of Philo's history of his embassy to Caligula.

² "Titus Flavius Vespasianus, with all his faults, was the true restorer of the State, a fact which has never yet been sufficiently acknowledged."—NIEBUHR, *History of Rome, from the Punic War to Constantine*, vol. ii. (Ed. 1st) p. 231.

made more terrible by the religious motives which were not only put forward as pleas for them, but which, in very many cases, prompted the commission of them. It is evident that the faith of the Jew in his Covenant and Law was not extinct. At times it could awaken a courageous resistance to direct outrages of the Imperial power; as for instance, when Caius Caligula wished that his image should be set up in the Temple, and that sacrifices should be offered to it. But this faith was itself turned into a lie, the most malignant of all lies; for the God of Abraham became to the darkened minds of the children of Abraham, a concentration of the evil qualities which were scattered through all the Gods of the heathen world. It is impossible not to feel, as one reads the accounts of Jerusalem and Palestine in those last days, that the villany of the rest of the world, and all that was most devilish in the religions of the world, was represented in its rulers and teachers. It was the same wickedness, the same exaltation of the Evil Spirit into the place of the God of Righteousness and Truth, which one sees elsewhere; but in Jerusalem it seems as if wickedness were chosen deliberately and in preference, as if its citizens bowed to the Prince of Darkness, not for any bribes he offered them, but for his own sake. It is a horrible story, yet we ought not to shrink from reading it. We learn from it what a called people must become, when they cease to believe in their calling, when they become haters of the world which they are sent to bless; when they think they are possessors of the blessings of which they are the stewards. Such a body cannot throw off its trust; but it serves as an example of the portentous crimes against which it was appointed to protest, and of the eternal truth, that in the punishment of those crimes, God is no respecter of persons.

The Festus before whom St. Paul pleaded, had redressed some of the evils which the administration of his predecessor had augmented. In the interval between him and his successor Albinus, the priests in Jerusalem showed how much worse crimes might be committed by natives, than by the worst Roman rulers. The high priest was then a Sadducee. To him Josephus attributes (in a passage generally admitted to be genuine) the death of James, who had earned the name of the Just, or Righteous, in spite of the prejudice against him as a Nazarene. Hegesippus, as quoted by Eusebius, says, that he was thrown from a pinnacle of the Temple by Pharisees, who professed the greatest respect for him personally, and who had brought him to that place with the hope of inducing him to undeceive the people about Jesus. The story, as he tells it, is a confused one, and Josephus must be the better authority. But the substantial parts of the two narratives may be reconciled, by supposing that the object of the Pharisees was to obtain an acknowledgment from St. James, that he did not look upon Jesus in the way in which Saul of Tarsus looked upon him. They could have no dream of making St. James renounce Jesus; they might have half persuaded themselves that he held the

Lect. VIII.

Festus.

Albinus.

Death of St. James, Antiquities, lib. xx. c. 9.

Eusebius, Hist. Eccl. lib. ii. c. 23.

faith of Him in some sense, which was compatible with not thinking of him as the one 'door' into the sheepfold. But St. James declared that the Son of Man was sitting on the right hand of the Majesty on High, and would come in clouds; thus accepting what they considered the blasphemy of Stephen and Paul. Probably they gave him up to their opponents to be stoned; so the statement of Josephus would be sustained, and the story would be in keeping with the proceedings of the two sects on many other occasions. Hegesippus has introduced some evidently legendary matter into his narrative, but I think it is entitled to more attention than it has of late received. This was at all events an act of purely Jewish fury. Albinus, though an evil ruler, was in no way a party to it. The more intolerable government of his successor Gessius Florus, was felt by the Jews to be a requital for it.

Florus evidently sought to provoke the Jews into a war with Rome. The fanatics among them were eager for it. King Agrippa, before whom St. Paul spoke, who was in favour at Rome, and who was attached to the people, pointed out to them in an eloquent speech, if we may trust Josephus, the madness of the attempt. At length Cestius, the governor of Syria, besieged Jerusalem. To the extreme surprise of the Jews, and of his own army, he withdrew just when the city was ready to fall into his hands. Nero sent Vespasian to conduct the war. He had subdued most of the cities in Galilee and Samaria, and was on his march to Jerusalem, when the news of the commotions in Italy that followed the death of Nero reached him.

Marginalia:
LECT. VIII.
This I suppose is the meaning of the words ἀπάγγειλον ἡμῖν τίς ἡ θύρα τοῦ Ἰησοῦ.

Neander (Geschichte der Pflanzung, Band 2, p. 442, Note) dismisses it with entire contempt.

Gessius Florus.

Bell. Jud. lib. ii. c. 16.

Vespasian.

Either in Judæa or Egypt he was first proclaimed Emperor by the legions. The care of the siege was left to Titus.

There was, then, both an outward and an inward connexion between the events which were precipitating the judgment on Roman tyranny, and those which were filling up the measure of Jewish iniquities, and the wrath that was in store for them. What, in the meanwhile, was the condition of the baptized community? I cannot read the Second Epistle of Peter, the Epistle of Jude, the Epistle to the Thessalonians, but, above all, the Epistle to the Hebrews, without perceiving that the Apostles saw in the condition of their own disciples, the signs of a coming Apostasy, which the events that were passing in the Roman world, and in the Jewish world, would develope and bring out into full manifestation. It is usual, I know, to suppose that these intimations belong to a much later period; perhaps to one that has not yet arrived. They may belong to times of which we shall hear in future Lectures; and to times which are at hand; I would express, with trembling, my conviction that they do. But I cannot explain away distinct and positive words which declare that it was impending, and which point out the perils of it to those whom the Apostles were exhorting at that time. Above all, I cannot explain away the whole of that great Epistle, which is addressed expressly to Jewish believers.[1]

[1] In some Lectures on the Epistle to the Hebrews, delivered at Lincoln's Inn in 1846 (Parker), I have spoken somewhat more at large on this approaching Apostasy, and the signs of it.

ON CHURCH HISTORY.

LECT. VIII.

Followers of St. James.

I will tell you what I think the writer of it feared for them. A good and great man may leave a set of followers, who turn all that was in him the most precious truth, into falsehood. St. James, we have seen, asserted the dignity of the Jewish calling. Disciples of St. James might make that calling an excuse for declining all fellowship with Gentiles. St. James had spoken of Jesus as bearing witness to the Jewish nation of their God and Father. Disciples of St. James might say that he was a very high witness of God indeed, perhaps a great prophet, perhaps even an angelic person, but that He was not actually the Son of God. We know that there were such disciples of St. James; that a set of men, called Ebionites, or poor men,[1] existed in this century and survived into the next, who maintained the greatest exclusiveness towards Gentiles, preferring a circumcised disbeliever in Jesus to an uncircumcised man who confessed Him. We know also that some of these Ebionites regarded Jesus as merely of the Jewish race, some as having a certain divinity, because he was miraculously conceived by the Virgin, some as having an angelic nature, which was neither human properly, nor properly divine. You will see, as you read the Epistle to the Hebrews, how much the writer sets himself from the first to establish both sides of the truth, which these teachers were denying. But you will see

Ebionites, Eusebius, book iii. c. 27.

Bearing of the Epistle to the Hebrews on them.

---

[1] Eusebius says, τούτους οἰκείως ἐπεφήμιζον οἱ πρῶτοι πτωχῶς καὶ ταπεινῶς τὰ περὶ τοῦ Χριστοῦ δοξάζοντας. "These the early Christians aptly described (by the name Ebionites) as holding poor and mean notions in reference to Christ." Probably they dwelt on Him with extreme delight as the poor man, the friend of the poor, till every other notion of Him was lost in that.

also what fear he had that those who had no stronger faith concerning Christ than this, would be unable to bear the shock of the coming time, which would certainly overthrow the institutions in which they were trusting, and would leave nothing behind, if Christ were not indeed the ground, and root, and centre, and corner-stone of the whole universe, if all men and all society were not upheld by Him.

LECT. VIII.

The traditions of the Jerusalem Church, after the death of James, became very vague indeed. Symeon is said to have been chosen his successor as overseer of the Church; chiefly, it would seem, because he too was supposed to have some relation to our Lord, according to the flesh.[1]

Eusebius, Hist. lib. iii. c. 11.

I have observed already, that we have no account of any *election* of St. James to be the overseer in the Jerusalem society, and that it is not probable there was any. If we are to assume the report respecting Symeon as authentic, it would indicate that offices in the Community were now beginning to be sought after. There is an obscure story of one Thebuthis, who was a rival candidate to Symeon, and who seems to have coveted the government from motives of personal ambition. Eusebius, speaking afterwards of the election of Justus to succeed Symeon, reports him as " one of the tens of thousands of the circumcision that had believed in

Book iii. c. 35.

---

[1] The importance attached to this circumstance in the Jerusalem community, ought by no means to be overlooked. The chapter in Eusebius, from which I have quoted, should be compared with the twentieth of the same book, where he quotes from Hegesippus the story of the relations of our Lord who were called before Domitian. It should be remembered that the Origenian tendencies of Eusebius would incline him *not* to dwell on a circumstance of this kind.

Christ;" a phrase which conveys the impression that the Christians in Jerusalem acquired numbers and reputation, as they lost purity. With these imperfect records is joined the express assertion, that the Church continued pure till the death of the Apostles, but that afterwards it became full of all strange opinions and heresies, and utterly corrupted. These words are drawn from some old author; they must apply to the first century. Some would restrict them to the Church of Jerusalem. I have no doubt that they apply first to that, as the Epistle to the Hebrews in all probability does. But as that Epistle bears also upon the condition of the whole body of Jewish believers in Jesus, I cannot doubt that the mighty convulsion which destroyed all the outward signs that separated them from the Gentile world, caused the love of numbers to wax cold, some sinking into actual idolatry, some into that recklessness of all moral law, of which St. Jude and St. Peter speak, some into declared atheism.

Eusebius, Hist. book iii. c. 32. But a far more important passage occurs in book ix. c. 22, where the quotation is made directly from Hegesippus, and where there is the allusion to Thebuthis and to the sects.

Nor was the feebleness of the Ebionitic faith the only ground for fearing such a result. The Hebrews to whom St. Peter had spoken of Christ as the Head of a divine kingdom, might, when Jerusalem perished, expect Him to create another Society on a more glorious scale, which should outrival the splendours of Rome itself. We see from the Gospels how much the Jews had connected a thought of this kind with the appearance of the Christ; it was too plausible a notion,—too much akin to all the tendencies of the unregenerate heart, not to be reproduced again and

Cerinthus. Eusebius, book iii. c. 28.

See Gieseler K. G. 1st Period, Abs. 1, § 35.

again in the Church. It is connected in the first century with the name of Cerinthus. To whatever place he belonged, it seems clear that he was a Jew, and that there were many who dreamed his dream, of a visible throne on which Jesus should sit, while His ministers and subjects should be free to enjoy themselves, and to trample upon other men.

It would be an error to suppose that though this opinion had a Jewish origin, and a Jewish character, the Churches which St. Paul had founded in Gentile cities may not have been infected with it. They had also their own temptations, to which, at a crisis like this, they were especially likely to yield. The Ebionites were disposed to shrink from the thought of Christ's divinity; yet some of them, as I have told you, also lost sight of His actual humanity. The Churches which had learnt from St. Paul,—which had heard him say, "That he would know no man after the flesh, yea, that though they had known Christ after the flesh, now henceforth they knew Him no more,"—might easily pervert his doctrine to the denial that the Son of God had taken flesh. They might even think it a low, grovelling conception, that so pure a Being could come into contact with our earthly nature. I need not tell you how far such a doctrine was from St. Paul's meaning; and that though he apprehended Christ with his spirit, not with his flesh, no one would have been more ready to die for the truth that He took an actual body, brought it from the tomb, and ascended with it on high. But it is needful to show you, thus early in our course,

Pauline Churches.

Abuse of St. Paul's doctrine by them.

LECT. VIII.

General conclusion.

how the doctrines of Apostles, as well as of inferior doctors, may be corrupted and inverted by those who profess to take one or another of them as their guide. When once the party or sect spirit possesses men, they must turn sacred portions of truth to the denial of other portions of it, which are as sacred and as needful for mankind.

Christ's words fulfilled literally.

On the whole, I can use no other language concerning this period than that which Christ and His Apostles used. They speak of events in the nations generally, in the Jewish nation particularly, and in the Churches of baptized men, which would be signs of the coming of the Son of Man as a Judge. The events I have reported, which were accompanied with a number of physical portents such as our Lord hinted at, seem to me such signs. But I could not interpret them, or understand the issues of them, or how the kingdom of the Son of God and the Son of Man was to be manifested by means of them, if

Transition to S. John.

we had not the help of another divine Teacher, of whose person and whose writings I hope to speak in the next Lecture.

LECTURE IX.

ST. JOHN.

St. Luke does not tell us in what directions the majority of the twelve Apostles went to fulfil their Master's command. The traditions which report to what countries they travelled are, some more, some less, probable. Those which concern the East are many of them worthy of credit, and are confirmed by later investigations. Since the first business of the Apostles was to gather Jews into the fold, they would be likely to go wherever their countrymen had settled. It is not proved that they had many colonies in Western Europe; we need not, therefore, be surprised if we find that the notions which the different Churches in Gaul, or Spain, or Britain have cherished that their origin was apostolical, may be commonly traced to some mistakes in names, overlooked and favoured by national vanity. If you wonder that we have not New Testament information on this subject, you must learn once for all, that the New Testament is not written to tell us about the doings of men, but about the great purposes of God to the world, and how, by this agent or that, He has accomplished them. St. Luke has made occasional allusions to St. James the

[Lect. IX. *Traditions respecting the Apostles.*]

[*St. Paul's intended journey to Spain, mentioned in the Epistle to the Romans, was prevented by his imprisonment.*]

116   ON CHURCH HISTORY.

LECT. IX. Less; he has spoken much of St. Peter; he has given us a continuous narrative of St. Paul's labours up to a certain point. But he says nothing of St. James's death,—of St. Peter's journeyings, or how they terminated,—of the issue of St. Paul's imprisonment: upon all these points we must get such tidings as we can; when not supplied by the Epistles, they are very doubtful. St. Luke has given us such a view of the principles and development of the kingdom, which John the Baptist said was at hand, as we can find nowhere else. It is well that we should understand how precious that knowledge is; of how little worth, except for the satisfaction of curiosity, the other would be.

St. Luke's silence.

If you want a proof of the difference between the sacred historian and the later ecclesiastical historians, take this instance. There is scarcely any Apostle who is spoken of more frequently in the Gospels than that James, who was with our Lord on Tabor and in Gethsemane, whose mother desired that he and his brother John might sit, one on the right hand, and one on the left, in their Lord's kingdom. He was the first Apostle who died for the faith of Christ. What an opportunity for a long and eloquent discourse, for an accurate description of sufferings, for records of divine and mysterious succours afforded to the martyr! St. Luke says, "*And Herod slew James the brother of John with the sword.*" That is all. He fell fighting in the ranks where he was set to fight: what more could be said of him? But there is an omission which may seem to you more surprising

St. Luke as a martyrologist.

still. What has become of the other son of thunder? of him who leaned on Christ's breast at the last supper? of him who is called the beloved disciple? We hear of him as joined with Peter in the first miracle of healing, after the day of Pentecost. He stands with Peter before the Sanhedrim. He goes with Peter to Samaria. Then he vanishes out of the narrative; we have no more news of him. He is called, in the letter to the Galatians, an Apostle of the circumcision. But we are not told how he worked for the circumcision, or whether he had any connexion with the Apostle of the Gentiles.

LECT. IX.

The rareness of his allusions to St. John.

I believe that the failure of information in the sacred historian on this subject, is not merely owing to the general cause which I have assigned for his silence. St. John, it seems to me, *could* have no conspicuous place in St. Luke's narrative; his work belongs to a later time. We could not understand what it was, and why it was needed, if we had not that narrative; if we had not the Epistles of St. James, St. Peter and St. Paul; nay, if we had not those notices which general history supplies us with of the convulsions in the Roman empire, and its progress to perdition, till the time of Vespasian,—of the strifes and crimes by which the Jewish nation was hastening to a still deeper ruin,—of the way in which the Church in Jerusalem, and the baptized Jews generally, were shaken by the catastrophe which their guides and teachers had predicted.

How it is to be accounted for.

The traditions which have come down to us respecting St. John are even more uncertain, and have

Notices of St. John by

more the air of fables, than those respecting the other Apostles. I am thankful, for my own part, that it is so. The more Christians are driven, by the unsatisfactory character of other documents, to study the books of the New Testament, and to derive their knowledge of the Apostles from them, the more, I believe, they will understand this period, and the more light will fall from it upon the history of later periods. Still a story is not worthless, because we do not accept it as a statement of facts. It may indicate some current belief, which more consistent records will test, and either confirm or reject. There is a tale of St. John rushing out of a bath in which Cerinthus was, lest the roof should fall on a heretic. The details of this story are very confused, and it rests on very weak authority. Eusebius, in two places, quotes Irenæus as quoting Polycarp in support of it. Epiphanius, writing in the fourth century, puts Ebion (who probably never existed) in place of Cerinthus, and tells the story with many additions. On such evidence one cannot believe a story, which is so like a hundred that happened, or were invented, in later times. But the very inconsistencies in it serve to show, that St. John was regarded as in some sense an especial protestant against Cerinthus, and also against the Ebionites. It is said that St. John wore the *insignia* of the high-priest. It is quite incredible that he did so; but I believe we may perceive in the story the indications of a very important truth, viz., that St. John lived in the transition period between the passing away of the Jewish dispensation, and the coming in of the

ST. JOHN. 119

Christian; and that it was he who, when the Jewish priesthood had ceased, showed how the substance and principle of it still survived. He is said to have been taken to Rome in the time of Domitian, to have been thrown into a cauldron of boiling oil, and to have come out unhurt. The story rests upon a most suspicious authority, that of Tertullian[1] in the end of the second century; it is adopted by no one before Jerome in the fourth. There is no probability that St. John ever saw Rome. Nevertheless the existence of such a story confirms the opinion, which we derive from a better source and from internal evidence, that the Roman emperor had an undefined dread of St. John, as of one who was still speaking of a kingdom which might interfere with the monarchy of the Cæsars, after it was supposed that such hopes were buried in the ruins of Jerusalem.

I cannot venture to give you any decision about the exact chronology of the books which are attributed to St. John.[2] There have been long disputes about it, which you may study hereafter, if you have time.

Tertullian, dePræscriptionibus, c. xxxvi. &c. Jerome adduces the story (Comment. on Matt. xx. 23) with the words, Si legamus historias ecclesiasticas in quibus fertur, to prove that St. John really drank our Lord's cup.

The writings of St. John.

---

[1] "Felix Ecclesia (Romana) cui totam doctrinam Apostoli cum Sanguine suo profuderunt; ubi Petrus passioni dominicæ adæquatur; ubi Paulus Johannis (*Baptistæ*) exitu coronatur; ubi Apostolus Johannes postea quàm in oleum igneum demersus, nihil passus est, in insulam relegatur." This is actually *the* warrant for a story, upon which some have been bold enough to rest the credibility of a Gospel, by which the very life of Christendom has been sustained for 1800 years!

[2] I have omitted any allusion to the celebrated story of the youth whom St. John recovered, and to many of the other tales respecting him, the chief value of which consists, I think, in the impression which they leave on our minds of the vague dignity which was attached to its person and position. To ascertain whence their real dignity arose,—what St. John's historical importance is,—we must turn to his own writings.

LECT. IX. I do not feel the question, whether they were all, or any of them, written after or before the destruction of Jerusalem, to be very important. What I do feel is, that they explain, as no books not contemporaneous, and not written by a divine teacher, could explain, the condition of a period which is otherwise most obscure, the period between the reign of Vespasian and the close of the first century. When I speak thus, I do not mean that the Gospel, the Epistles, or Apocalypse of St. John, are chiefly valuable because they interpret to us a little fragment of history. I believe they interpret the deepest mysteries concerning man and God; that they reveal to us the very ground of theology; that they show us the principles of all history. But I do not think they would accomplish these purposes if they did not, first of all, apply to a particular crisis in God's government of the world; to a crisis in which, I believe, the question was tried, whether mankind was to sink into utter atheism, or whether Christ's kingdom was to be manifested, as it had never been manifested before. This is my reason for speaking of them. I have no wish to give you a commentary upon them; that is not my office. I shall not set forth any theory about that which is in opposition to other theories. Hereafter you may, perhaps, find that it is possible to do justice to all the theories of good and learned men about the prophetical books of Scripture, and to perceive that their different expectations have had a fulfilment, and may have a fulfilment, in the history of the Church and the world. But that you may do this, you should first try to

Their relation to all times not affected, by investing them with a special importance in relation to this time.

follow the letter of those books. You should strictly believe the writers, when they say that they are speaking of things that are, or of things that are very shortly to be; then you will understand how truly they foretel what God would accomplish in other circumstances and distant generations.

The Apocalypse has seemed to many to be so different in its character from the Gospel and the Epistles of St. John, that they have thought it could not proceed from the same writer. Eusebius hints that it may have been written by John, a presbyter, of whom Papias makes mention as living in Asia about the time of St. John's death; but he does not offer the least argument in support of the hypothesis. Some later writers have taken just the opposite view. They have said the Apocalypse belongs to the first century, and has all the characteristics which one would expect from St. John, an Apostle of the circumcision; but that the Gospel evidently belongs to a later time, when Judaism was at an end, when people had been much in the habit of talking of Christ as the Word of God, and when the simple faith in Him had given place to a refined theology. I think that the hypothesis upon which both these opposite opinions rest is a false one; that the Apocalypse and the Gospel have the same object, and are in all essentials of the same character; that one as much as the other has clear marks of belonging to the end of the first century, and could belong to no other time.

Theories concerning the Gospel and Apocalypse.

You remember that the Gospel opens with the words, "*In the beginning was the Word, and the Word was*

Opening of the Gospel.

with God, and the Word was God. The same was also in the beginning with God. All things were made by Him, and without Him was not anything made that was made. In Him was Life, and the Life was the Light of men. And the Light shineth in the darkness, and the darkness hath not comprehended it." These words evidently give the character to the Gospel. They led the Church to call St. John, above the other Apostles and Evangelists, The Theologian. They afford the excuse for saying that he must have belonged to the second century, when the earlier belief in Jesus had given way to theories and speculations about His divine and mysterious nature. I quite admit that the words I have quoted do lead us into the very heart of theology; that we shall never be theologians if we do not think of them, study them, live upon them. But those who say, that therefore they must have been written in the second century, and not in the first, overlook one or two facts, with which, as they are learned men, they must be perfectly familiar.

The first is, that there never had been more discourses respecting the Logos, or the Word of God, than there were in the early part of the first century. I have mentioned the name of Philo, the Alexandrian Jew. I did not dwell upon his writings, because the time was not come when I could make you understand how important they are to ecclesiastical history. Nor shall I speak of them in any detail now, because they would keep me from a still more pressing topic. But I must tell you that Philo, being a deep student of the Old Testament, discovered in every part of it, in the History, the Law, in the Psalms, the Proverbs, but above all in the Prophets, continual allusions to One by whom God had spoken to men, in whom He was marvellously united to the creatures whom He had formed in His own likeness. All that is most interesting in Philo—all that is most practical —bears directly upon this subject; it is the key to every one of his thoughts. He desires to know how this Divine Person is related to God; how he is related to man. He sees that all light must have come into men's hearts from Him. He cannot doubt that the Gentiles must have been instructed by Him as well as the Jews, else how could they have known anything, or ever have turned away from vain things, to seek after what is substantial and good? Philo built a number of allegories and conceits upon this belief. He made the apprehension of this Divine Teacher the test of the wise man, and he was much inclined to despise all people who were not wise. He could, therefore, have very little sympathy with those who came preaching of a Lord who had spoken to publicans and harlots while He was upon earth, and who was drawing the most ignorant and the most sinful to Him, after He had ascended on high. The thought of a crucified King and Son of God was, I suppose, more offensive to the Jews of Philo's school than even to the Pharisees. I have hinted already, that they had probably a chief part in Stephen's death.

His school, why opposed to the Gospel.

Yet this class of men at last supplied as many disciples, and as many teachers of the Cross, as any

Christian Teachers from it.

class in the Jewish or the Roman world. Apollos is a specimen. When you read the First Epistle to the Corinthians attentively, you will find what kind of effect he produced on that Church, and how thoroughly St. Paul recognised the truths which he taught; though he saw how they were likely to be perverted, and were perverted, by the self-conceit and the party spirit of the Greeks, and how needful it was that he should declare to them that in Jesus Christ, and Him crucified, God had manifested His Wisdom and Power. To connect these two truths together, the glory of Christ and His humiliation,—the truth that all God's righteousness and wisdom had been revealed in Him, but that they were revealed in His weakness, poverty, and death; to show the Corinthians how impossible it was for them to form a united body except in Christ,—here we have the aim of St. Paul's teaching. The necessity for such teaching became more and more apparent afterwards. I have told you already, that the disciples of the Apostles were inclined to rend asunder the truths which they had been appointed to proclaim, and to set them in conflict with each other. These strifes took various forms in various places; Cephas, Apollos, Paul, were the Shibboleths at Corinth; James and Paul elsewhere. But this cardinal difference lay at the root of them all: one set of men were inclined to contemplate Christ as divine, and to deny that He had taken flesh; the other were inclined to contemplate Him as merely the great human Teacher, who had come at a certain time on a certain mission into the world, and had no eternal relation to the Lord God, whom eye had not seen, nor ear heard. We have seen how this kind of feeling was at work, especially among the Hebrew Christians, and how the only way to prepare them for the crisis that was at hand was to lead them to a deeper foundation,—to the acknowledgment of Christ as the express image of the Father, in whom alone God could look upon them as children, who, because the children were partakers of flesh and blood, Himself also took part of the same. And it was, I conceive, that men might pass safely through this crisis that St. John, in language more broad, simple, and distinct than that of the Epistle to the Hebrews, proclaims his theology.

How the Epistle to the Hebrews is related to the Gospel of John.

For this is the other fact which I alluded to as being overlooked by the learned men, who will throw St. John's Gospel into the second century. They first assume that he could not have talked as he does of a Word of God in the first century, though no language was so familiar and widely diffused as that was in this very century; they next assume that he is not as simple as the other writers of the New Testament. Here they are at issue, not with history, but with the heart and the common sense of humble readers. They feel and express the conviction, in a number of ways, that St. John is the most simple, the most childlike of all the writers in the New Testament—the one who brings our Lord, as a man in his acts and sympathies, the most thoroughly before them. Instead of writing like a man who, in a dis-

St. John the simplest of the Evangelists.

LECT. IX. tant day, was looking back and speculating about His nature, he writes like one who had seen His acts on earth, and had stored them in his heart; who had felt the meaning of them a little at the time, and who had entered into the whole sense of them afterwards, as being the manifestation of the only-begotten of the Father, full of grace and truth.

Depth and simplicity.

If you have a fancy, any of you, that these two qualities are inconsistent with each other,—that a man must give up his simplicity if he is to be a deep theologian, or must be a shallow theologian that he may be simple—no one will clear your minds of it like St. John. And, be assured, you have need to clear your minds of it. You will have to work among very ignorant people. You ought to be thoroughly direct, and straightforward, and childlike in your addresses to them. But if you are *childish* instead of childlike; if you pour out froth to them, or give them empty, wordy truisms, when you should open to them divine truths, you will be utterly useless, and God will call you to account for such trifling. The poorest, stupidest, wickedest man you can meet with, seeing he is a man, wants to know what he is himself, and what God is, and how he is related to Him. If you tell him less than that, he will never be satisfied, and you have not fulfilled your commission. If you tell him that, you must go down to the very root of theology. Superficial thoughts may do for lazy, comfortable people, who want a religion to set them at ease with their consciences, and to enable them to go on worshipping God and Mammon together; they

Deep theology needed for the poor.

will not do for suffering people, with whom it is a question of life and death, whether there is any one in whom they may believe, and how they may find Him, and what He has done for them.

Do you want some interpreter of St. John's Gospel? I believe the more you know of your own hearts, the more you know of human beings, the more you will find that you want St. John's Gospel to interpret *them.* Those first words that I repeated to you, so distinct, decisive, authoritative, how they meet the hearts and consciences of human beings! how they tell them of the very Guide and Teacher, they have been feeling after, and trying to find, whom they confess every day, and deny every day, whose light comes to them, and whose light they try to hide in their darkness! Do you want to convince them that this Person is God, and with God? Tell it them as St. John tells it them: try whether they do not perceive more of what you mean through God's own teaching, than by all your arguments. But they *do* want to hear whether this Person, their Lord and King, has always been hidden, or whether He has come forth and manifested Himself as He is. And if you will go on with this first chapter, you will see how St. John says, in the same simple, decisive manner as before, "*And the Word was made flesh and dwelt among us; and we beheld His glory, the glory as of the only-begotten of the Father, full of grace and truth.*" It is not, you see, that he is unfolding to us a great theory; he is telling us of a living Being whom he saw, with whom he conversed. Then, in all the

LECT. IX.

When St. John's Gospel becomes intelligible.

The Word.

The Word made flesh.

Gospel afterwards, you will find him showing by what acts and words, to what different classes of persons, He made His light and glory manifest, never for a moment being less an actual, suffering, sympathising Man, that He might display His divine might and character, but making the one visible through the other. At the marriage-feast of Galilee, where He is eating the same food with His disciples, sharing the same joy, He manifests forth His glory, and they believe on Him. In the Temple, where He manifests that zeal for God's house which all the old prophets had felt, they discern that it is from Him all had received that grace. And though the disciples did not understand at first what He meant by saying that if they destroyed that temple, He would raise it again in three days, yet, after the resurrection, they perceived that His body was the true temple in which God dwelt. In this way, as St. John explains it to us, the conviction of what He was, sometimes flashed into their minds at the moment, sometimes awoke up afterwards when events explained His dark sayings. So likewise the Pharisee Nicodemus, who came in secret, puzzled by Christ's miracles, to question Him about the kingdom of which He spoke, heard words to which at first he could affix but very little meaning,—about a birth from above, and water and the Spirit, and the Son of Man being lifted up, and the Son of Man having come down from heaven, and being in heaven; but by degrees, as he sought for light, and came to it that his deeds might be made manifest, these things interpreted what

The marriage-feast.

The Temple.

The birth from above.

he had been studying before, and teaching others as a *Lect. IX.*
Master in Israel. So He makes the Samaritan woman *The Well of water.*
understand, as He sits by the well, that He knows all
that ever she did, and that she needs a spring of
living water, which He alone can call forth in her. So
by healing a man on the sabbath, at the pool of Bethesda, He leads the Pharisee to questions and complaints, which bring out the assertion, that He works,
as a Son, His Father's work; that it is His voice *The Son and the Father.*
which quickens the dead, and that it is He by whom
all will be judged. So the feeding the multitude brings
out the lesson that He is the Bread of Life, that He
came down from Heaven to give life to the world;
that His flesh is meat, and His blood drink indeed.
So at the feast of Tabernacles, while the women were
carrying the pitchers of water to celebrate the striking
of the rock in the Wilderness, He speaks of the well of
water which He would open, of the Spirit which those *The Spirit.*
who believed on Him should receive. So the assertion
of the Jews, near the same time, that they were never
in bondage to any man, leads to His teaching, that
those who had committed sin were the servants of sin, *Slavery and Freedom.*
and that only the Son could make them free. So the
giving light to the eyes of a man who had been blind
from his birth, leads to a revelation of Him to the
heart of this man, as the Son of God; and to a new
declaration of the reason why the Pharisees were
blind, because they thought they had light, and *The Blind.*
did not come to the light, that it might show
them their darkness. So the pride and selfishness of
these shepherds leads Him to speak of the true

K

LECT. IX.

The true and false Shepherd.

The Resurrection and Life.

The corn of wheat.

The discourses at the Feast.

The Vine and the Branches.

Shepherd, and of the test of His character, that He gives His life for the sheep; so this test leads to the assertion of His own oneness with the Father, who knows Him as He knows the sheep. So the death of Lazarus leads to the manifestation of Him as the Resurrection and the Life. So the coming up of a few Greeks to the feast, who desired to see Christ—the first-fruits of the Greeks that should afterwards be called in—leads to a foretaste of His sufferings, and to the deep saying, which after times were to expound, that, if a corn of wheat fell into the ground and died, it would bear much fruit; that Sacrifice and Death must always be the root from which life comes.

I have run hastily over those chapters which contain St. John's account of our Lord's public ministry, that you may see how livingly they exhibit the Son of God in all the different aspects of His character, through the Son of Man. Then if you proceed to the latter chapters, which contain His discourses with His own disciples, (between the 12th and 18th,) you will see how, in the like living manner, they bring forth the name of the Father, and the Son, and the Holy Spirit. There is no doctrine formally enunciated; but the disciples are led, in their sorrow and approaching desolation, to feel that He, from whom they are going to part, will be with them still; that they are attached to Him as the branches are attached to the vine; that He is going to the Father with whom He is one, and who is watching over them; that a Comforter will be sent from Him to testify of Him and the Father, that they also may be able to bear witness;

which witness will expose them to hatred and death, the shepherd being first smitten, the sheep afterwards. Finally, that when our Lord prayed to His Father, He could not separate Himself from them, or from those who should come after; that what He had asked for them, and asked then, and would ask for ever, was, that, " as Thou, Father, art in me, and I in Thee, so they may be one in us." This prayer, and the discourse which has introduced it, you must never separate from the history of the Betrayal, and Trial, and Crucifixion, and Resurrection. Those events express the sense of all that has gone before. There we see the Sacrifice, without which the prayer would have had no reality. The record of them, so St. John concludes, was written, that all who read might know that Jesus is the Son of God, and that, believing, they might have Life through His name.

LECT. IX.
The Comforter.
The Prayer.
The Sacrifice.

If you pass with these words on your minds to the first Epistle of St. John, which begins thus: " *That which was from the beginning, which we have heard, which we have seen with our eyes, and which our hands have handled, of the Word of Life; for the Life was manifested, and we have seen it, and we declare to you that Eternal Life which was with the Father, and has been manifested to us;*" you will have a sense of the connexion between these two documents, and a perception of the thought with which the writer of them was occupied, such as no arguments of mine, or of any one else, could give you. But you must also consider that Epistle in relation to the Epistles of the other Apostles, to whom I referred in my last

The Eternal Life manifested.
St. John's Epistle.

K 2

LECT. IX. Lecture. You heard how the disciples of St. James, St. Peter, and St. Paul, were attempting to set up the doctrine of one against that of the other; how the honest preference which they felt for him who had been their own guide in the path of righteousness, *Cause of Division.* made them dividers of the Truth, and therefore perverters of what he had told them. All such divisions arose from their magnifying some thought or feeling of theirs about God into the place of His Revelation of Himself; from their notion that they were choosing Him, not He them; from the dream, that their faith, or good works, or knowledge, or graciousness, or love, was the ground upon which they were to build. *Truths inverted.* Then when they had once assumed this false starting point, Christ's appearing and His acts became themselves the pleas for fresh disputings. 'He had come to confirm the Law, or to set aside the Law. He had merely asserted the old Covenant against those who were forgetting it, and setting it aside, or He had come to introduce a new Covenant, which was to abolish the old.' Each side in those controversies felt it had hold of something, which the other was refusing to acknowledge. Each became more impatient of its adversary's conviction for that very reason. Each was making Christ Himself the author of strife.

Return to the Divine ground. Now St. John did not undertake to reconcile these quarrels by conceding a little to one of the parties, and a little to the other. He went to the root of the matter. Leaving the notions of men, he returned to the revelation of God. He affirmed boldly that He whom they had heard, and seen, and handled, had manifested forth God as He is, had shown Him to be the Light, with which no darkness at all is mingled; the Love in which there is no one element that is contrary to Love. Painters have had silly, childish, mischievous notions, that because St. John speaks of Love more than the other Apostles, he had a soft, feminine, sentimental countenance, without the wrinkles of age; betraying no conflict; capable of no indignation or sternness. Do not believe them. Every word in this Epistle refutes such a fancy. There is as much severity in this letter as in any in the New Testament. He calls those who pretend that they love God and hate their brother, liars and murderers. He says that they abide in death. He says that those who commit sin are of the Devil. These are broad, plain words, and instead of being qualifications of those which went before, they arise out of them. God is absolutely good; God reveals Himself to us in His Son, that we may have fellowship in Him. God sends His Spirit into our hearts, that we may be His children, and have His likeness, and acknowledge His features in our fellow-men. To be separate from this God, to have a will at war with His, must be misery, must be death.

Observe what follows from this method of the Apostle. He is able to reconcile that strife of the Old and the New, which, at this time especially, was becoming so violent. That which I tell you, he says, is what you have heard from the beginning. I am proclaiming the same God who gave your fathers the Covenant and the Commandments; the law of Love

Lect. IX.

The Apostle of God's Love no Sentimentalist.

His severity.

The Old and the New.

was always the law of His being. It was this law which was implied in all His dealings with His creatures, in all that He demanded of them. But now this is *true in Him and in you.* This Law has been kept. The Word of God, who was from the beginning with God, has taken flesh and fulfilled it. For you then it is a new Law, a new Commandment. It is revealed to you in a Person. It has become in Him a power enabling you to act rightly, not only a decree which makes you feel that you have acted wrongly. In this way St. John realizes His calling as an Apostle of the Circumcision. He vindicates the ground on which his fathers stood. He says that their revelation of God was altogether a true revelation. But in this way he also fulfils his calling as the herald of a new age that was to supersede the old. He shows that the old must pass away; because it has done its work so thoroughly. St. John's Epistle is Catholic, as St. James's and St. Peter's are Catholic. It assumes the calling of the Jews to be the ground of the divine Ecclesia. But he is Catholic in another sense. He does not speak of Twelve Tribes. He speaks of that body into which the Twelve Tribes had been expanded. He speaks to those who were united in the Name which his Gospel and Epistle alike are setting forth, the name of the Father, of the Son, and of the Holy Ghost.[1]

---

[1] I do not mean, of course, the slightest allusion to the verse upon which there has been so much valuable criticism expended, and which defenders of the Trinity were, for awhile, so foolishly set upon supporting. I believe the effect of the whole Epistle, as a declaration of the Divine Name, is weakened, not strengthened, by the passage in which

ST. JOHN. 135

If you have understood me so far, you will be LECT. IX.
prepared to follow me in what I have to say of the
Apocalypse, which I reserve for the final Lecture of
this Introductory Course.

some marginal annotator, probably with the most innocent intention,
endeavours to sum up the doctrine of it.

LECTURE X.

THE APOCALYPSE.

THE book[1] of which I am to speak opens with the words: *The Apocalypse or unveiling of Jesus Christ, which God gave to Him; to show unto His servants things which must shortly come to pass: and He sent and signified it by His Angel to His servant John; who bore record of the Word of God and of the testimony of Jesus Christ, and of all things which he saw.* The writer immediately explains his title. On the island of Patmos he had a vision of the Son of Man

---

[1] Dionysius, the Bishop of Alexandria, according to Eusebius, considered the style of the Apocalypse evidence against its proceeding from the same writer as the Gospel. The force of his objection may be felt more strongly by those who read the text of Lachmann, than even by those who follow that with which we are familiar. The offences against the rules of Greek grammar are greater in that which we are warranted, perhaps, in considering the more accurate collation. But every one, I suppose, will allow that the Gospel and the Epistle are very Hebraic in their form and construction; much more so than the Gospel of St. Luke and the Epistles of St. Paul. Hence their simplicity. Imagine a writer who,—by divine ordinance, as we believe, using his circumstances and education,—had *always* been led to look at Greek through the forms of his country's language, called upon to record visions of that which is not under the laws of Time. Might we not expect from him in such a case, a disregard of tenses,—the peculiarity of the refined Indo-Germanic tongues,—a recurrence to the freedom of the older prophets?

walking in the midst of seven golden candlesticks. I use the word "vision," because it is the one which would be generally used to denote such an appearance as is there described. But I must tell you that the other word, "unveiling," or Revelation, is an immeasurably better one, and for this reason. By a vision we are apt to understand a momentary impression made upon the eyes or upon the mind of a particular person, of something that has been, or that is, or that is about to be. We associate it with what is transitory, with what belongs to the feelings and circumstances of an individual. Now a revelation, whether we look at the origin of the word or at the use of it in Scripture, suggests a meaning that is precisely the opposite of this. A veil is withdrawn that we may know that which has always been, though it has been hidden from us. That which is true and permanent, but not visible, is laid bare. As the Psalmist expresses it, the foundations of the round world are discovered. And though the discovery is made to a particular man, the truth which he learns is for all just as much as for himself.

In what sense a Vision.

The word Apocalypse better.

If you read the first chapter of the Apocalypse considerately and devoutly, you will see how unlike it is to a mere dream. There is the profoundest reality in it. And it is not a case of what the Scotch call "second sight." It is not the apprehension of something that may come to pass hereafter, *as if* it were present. The unveiling of Jesus Christ is that final discovery for which all God's previous discoveries had been preparing. It gathers them up; it explains their

Not a mere book of Predictions.

purpose; it shows what that truth is which was beneath them all.

The Candlestick.

The form of the Revelation is connected with the Candlestick in the Jewish Tabernacle. It tells us what that Candlestick was teaching the people. A centre of light there was, from which all partial light proceeded; all creatures were dark when that was withdrawn; each fulfilled its own work and illuminated its own sphere, while it was drawing light from the source of light. Jesus Christ here, as in the Gospel of St. John, is declared to be this Centre of Light, and to be ever dispensing it. He is walking in the midst of the seven golden candlesticks. The old Tabernacle has passed away; the Temple has either perished or is about to perish. But the meaning of the Tabernacle and of the Temple remains. The living Person of whom they have been testifying, is now unveiled. And the old witnesses of His presence,— not only the Tabernacle and the Candlesticks, but the Nation whose office was to diffuse light through the world,—have left other witnesses behind them. *The seven Candlesticks are the seven Churches.*

Translation from symbol into reality.

The new witnesses.

Here, as in the Epistle, we find St. John reconciling what seemed the opposite views of the Church, which are presented to us by the Apostles of the Circumcision, and by St. Paul. We start from the Jewish ground, from the Tabernacle and the Candlestick. But the truth contained in these is now realized and exhibited in a number of distinct bodies. These bodies, we shall see, differ as much from each other in their characters, circumstances, dangers, as those which St. Paul makes us acquainted with. Though they were near to each other, there is no obvious fellowship between them; the Unity is beneath. And St. John goes on to show us, how He who is walking in the midst of them, and is their common Centre, is, at the same time, acting upon each one of them, speaking to each one.

LECT. X.

The Apostles were now all of them dead, except St. John. I have explained to you what kind of government they exercised while they were alive, how fatherly a government it was, how severe it often was, yet how gracious, how little it was defined by rules, how it reminded those who were subject to it of their Divine Father and of His government. What was to become of the Churches, when the Apostles passed away? The Epistles to Timothy and Titus tell us how St. Paul ordained overseers in Ephesus and Crete, to correct evils which were working in the Churches there, and to set them in order. The worth of these Epistles cannot be overrated. They teach us much respecting that age; they are guides to all after ages. But the Jewish polity was then standing. St. Paul did not desire to set up another in the place of it. It might be said that Timothy and Titus were both exercising their functions in subordination to the Apostle. We could not conclude what would happen in the new state of things after the great overthrow. The same writer who tells us that the seven candlesticks were the seven Churches, tells us that the stars in Christ's right hand were the Angels of the seven Churches.

Government of the Churches.

The Stars in Christ's right hand.

140   ON CHURCH HISTORY.

LECT. X. And then he interprets his own words, by delivering a message, not in his own name, but in Christ's Name, to these Angels.

The Angels. The name Angels is not defined, as words are defined in a dictionary. But there could not be a word which is equally significant to those who read the Bible, and especially to those who read this book. The Angel is the messenger between the invisible and the visible world. Each Church exists as a witness that there is an intercourse between these worlds, that Christ has broken down the barrier between them. He who presides over each Church testifies in his own person of this fellowship. His position declares that he has no light in himself, no authority of his own; that any good he does, any power he exerts, comes from One who is not seen, but who is really present, the Guide of his spirit, the true Shepherd of his flock. I must beseech you to keep this principle steadily in recollection. I cannot tell you what mists have gathered round the Church from the forgetfulness of it, or how much it may help us in seeing our way through those mists.

The Messages to the Church; how they are often interpreted. The messages to these seven Churches, which are contained in the second and third chapters of the Apocalypse, have seemed to some persons so wonderfully descriptive of different periods in the history of the modern world, that they have talked of the Sardian age, and the Philadelphian age, and the Laodicean age, as if the Apostle's object was to point out conditions of society which were to succeed each other in some predestined order. I do not know any thing which affords one a greater test of the truthfulness of the book and of the inspiration of the writer, than this. Every one sees allusions in the words to something which he has read of or met with. And he is not wrong. These applications, and multitudes which have not been observed, may all be admitted, if we do not try to bind the divine Teacher with our withes; if we will take the words as we find them, and believe that Christ was actually speaking through His servant to different Churches, which were existing in that day. For my purpose, I must adhere resolutely to that simple course.

Ephesus.

The Angel of the Ephesian Church may, or may not have been Timothy, whom St. Paul set over it. Whoever he was, he is described as very earnest in trying *those who say they are Apostles and are not;* as being patient and laborious; as *hating the deeds of the Nicolaitans;* but as having *fallen from his first love.*

False Apostles.

You will easily suppose that there were many at this period, who pretended that they were Apostles, in the sense in which St. Paul said he was an Apostle,—who boasted that Christ had called them; who affirmed that they had received a divine illumination, and must therefore be heeded by all people who cared for their salvation. The overseer of the Church in Ephesus appears to have been a bold, sensible, clear-sighted teacher, who was not daunted by these fanatics, but brought them to plain tests, and proved that they were not righteous men. There were also those who talked of the Gospel as being spiritual, and as having nothing to do with the Law. The flesh, in their

Nicolaitans.

Loss of first love.

The punishment and the blessing.

judgment, was utterly contemptible; they might use it as they liked.¹ Nicolas, one of the Deacons, is said to have maintained a doctrine of this kind; and either he or his disciples deduced from it the lawfulness of a community of wives. This doctrine, the like of which we shall hear of often in the Church, had found its way to Ephesus. The angel of the Church there hated it, and tried to put it down, as he was bound to do. You see he was a strict upholder of straightforward honesty and morality, against those who would subvert them. But, as often happens with people of his class, he appears to have become somewhat indifferent to spiritual principles, in his zeal against the abuse of them. Coldness and hardness were creeping on him, in the midst of his eagerness to assert the true, and to get rid of the counterfeits; he is bidden to repent, or his candlestick will be removed out of its place. The Spirit, who is speaking to him, tells him, that if he overcomes his besetting evil, he shall eat of the tree of life, which is in the midst of the Paradise of God. You must observe here, once for all, that in speaking to the Angel of the Church, the Spirit speaks to the Church. Its overseer represents it. His habits of mind, his temptations, the threatenings and promises which most concern him, belong to the society which he

---

¹ The passage in Clemens, Στρώματα, Book III. (from which Eusebius quotes, Book III. c. 28), if it cannot be assumed as strictly historical, has considerable internal evidence in its favour. Nicolas, it appears, wished to make a display of his amazing power of self-restraint. His followers converted his teaching into a plea for unlimited self-indulgence. The story has been repeated again and again in Church History.

guides. Observe, too, that the great punishment of all, is the extinction of Light. The candlestick shall be taken away. *Lect. X.*

The Angel of the Church in Smyrna was exposed to severe persecutions. The Apostle indicates clearly whence they came. There were some who said they were Jews, but were not. He maintains the believer in Jesus to be the true Jew, the true assertor of the covenant with Abraham. The other Jews, though they might be numerically stronger, were *a synagogue of Satan*. But they had the greatest power of annoying their countrymen, who clung to the right king, either directly, or by their influence with heathen magistrates and mobs. The Smyrna angel and Church had need to remember Him who had been dead and was alive; if they clung to Him—whatever befel their bodies—they could not be hurt by the second, the spiritual death. *Smyrna. The Synagogue. The second death.*

I imagine that *nearly* all the persecutions of this time still proceeded from the Synagogue; for the bitterness of the Jews against those whom they regarded as their worst enemies, both a little before the fall of Jerusalem, and (as we shall find) for many years afterwards, became intenser, from their own calamities and disappointments. If so, "*the throne of Satan*," which is alluded to in the message to Pergamos that follows, must be interpreted by "the synagogue of Satan," in the one to Smyrna. There the Jewish influence was probably stronger than in the other Asiatic cities. This Church is said to be infested by a set of men *holding the doctrine of Balaam*, *Pergamos. Balaamites.*

which the angel of the Church had not sufficiently discouraged. Balaam represents in the Old Testament History the prophet who had abused divine inspirations, to the accomplishment of covetous and sensual purposes. St. Peter had already used his name to denote a class which would appear in his—the latter—days. Simon, the Jewish enchanter, whom we met in Samaria, and who, after he was baptized, is supposed to have made his knowledge of the Gospel an instrument of his trade, is a specimen of the class. St. John speaks of them as bringing idolatry and sensuality into the Church; the confusion of the flesh and the spirit being the beginning of both. The Nicolaitan doctrine was another form of this tendency; the two appeared together in Pergamos. The angel of it was brave and unflinching in his conflict with external foes. It was in the power of distinguishing between the true and counterfeit within the Church, that he was deficient. He who had the sharp sword with the two edges calls upon him to repent of the moral confusion which was in him and in his flock, and to seek for the blessing of clearness of conscience, that white stone of absolution which no man knoweth but he who receiveth it.

The Flesh and Spirit confounded.

Thyatira.

The Angel in Thyatira, amidst higher praises than those bestowed on Ephesus or Pergamos, is blamed for suffering a prophetess, who is called Jezebel, *to teach and to seduce the servants* of Christ *to eat things offered to idols, and to commit fornication.* This tampering with idolatry and with the sins of which idolatry was at once the sign and the promoter, is, as we might expect, the great peril of that time; it has been the peril of all times; the peculiarity of Thyatira consisted in this, that a female enchanter or prophet was the instrument in the temptation. The name given to her, like that of Balaam to the other deceivers, is, of course, intended to connect the later history with that of the Old Testament. The Phœnician wife of Ahab, it has often been supposed, was more than a mere worshipper of Baal. She may have been his priestess; at all events, she had a fixed design of alienating the people of Israel from the worship of the unseen God of Righteousness, to the worship of a mere Lord of Power, a visible Ruler. The same kind of effect we may assume was produced by the teachings of the woman of Thyatira upon the Church there. They were led to substitute the visible for the invisible; and this from a notion that they had sounded some "depths" of wisdom which their ordinary instructors had not reached. A loss of moral strength, the commission of gross sins, was the consequence. He whose eyes are as a flame of fire declares that He will search out these secret evils, and bring them to the light of day; He promises to him who overcomes this temptation to be like the nations round about, —to mimic their worship and covet their splendour,— that he shall rule the nations.[1]

Lect. X.

The false Prophetess.

Why called Jezebel.

Ruling the Nations.

---

[1] It is added, "*And I will give unto him the morning star.*" The words must refer to the celebrated passage in Isaiah, respecting Lucifer, the Son of the Morning. The Jews, who were always aiming to be like the Babylonians, are told how their Man-god shall be cast down. If they will follow their own true King, the God-man, they shall triumph

L

Sardis.

No special deceivers are pointed out in the Sardian Church. It is simply declared with its overseer to be in a low torpid state. It has a name to live and is dead. He in this falling Church that overcometh its temptations will be clothed in white raiment; his name shall not be blotted out of the book of life. Christ will confess him before His Father and the Angels.

Philadelphia.

The Philadelphian Church, like those in Smyrna and Pergamos, was exposed to the special opposition of the pretended Jew. But it had clung in weakness to its true strength, and He that is holy and true, that hath the key of David, promises to keep it and its Angel from the hour of temptation, which shall come upon all the world to try them that dwell upon the earth. He is coming quickly. The Philadelphian Angel is bidden to hold fast that which he has, and to let no man take his crown. If he overcomes, Christ will make him a pillar in the temple of His God, and will write upon him the name of His God,

The new Jerusalem.

and the name of the city of His God, the New Jerusalem, which cometh down out of Heaven from God.

Laodicea.

The Angel of the Church of the Laodiceans is discovered to be neither hot nor cold. He thinks that he is rich and increased in goods, and has need of nothing. He knows not that he is wretched, and poor, and blind, and naked. Christ is standing at the door and knocking. If any one hear His voice

---

over all mere earthly powers, and over the spiritual powers which defy Him. The lesson is carried out and expanded by St. John.

and open the door, He will come in to him and sup with him. He that overcomes the lukewarm spirit shall sit with Christ on His throne, as He has overcome and is set down with His Father on His throne.

You will feel more and more, as we proceed in our history, how serious the words are, " He that hath an ear, let him hear what the Spirit saith unto these Churches." But there are one or two points which you should take notice of, in order that you may appreciate the force of the words to the generation for which they were at first designed. Observe, then, that these seven Churches all belonged to Asia Minor, to the region with which St. John appears to have been himself conversant during his later years. They are not Churches connected with Palestine, they are not Macedonian or Greek Churches, they are not Latin Churches; nevertheless, as their number seven indicates, they are evidently intended to set forth the Church as one complete body consisting of distinct portions. Though the Apostle exercises a kind of oversight in each of these societies, he does not pretend for a moment that it is he who unites them; he does not even pretend that he knows what is going on in them, or can speak to them, or judge them. The kind of deference which was paid him by the Asiatic Churches, both in his life-time and after his death, must have been very great indeed. We shall find that they appealed to traditions which they supposed they had received from him, in opposition to traditions which the western Churches followed. But he disclaims any such dignity himself. His revelation

Lect. X.

The Seven Churches, in what respect Johannine.

How they represent the whole Church.

is of another and diviner Overseer, who will remain for ever, and to whom the overseer of each Church is directly responsible. Another observation is one which you cannot have failed to make for yourselves, but which I must not be weary of repeating to you, viz. that each one of these messages supposes a great crisis or judgment to be at hand, through which some of the Churches would pass well and some ill. I want you to understand that whether Jerusalem had yet fallen or not, the whole of this time was one of tremendous sifting, one in which the pure gold would have to be proved in the fire and in which the dross would be consumed. You will remark, at the same time, how many allusions there are to a New Jerusalem, a better and diviner society of which the world in general would be ignorant, but which the hearts of true and faithful men would enter into, and of which Christ would make them citizens. This you must bear in mind, in what I have to say about the rest of this book. I wish to pass it over as rapidly as I can, for I would not have you think I am giving you any new theory about it. But I must show you that whatever other meanings it may have, it has one which makes it the best of all introductions to Ecclesiastical History.

When you read in the fourth chapter of a door being opened in Heaven, you may think that we are carried into some distant region, with which we may have to do after death, but which stands apart from the common events of this earth. If you adopt that notion, I believe you will never understand this Revelation, nor any of God's revelations, nor Church history which rests upon them. The vision which the Apostle has of a throne, and of One who sat upon it, and of the seven Spirits before the throne, and of the four beasts and the Elders, and of the Lion of the tribe of Judah, who is also the Lamb that has been slain, and who has seven eyes that go through the earth, and seven horns of power—is the vision of those divine and substantial realities which the eye cannot see or the ear hear, which are objects of faith not of sight, but which do not belong to the future more than to the present or to the past. They are always present. They constitute that Heavenly Kingdom which Christ came to reveal, which He declares is for the poor in spirit, which it will be the blessing of every one to apprehend hereafter, the misery to lose, but which the Apostle would tell us is with us here. This is that state of things which abides amidst all the changes and fluctuations of this world's history and policy. And that Book, sealed with seven seals, which was in the hand of Him that sat upon the throne, was, I apprehend, the book which showed how this perfect and eternal world is connected with the world of time and change; how all the dark and sad events which men witness, those that had been going on since the world began, those that were passing when the Apostle wrote, those with which different generations should be acquainted after he had gone away, are dependent upon Him who governs in this higher world, are subject to His laws which are obeyed there, and will

LECT. X.

The eternal present, not future.

The Book with seven seals.

serve for the manifestation of His righteousness. If this is the case, you will see why only the Lamb that was slain could break the seals of this book; for it is He who binds the two worlds together, it is He who is alive and was dead, who, as the Apostle speaks, has the keys of death and hell. This was the new and divine revelation which had been made by His death, and resurrection, and ascension. But that revelation did not supersede the old truth which the Jewish nation had been proclaiming. That chosen nation had existed to testify of a Son of God, who should be born of the tribe of Judah, and who was the Prince of all the kings of the earth. St. John says this Prince of the kings of the earth is the Lamb that was slain. His sacrifice marks Him out for the true King. All power which stands on any other ground than this, is rotten; it is falling to pieces now; it shall perish utterly.

Keep these thoughts in your minds, and then I have no doubt that you will be able by degrees to see a meaning in each of those seals, which the Lion of the tribe of Judah was able to break; a far better meaning than I could give you. I have felt the exceeding value of that passage of Scripture, as I have read different pages of civil and ecclesiastical history. But I am afraid to confine it by partial notions and apprehensions of mine. I have no doubt that they are true as far as they go, but other men's apprehensions of it, though very different from mine, may be true also. God's revelation, we may be sure, is infinitely wider and deeper than our thoughts of it. All I wish is, to put you in a method in which I think you may proceed safely. And by explaining to you, as I have tried to do, what an earthquake there was at this time; how, as the Apostles speak, it was one that not only shook earth but also Heaven, which caused all the dynasties of the world and all the powers above, to which they had been doing homage, to tremble and be moved from their seats; I think I have helped you to see that the convulsion when the sixth seal was opened, though it may have often occurred since, and though we may look for it in a more terrible form to occur again, is yet exactly what did take place while the last of the Apostles was tarrying till his Lord came.

The Earthquake.

You will perceive also, I think, that when St. John speaks of God's sealing 12,000 of each of the tribes of Israel with His Name, he teaches us that the divine purpose in setting apart a nation was not in any way frustrated by the unbelief of those who said they were Jews, but were not; that Israel was preserved though Israelites fell away; that the existence of a Christian Church is a testimony to the fact that the calling of God is without repentance. At the same time, you will learn from the magnificent conclusion of the seventh chapter, that we are not to confine God by the limits of any tribes or nations, by any thing that we see on earth or read of in history; that the visible world is surrounded by an invisible one; that in that there are multitudes which no man can number, of all nations, and kindreds, and peoples, and tongues, who have come out of great tribulation, and have washed their robes and made them white in the blood of the Lamb.

The sealed Tribes.

The multitude that no man could number.

LECT. X.
The prayers of the Saints.

You will read in the allusions to the altar and the golden censer, and the incense and the prayers of the saints, and what followed them, how close and inseparable is the connexion between prayer and sacrifice; how both suppose a real connexion between the visible and the invisible world; how unreal that connexion would be, if there were not a Mediator between God and man, One who is both the Priest and the Sacrifice, One who has offered Himself up that God's will may be done on earth as it is in Heaven.

The Trumpets.

You will see how the Apostle adopts the language of the Old Testament, and explains its meaning, where he speaks of the seven Angels with the seven trumpets. As those which were blown, when the children of Israel went round Jericho, announced the approaching fall of an accursed city, so all the different forms of God's judgments, whether they fall on sea, or earth, or air, whether they destroy the things in which man has delighted or come directly upon himself, whether they are plagues to his body or terrors and torments to his conscience, whether they affect the mass of a people or its heads and rulers, are always forewarnings that a false state of things is doomed and coming to an end, and that a righteous King is declaring His own power and government. If you ask me whether the city, on which the trumpets in St. John's day pronounced the sentence, was the city of Jerusalem, I can only answer by what I have told you already. It seems to me that the whole Roman world at that time had come into an accursed atheistic condition; that that Babylonian principle

What was the accursed City?

which the Jewish nation existed to denounce was the only one any longer recognised; but that the very heart and core of the evil was among the chosen people themselves; that Jerusalem was the centre of the crime and wickedness of the earth; that all the surrounding nations shared in the revolution, the most tremendous effects of which descended upon it. I think St. John teaches us this truth as we go on with his book, and it is one which we ought earnestly to lay to heart.

LECT. X.

He seems to tell us very clearly in the 10th chapter, that the book which had been sealed with the seven seals was opened, and that the mystery of God, which He had declared to His servants the prophets, was about to be accomplished. This is exactly what I have been trying to show you, that the period we are speaking of was one in which the iniquities of all previous times were gathered up, and in which that mystery of the divine Love which had been revealing itself in all previous times, was also fully declaring itself.

The open book.

In the hour of utter darkness which is spoken of in the next chapter, two witnesses are said to be prophesying in the midst of a great city, which is spiritually called Sodom and Egypt, where also our Lord was crucified. You will hear of many attempts to find out who these two witnesses were. Some of those attempts greatly confuse, I think, the course of ecclesiastical history, and make the records of God's dealings with men unintelligible. All I would say to you on the subject is this: that as these two witnesses

The two Witnesses.

ON CHURCH HISTORY.

LECT. X.
Hints concerning them.

are affirmed to be the two olive-trees and the two candlesticks standing before the Lord of the whole earth, which the prophet Zechariah speaks of, there must have been two such witnesses in the old times. As Moses and Aaron represented the law and the priesthood of the Jews—as Zerubbabel and Joshua represented the same law and priesthood after the captivity—we may suppose that there have always been some men, or some forms and institutions, who have asserted the great principles of God's order and of His fellowship with man. The particular men may have been killed; the forms may have perished for a time; there may have been a sense of triumph in the world, as if it had been rid of tormentors. But the principles could not die. They have revived, and have been found more terrible than ever, to the exulting wickedness which they denounced. That this should have been so in the city where our Lord was crucified, in its worst state, is according to all reason and probability. It is not very important for us to know who or what the witnesses then were: it is very important to understand the course of God's dealings with His creatures in every fearful crisis—in every hour of darkness.

The Woman and the Child.

We are told in the 12th chapter, that there appeared a great wonder in *Heaven*. A woman is travailing in birth; she brings forth a man-child; a dragon is seeking to destroy it; there is a battle between the hosts of heaven and the powers of hell; there is a great victory of the one over the other. All this passes behind the veil. These are great truths and principles, of which the *effects* are to be manifested in this world. God has redeemed humanity; Christ the Son of Man is to rule over the nations; the powers of evil have struggled against Him. He *has* vanquished. The loud voice *has* declared in heaven, "Now is come salvation and strength, and the Kingdom of our God, and the power of His Christ. For the accuser of our brethren is cast down, which accused them before God day and night." The Apostle goes on to intimate, that those who understood and believed this—who perceived that man was redeemed, and that a Brother, and not an accuser, was between them and God, were able to overcome the tempter by the blood of the Lamb and the word of His testimony. On earth they understood the mystery of heaven, and so they loved not their lives unto the death.

The hosts of good and evil.

But there is another vision upon *earth.* Though Humanity is redeemed—though the Child is caught up to heaven—the Woman is still on earth, persecuted by the dragon. Do you ask me what this woman is? The interpreters will all say, the Church. I would say the same. But yet I believe St. John's words are better than ours—that they teach us something which our substitutes for them do not teach. The Church is a true Church while she feels that she is the representative of Humanity as redeemed in Christ, when she looks up to Him and acknowledges that the *Son of Man* is at the right hand of God. She has to endure persecution for this witness so long as she bears it. But God preserves her. The wings of a

The Woman persecuted.

great eagle cover her. She is safe in any desolation. This principle is, I believe, true universally. But as the Apostle speaks of a time and times and half a time, I take it for granted that he alludes to the special tribulation through which those who believed in Christ and testified of Him were passing at that period.

The forms of animal and of spiritual wickedness.

In like manner, the beast that came out of the sea —the image of brute force—to which the evil spirit gave his dominion, will, I doubt not, be found the great antagonist of the Church and of man in all days. This is the godless, inhuman power, which sets itself against the Prince of the kings of the earth—against Him whose kingdom is based on sacrifice. And the other image of lying spiritual power which works miracles beside him, and draws men away to pay him homage, has, I am sure, been found doing the same work from age to age. But I cannot get rid of plain words, which seem to show that this brute-power was gathered up into some person,—I should suppose, a Roman Emperor—most probably Vitellius,—and that all the enchantments and lying wonders which we have heard of as so prevalent in the empire, were likewise conspiring, perhaps through some one insignificant agent, to deceive and degrade the world which the Emperor

The mark of the beast.

ruled. To be subject to this beast was the appointed lot of Christian men as of other men. Their patience and faith were to be shown in not joining in the conspiracies and revolutions of the empire. But what they had to beware of was, lest they should receive the mark of the beast on their forehead and on their hands, lest they should inwardly reverence this brutal force and think it divine.

The world in general, it is intimated, did this. There were some who could not do it. For they had another Name marked upon them, the name of a Father. They followed the Lamb that was slain; they stood as redeemed men, singing a new song before the throne. They are described as a guileless band— unlike, you will say, any of those Churches exhibited to us in the Apostolical Epistles; for in them there was much of division, unbelief, and evil. Unlike, only in this respect, that these who are said to be gathered on Mount Sion, (they may have been scattered, as far as place and fleshly intercourse went, far and wide,) understood their privilege as baptized men; that they *claimed* to be what St. Paul declared the Churches that he blamed most, *were*—elect in God the Father, and in Jesus Christ. Such songs as these have been sung in all, even the darkest, times. With them the Apostle teaches us to connect a proclamation going forth from an angel's voice in the midst of Heaven, and reaching to every nation and kindred of the earth. Fear God and give glory to Him, for His judgments are come, and worship Him that made Heaven and earth, and the sea, and the fountains of water. This summons to turn from all divided worship, all devil worship, and to confess the living and universal God —the God in whom is Light and no darkness at all, the God whose Life Christ had revealed—is called an everlasting Gospel. Upon it follows the shout of an angel. Babylon—the Babel city, the city of con-

The mark of the Father.

The band on Mount Zion.

The Gospel.

LECT. X. fusion,—the city of divided Gods and lawless tyranny,
The fall of Babylon. is fallen. And then the decree of another angel, "If any man worship the beast and his image, and receive his mark in his forehead, or in his hand, the same shall drink of the wine of the wrath of God, which is poured out without mixture into the cup of His indignation." How closely these proclamations are linked to each other, how wonderfully the history of the Church and of the world has at various periods confirmed them, I believe you will know better hereafter. But St. John was permitted to see in the events of his own day the clear and authentic testimony of them. The judgments on Jerusalem and on Rome, the miseries of Jewish and heathen beast-worshippers, connected as they were with the preaching of the everlasting glad tidings, of the true Father and the righteous King, announced emphatically to his purged ears, however few might understand the message, that Christ was putting His sickle into the earth, and gathering the vine of the earth.

The true King perceived by the true Prophet.

The Song. If in this spirit you read that song of Moses, the servant of God and of the Lamb, which is contained in the 15th chapter, and the description in the 16th,
The Vials. of the seven vials, and of the voice which said, "*It is done,*" and of the division of the great city; though you may find many things too deep for you, much about which you must in ignorance and patience desire to be enlightened—you will feel that you are not reading a book of tricks and puzzles, but a book full of awe, and wonder, and reality, which we want a child's heart to enter into, but which becomes most

needful, as the plot in the great drama of the world thickens, and its catastrophe draws nearer. You will then, I think, approach the account of the judgment of the great harlot, *the woman who was arrayed in purple and scarlet colour, and decked with gold and pearls, having a golden cup in her hand, full of abominations and filthiness of her fornications; upon whose forehead was a name written, Mystery, Babylon the Great, the mother of harlots, and abominations of the earth,* with a full readiness to profit by all the suggestions which great and learned men have offered respecting it—with an assurance that what they have said must have much worth, and be entitled to the most serious reflection—but also with a determination to let the divine Teacher Himself open the book, and tell you its meaning. And then I apprehend that the mystery of iniquity described there will be found indeed to have worked most mightily in Christendom, and to have called forth the protests of reformers and martyrs, whose names should be unspeakably dear to us, in this country and in all countries; but that it is not safe to limit its operation to any time or place or Church; and therefore that it is better, and more hopeful, to perceive how deeply the evil principle had penetrated in St. John's own day, how widely it had diffused itself, how fully he believed that a principle had been revealed which was mightier, which was going forth against the other, to battle and to victory.

If you study the 18th chapter of the Apocalypse well, you will find how many aspects of evil are dis-

The Harlot.

Modern applications of it, how to be regarded.

closed to us there—sensual, commercial, spiritual. It reads, certainly, like a picture of the breaking up of a whole complicated system of society, that had been sustaining itself upon an unrighteous, anarchical, selfish, anti-christian principle. It is a prophecy, I doubt not,—a prophecy of which we shall find many fulfilments, and may yet find more perfect fulfilments; but it is also a most accurate history of that overthrow of all social order which affected the city of Rome itself, the great mercantile cities which Rome had adopted into its huge empire, and the city which was so holy in its own eyes, and which is so horrible in ours, whereof Rome was the predestined scourge and destroyer.

The spectacle of such a judgment—in spite of the awful righteousness which we feel to be in it, and which makes us rejoice, because the evidence it bears is so clear and decisive, that the righteous God is the King of the earth—would be too appalling, if it were not for the last chapters of this great Revelation; if there were not the vision of the marriage of the Lamb with the Bride who had made herself ready; of Him, the divine Word of God, by whom all things were made, in whom is Life, and whose life is the Light of men,—as the Conqueror and Judge, followed by the armies of Heaven, clothed in fine linen, white and clean; of the utter overthrow of the beast and the false prophet; of the binding of Satan—though afterwards to be loosed for a season; of a judgment of the dead as well as of the quick; of a new Heaven and a new earth; of a city which had no need of the sun,

neither of the moon, to shine in it; for the glory of God *Lect. X.*
did shine in it, and the Lamb was the light thereof: *The Holy*
and into which the nations should bring their glory *City.*
and honour; of a pure river of water of life proceeding
from the throne of God and of the Lamb; of a state
in which there is no curse, because His servants serve
Him, and see His face, and His name is in their
foreheads. When are these things to be? St. John *The office*
answers, " Behold, I come quickly." He evidently *of the Church.*
believed they were *then;* that Christ was then coming
to make it evident that these sayings were faithful
and true. On their truth and faithfulness, I believe,
our Christendom, our modern world stands. I cannot but believe that the Church of God has existed,
and does exist, to bear witness of a Father, a Son,
and a Spirit, a one living God, who is mightier than
all the gods whom men have made for themselves to
worship; of a kingdom of Christ, to which the kingdoms of the world are subject, and must at last confess their subjection; of a divine Word and Wisdom, *Transition*
from which all the wise thoughts and words of men *to the new*
have proceeded; of a spiritual unity which has made *age.*
itself good, and shall make itself good against all
divisions and separations. How the Church has
borne this testimony; how the Church has failed to
bear it; how God has borne it by her, without her,
in spite of her—is the subject of the Lectures which
I shall hereafter deliver to you.

Before I conclude, it may be convenient that I
should tell you what method I shall hereafter adopt.
The first division of my lectures will extend to

M

LECT. X.

General division of the History.

Division into centuries.

the death of Gregory the Great, Bishop of Rome, A.D. 605. The second division will extend from that time to the end of the Popedom of Boniface VIII., A.D. 1303. The third will extend to the commencement of the present century. The first period will be divided by the beginning of the reign of Constantine the Great, A.D. 306. The second, by the opening of the eleventh century. The third, by the commencement of the German Reformation, A.D. 1517. I cannot explain to you at present why I fix upon these epochs as boundary lines. I hope they will explain themselves to you as we proceed. I have given the subject some consideration, and I think the arrangement that I have adopted, is, on the whole, the most natural, and will prove the most convenient to you. Within each of these divisions, I shall follow the order of the centuries. It would be a good reason for doing so, that I am walking in a line which the experience of ecclesiastical historians has led them to choose. They knew well enough that there were some disadvantages in it, but they found that the advantages preponderated; and if you try any other method, I think you will find that it is so. As I wish my lectures to be guides to you in your reading, I would not willingly embarrass you by inventing new plans which you would not be able to reconcile with those which more learned men have struck out for themselves.

Lectures on the Second Century.

LECTURE I.

THE DIFFERENT CHURCHES IN THE SECOND CENTURY.

SOME of you have asked me about the books which I should wish you to use while you are listening to these lectures. If I could find a text-book that satisfied me, I should desire you to get it, for it is a considerable help in class-teaching. But I have not fallen in with one that would exactly suit my purpose. I must therefore do as well as I can without it. The manuals which are most in use among us are translations from French or German authors, some of whom have written in their own tongues, some in Latin. The exceptions are Dr. Burton's book, which only extends over three centuries; the sketch of Bishop Hinds, originally published in the Encyclopædia Metropolitana, which does not go so far—at least, the part which has been republished; the History of Milner; Dr. Waddington's History, published by the Society for Promoting Useful Knowledge; and the short one of Mr. Palmer, published in the Englishman's Library. Each of these has its own merits. Two or three of them are books of much care and learning. I hope I may assist you in profiting by them all, as well as in using the work of Mosheim, which is a most learned and

Summaries of Church History.

A few of those best known in England enumerated.

valuable index to Ecclesiastical History, drawn up by an honest, conscientious man, but from which I think you would hardly learn what the Church is, or what it has done in the world. If you read him in English, you must get the latest translation, revised by Soames.

Gibbon. Gibbon, though he hated Christianity, will make you feel the reality of the Church, and its influence on the politics of the world, far better than the regular Ecclesiastical Historian. What he will not tell you, how the faith of the Church moulded the hearts of its

Neander. members, you will learn from Neander, considerable portions of whose deeply interesting work have been

Gieseler. translated into English. You will find Gieseler's Manual, of which there is an American translation, an invaluable book of reference, when you want to study the literature of the Church as it bears upon any particular topics. He illustrates questions by quotations from original authors, with remarkable fairness

Men, more than books. and skill. But you must beware of trying to ascertain the convictions and mind of a writer, even from passages that are chosen most impartially to explain his opinions. You must know the battles he has fought with himself, the men he has mixed with, the work he has done, if you would know him, or even understand his words. I shall be most thankful if any hints of mine should put you in the way of getting this kind of acquaintance with the persons of whom I shall speak to you, and with the times in which they lived. Most of you will be too much occupied hereafter, to have much leisure for antiquarian investigations. But I should like you to feel that the facts of Ecclesiastical History concern yourselves and your flocks; that the people whom it brings before us were men of our own flesh and blood; that He who called them to their work is calling us to ours. I do not think it is our business, but our laziness, which keeps us from understanding God's world and God's Church. If we were more alive, and more interested in all the men and things that are passing around us — in all that we and other men have to do and to suffer—the history of past times would become infinitely more clear to us. At all events, that is the way in which we Englishmen must get to know any thing about it. The study of books and manuscripts may be pursued more diligently elsewhere than here. We ought to be most grateful to those who have pursued it, or are pursuing it, in any part of the world. All their studies, their discoveries, their mistakes, are of exceeding worth. *We* are to discover their worth by life. Instead of complaining that God has put us into the midst of a bustling, working nation, we are to make use of that bustle and work, to explain thoughts and desires, fears and hopes, which men have cherished in their closets, and uttered in their prayers. Then, what was spoken to them in the secret ear, will likewise teach us what we have to proclaim on the house-tops.

<small>LECT. I.

Ecclesiastical History for workers.</small>

The method I have adopted in my introductory lectures—or rather, the method which the Acts of the Apostles and the Apocalypse have pointed out to us —will be the best for us in future. I shall consider what information we have about those Churches which

<small>*History of Churches during eight reigns.*
Trajan, A.D. 98.
Hadrian, A.D. 117.</small>

the Scripture History brings before us, when we lose sight of it, and what new Churches arose out of these. I begin to-day with the reign of the Emperor Trajan, A.D. 98. I shall follow out the information to the end of the century.

Our first interest is, of course, about Palestine. From the hints I have given you, you will be prepared for much vagueness in the reports upon this subject. Eusebius, who lived in Palestine, and must have had access to written memorials, if any were to be found, acknowledges that he knew of none: he only believed from tradition that Justus succeeded Symeon; that circumcised men ruled the Church till the time of Hadrian; that then a number of men, indifferently circumcised or uncircumcised, followed each other at very short intervals.

These reports tell us something by their very obscurity. The Palestine Church clung to the city and the Temple: they were gone. It had tried to assert the sanctity of the calling of the Jews: God seemed to have disowned that calling. The Christians may have striven hard to preserve their character. They may have put themselves under the guidance only of those who had the sign of the old Covenant. They may have even resolved only to acknowledge as their legitimate guides, those who were of the house of David. I suppose there may have been great party conflicts; many of the old sects may have appeared with new faces; there may have been questions not only who should govern them, but about the form of government they should adopt. But the Ebionitic party was probably in effect predominant — the one which boasted that it followed the tradition of St. James.

Then came what we may always expect in such circumstances—a time of persecution. There arose a false Christ—Barcochba was the name which he bore —who stirred up the Jewish people to revolt. It is the common opinion that the Roman ploughshare had not yet gone round the city of Jerusalem. The Temple had perished, against the wish of Titus. Who could tell that both might not rise out of their ruin? There was such a hope always latent in the Jews everywhere. It was likely to be strongest in Palestine. They only wanted a leader. When one appeared with the old characteristics—a fanatic and a brigand —using the Name of God and the words of Scripture —ready to die and to murder in that Name, and for the accomplishment of those words—multitudes were sure to gather about his standard. The revolt of desperate people, who have ties of blood and religion to each other, is always very formidable. Through a great part of the reigns of Trajan and of Hadrian, this Jewish war troubled the Roman empire, and required the serious efforts of the legions to put it down. It is not unimportant in that point of view; but it is most important in the history of the Church. The insurgent Jews, who were often triumphant— who were in possession of towns and districts in Palestine for a long time—regarded, as you will suppose, the followers of Jesus with especial hatred. I should not think that any organized persecutions which they suffered afterwards could have been worse

The Jewish insurrection.

Persecution of Christians by the Insurgents.

than the sufferings they underwent from these anarchists; though they are not of a kind that are likely to be recorded, and though the Palestine Church was in too unsettled a condition to preserve records. The trial may have been temporary, but the effect of it was permanent. This war seems to have been the great means of severing the Church, there as well as elsewhere, from the synagogue. After it, there could be no question whether the disciples of Jesus were a Nazarene sect or no. Those who were still inclined to acknowledge that name, and to cling to their Jewish distinctions, were now regarded as separatists. The Ebionites were treated as a party outside of the Church.

The end of this war in the reign of Hadrian was memorable for another reason. Jerusalem, the holy city, the city of David, the city of Jehovah, acquired a new name. It was called Ælia Capitolina. The first name was taken from the emperor, Ælius Hadrianus; the second declared that it was dedicated to the Jupiter of the Roman Capitol. There is something more significant in this change than even in the overthrow by Titus; or rather, one was the consummation of the other. That mighty witness that the earth has an unseen God over it, a righteous King ruling over the inhabitants of it, was now utterly gone. The Jew might approach the city once a year, and only once, to think of what it had been. Two centuries hence we shall hear of the old name again. It will meet us in various passages of our history; it will never lose its power over the heart of

Christendom. But at this time Christians rather [LECT. I.] pointed with a kind of exultation to the witness which was borne by its downfal to their King. They preferred long afterwards to speak of Cæsarea as the chief city of the Palestine Church.

Samaria, you will remember, had a different cha- [Samaria.] racter from Judæa in the Apostolical records, as well as in the earlier times. Simon the enchanter presented himself to us there in conflict with St. Peter. I have hinted at various traditions that became current respecting him, all of which turn more or less upon the belief that his doctrine was in some way especially opposed to that of this Apostle. St. Peter sets forth Jesus Christ as the centre and corner-stone of all fellowship among men; Simon believed in *a* Christ, [Simon.] one among many who exercised great powers, and had some mysterious divinity. This distinction becomes more and more important, as we proceed in the history of this century. I speak of it here, because Samaria is always regarded, by old historians at least, as the starting-place of the debates to which this radical difference gave rise. Menander is said to have [Menander.] been Simon's successor. You must not infer from the word "successor" that they were necessarily related to each other as pupil to teacher, though that may very possibly have been the case. The phrase only intimates that Menander had the same habit of mind as Simon; that they both looked upon the Christ mainly, either as One possessing miraculous powers, or as an emanation from the Divinity—that they both separated Jesus the humble Man from Christ the divine Power. They

LECT. I.

did this probably in a more Jewish way than those we shall hear of afterwards. I think there is no doubt that we may trace in Samaria the rude form of a system which became refined and complicated in Syria and Egypt.

Justin, a Samaritan.

As I wish you always to associate eminent men with the countries from which they sprung, when we can know them, I will add, before I leave Samaria, that Justin, of whom we shall hear much hereafter, was born in one of its villages. His after life is connected with the Greek cities and with Rome. I do not suppose that he had anything to do with the Church in Samaria; he was probably an unbeliever in Jesus while he dwelt there. Nor is there an evidence that he was a Jew by birth; it seems to me clear that he was not. Nevertheless, his Samaritan origin must have affected his thoughts and character not inconsiderably, the more as he must in his childhood have heard much of the war under Barcochba, if he did not witness some of the later events of it.

Syria.

We will now go to Antioch. Here we find ourselves in quite a new region. There is evidently a settled society; a father or overseer is at the head of it: there is fellowship between it and other societies that we have heard of already in the Apostolical records; the Heathen people wonder what it means, and begin to regard it as troublesome, even formidable. I told you that there was a tradition of St. Peter having presided over this Church, in the same way as St. James did at Jerusalem, and that there was very little justification for the opinion in the facts of his history.

THE SECOND CENTURY. 171

We know nothing of the society, after the story in the Acts of the Apostles leaves us, till we find Ignatius there in the days of Trajan.

There has been a great controversy about his letters, one in which our Bishop Pearson took a conspicuous part. A number of epistles had been passing under the name of Ignatius, which were manifestly forgeries, and which had brought the rest into discredit. Pearson maintained the genuineness of the letters to the Churches of Ephesus, Magnesia, Rome, Philadelphia, Smyrna, and of one to Polycarp. These epistles contain some very strong passages respecting the authority of the Bishop or Overseer, and the impossibility of a Church acting without him. The question, therefore, whether they are genuine, has been mixed up with the opinions of men upon this subject. However much they may have wished to look fairly at the evidence, their wishes to find, or not to find, something in so early a document which might support their previous conclusions, have more or less affected their judgments of it. The recent discovery of a Syriac version of these epistles, greatly reduced in size, has given a new turn to the controversy, some maintaining that this version enables us to make out a consistent original text, some that it was garbled to suit the purposes of persons who did not like the sentiments of Ignatius.

I am not going into this dispute. But I have said thus much to you about it because I desire to point out to you a good and an evil which has followed from the argument. The good is, that documents are

Lect. I.

Ignatius.

His Letters.

Controversy respecting them.

Advantage and mischief of it.

sifted—that each person, on whatever side he writes, brings out some fact or observation which others had overlooked—that between them some maxims and rules of evidence which may be applied to different cases are established. The evil is, that the readers, and still more, the disputants, begin to form quite a false notion of the man about whom they are talking. Some of you have fancied, I dare say, because I have alluded to statements respecting the authority of the Bishop, that Ignatius was a polemical author, who was maintaining some doctrine or theory about Church government. You could not make a greater mistake. He is the simplest, most child-like man, one can meet with anywhere. We call him one of *the Apostolical Fathers*, and we could not give him a better name. Whichever text of his writings is the true one, that character comes out most evidently in him. He is a shepherd watching over a flock, a father looking after a family. There are other flocks under different shepherds, distinct families under distinct fathers. These he claims fellowship with, because he confesses one chief Shepherd, one Father that is over them all. But he is as little of a debater or of a speculative man as it is possible to conceive. His only thought is how to keep his sheep together; what is likely to tempt them to wander and choose ways of their own. Even on this point he does not go into any refinements. He knows very little about the thoughts that were stirring in men's minds at that time, or how to bring out the truths of the Gospel in reference to them. He has no calling

Ignatius a pastor and father.

to that work, and he does not pretend to do it. If you fancy that because he lived so near the time of the Apostles, and because he was, perhaps, the disciple and friend of the Apostle John, there must be some danger of confounding his letters with those in the Bible, you have only to read them, and you will find the difference. All that wonderful and various wisdom which was brought out in the Apostle Paul, to meet the various circumstances of men in different nations and churches of the world, is entirely wanting in Ignatius. The deep theology of the Apostle John, which reconciles so many different and opposing thoughts, and which remains a treasure for the peasant and the sage in every new period, has nothing which corresponds to it in his pupil. Yet in one sense the mantle of his master has fallen upon him. The affectionate, loving, uniting spirit is with him. That was wanted for the new time as for the old. In every other respect the Apostolical Fathers were to offer the most striking and lively contrast to the writers whom they reverenced, and who were by degrees to be recognised as canonical.

Cannot be confounded with the Canonical Epistles.

Resemblance between them.

Yet Ignatius had a calling of his own, and I want you to see how great and noble a one it was. You must think of him as a man and a pastor, much more than as a doctor; and then you will understand what his doctrine was, how living it was, how entirely it meant faith and trust in a living Person, how, for that reason, it could sustain him in his work and in his death. He had certainly a weakness, and one which

Desire for martyrdom in Ignatius.

LECT. I.

Reason of it.

might afterwards do much harm in the Church, when it was indulged by men of another character than his. He had an intense craving to die for his Master. It was not that he attached the least merit to such an act; that thought never entered his mind, or, at least, never dwelt there. But the death of Christ was so present to him, he so much lived upon it and in it, that he could conceive no blessedness or glory like that of entering into it thoroughly and altogether. He could not feel himself much at home in the frivolous city in which his body dwelt; his home was elsewhere. And there was a certain impatience to get rid of his earthly tabernacle, that he might be ever with the Lord, which shows how real his faith was, but shows too, I think, that there was some great difference between him and that Apostle who was content to be a prisoner of Nero, that he might be a witness for God.

Trajan and Ignatius.

There is nothing, however, much more instructive, or more beautiful, than the story which is preserved to us of the interview between this old Father and the Emperor Trajan. Trajan had the kingdoms of the world in possession; he was adding to them by fresh conquests; he was ruling them, on the whole, wisely and honestly. He took the society of the Roman empire as he found it, with its beliefs and its unbeliefs, its vices and its gods,—the order which had come down from other days, the corrupt habits and passions which were threatening that order with destruction. He did not pretend to make this world better: he was to hold it together as well as he could. He felt he was bound to do that; and he did not shrink from the labour that was wanted for the task. He was a man of strong, clear sense, of kindly dispositions, covetous of power, but desirous to be just. Ignatius was a ruler, too, in his way,—a ruler on a very small scale, over a few sheep or children, such as I have described, in the midst of a city that was hungering after wealth, given up to pleasure, worshipping the gods,—in a great measure for the games and festivals with which their worship was accompanied. The Christian family was not one which left the inhabitants of this city quiet. It is not like those who frequented the Jewish synagogue,—a people with curious rites, which they have inherited from their fathers, and who leave other people to keep their own traditions, while they keep theirs. This family is intrusive, aggressive,—it claims all people as belonging to it,—it tempts them within its circle. If they come into it, they abandon their own.

It was impossible for Trajan not to take notice of such a society. You will easily conceive that when the two men looked each other in the face, they would understand each other very little. Trajan accused Ignatius of transgressing his commands, and of tempting many to their ruin. He called him κακοδαίμων, by which he meant much what a person would mean in our day, by calling one for whom he had a contempt, a poor devil. Ignatius took hold of the word, and said, "That one who bore God in him could not be called a demon or devil, seeing that the demons depart from the servants of God. But if the Emperor meant that he was evil towards the demons, he confessed it. Having Christ as his Heavenly King, he broke their plots in pieces." "Who is it," asked Trajan, "who carries God within him?" Ignatius answered, "He that has Christ in his heart." "Why," said Trajan, "do you not think that we have the gods in our mind, seeing that we have them as our allies against our enemies?" Ignatius said, "The demons of the nations, thou, in thy error, callest gods. For there is one God, He that hath made the heaven, and the earth, and the sea, and all things in them; and one Christ Jesus, the Son of God, the Only-Begotten, whose kingdom may I enjoy." "Do you mean," said Trajan, "Him that was crucified under Pontius Pilate?" Ignatius said, "Him that hath crucified my sin with the inventor of it, and hath put down all demoniac error and wickedness under the feet of those who bear Him in their heart." "Dost thou, then," said Trajan, "carry the Crucified One within thyself?" Ignatius said, "Yea. For it is written, 'I will dwell in them, and walk in them.'" Thereupon Trajan pronounced sentence: "We ordain that Ignatius, who says that he bears the Crucified within him, be led as a prisoner to Rome, there to be made the food of wild beasts, for the amusement of the people."

I shall not dwell as much as some have done, on the records of martyrdoms. Many of them are clearly of later invention. But this, and one or two to which

I shall allude in the second century, have not only a LECT. I.
real savour of antiquity in them, but make known to
us the innermost principles upon which the Church
was standing, and the secret of the power which it
was exerting in the world, a secret often misunderstood by those who glorified the Fathers of the Church
in after days. For instance, it became a custom in *Ignatius,*
the Church to call Ignatius Θεόφορος, 'the God- *in what sense*
bearer,' because he spoke of his carrying Christ in Θεόφορος.
him. So far as this name expressed merely the
respect and love of his own flock, and their conviction that he was living in close communion with the
spiritual world, there was no great harm in applying
it to him. But certainly he never meant to claim it
as if it were some special title. His quotation from the
Scriptures showed that he looked upon every Christian
man as a Θεόφορος, whether he was mindful of his
high and awful privilege or not. His exhortations
had no meaning, if this were not true. He had no
testimony to bear to Trajan against the visible gods
to whom he was bowing down, if he could not speak
of Christ having come to claim men as members of
Himself, and so, as children of His Father. The
limitation of the language was a dangerous symptom.
I cannot say how early it may have manifested itself;
but I have no doubt very soon, it is so natural. And
there was another bad symptom, which the history of *Search for*
the martyrdom of Ignatius makes known to us. His *relics.*
friends gathered up relics of his body after he was
killed, and preserved them; so the story says, and I
cannot see any reason for disbelieving it. The act

N

was a simple and innocent one at first, but, like the Ephod which Gideon made, it became a snare and a sin to the house of Israel. The antiquity of the practice makes no difference at all in this respect. There was peril in it from the beginning. We shall see by-and-by with what other perils it speedily became connected.

Intercourse between the Church and the Persian sages.

I spoke of Ignatius as knowing very little of the thoughts by which men were exercised in his time, though he fulfilled his own work so faithfully. You must not suppose that such ignorance was universal in the Church of Antioch. It was on the borders of the old Persian empire. The members of it met continually with men who had been nourished in that faith of which I spoke to you in a former lecture. It had not lost its power,—it could not, for it appeals to some of the strongest and deepest experiences in men's hearts.

The dark and bright world.

"Are we not dwelling in an evil world?" these Persians asked;—"Who can have made it?—Surely some dark and evil being. But there is a better world we think of and dream of. It may be in the bright stars over our heads, in the sun, or moon;— it may be in some region where spirits dwell, but which the eye does not see. No doubt that world must have something to do with ours. All the light that visits us must proceed from it. Doubtless from time to time some persons or spiritual beings come thence to do us good. How else could we account for any good men dwelling here, in the midst of all our evil? They must be the chosen favourites of Heaven, picked out from the rest, by these beings that descend to us, and act in a multitude of secret ways upon us."

Such thoughts were more distinctly and broadly expressed in the Persian faith than in any other. But they were diffused, in one form or other, through the Roman world. That passion for enchantments, that ready belief in all teachers who spoke of strange new influences, was a sign of their prevalence. The visible powers to which men paid a traditional, heartless homage, were not enough for them. There must be some unknown, mysterious agency, of quite a different nature from these. Nay, were not these their oppressors, from which they were crying to be delivered? *Wide diffusion of these notions in the second century.*

The preachers of Christ's Gospel said, in plain terms, that they were. They spoke of the rulers of the darkness of this world. They spoke of Christ delivering men from them. Those who embraced the Gospel heartily, in the love of it, soon found what these words meant. They felt they were not the servants of dark, malevolent powers,—that they were not the servants of visible things. They had found their true Father: they had arisen and gone to Him. Christ, by His acts of power, had claimed earth, and sea, and air, for Him. They could confess an unseen, heavenly, spiritual Lord of all. They could invite their fellow men to renounce any other worship, and serve Him. *Apparent identity with the teaching of the Gospel.*

This was the spirit in which Ignatius spoke to Trajan. But those who had not felt the true burthen of the world's evil on their hearts, or had not sought deliverance from it as he had, could easily draw from his *Inferences from that teaching.*

words the sense that this world was the possession of evil spirits; that it belonged of right to them; that Christ had come as an alien or intruding power into it; that He had chosen out a few favourites while He was down here on earth, whom He meant to be with Him in the world of Light; that their duty was to keep themselves out of all contact with material things which were utterly evil, and, as far as they could, from any intercourse with a world which was not only devil-tainted, but devil-possessed.

Attempts at a higher devotion.

For some time, those who held those thoughts would seem to themselves and to others more eminent Christians than the rest of the Church; stronger protestants against the surrounding heathenism; holding up a higher ideal of devotion to their brethren. They knew that St. Paul had striven to bring his body into subjection; they could invent devices for the purpose of showing their utter contempt for it, and of separating their souls from all intercourse with it. The further they carried these experiments, the more they appeared to ascend into an invisible region, and to acquire the power of investigating its secrets.

Doctrines founded on the ascetical practice.

By degrees, however, those who had admired these teachers for the sublimity of their virtue and of their aspirations, would be startled by very strange language from their lips, language which seemed not only at variance with all they had heard from Ignatius, all they read in the writings of the Apostles, but absolutely subversive of their doctrine. "Matter being essentially evil—the body being accursed—is it possible," these spiritual men would ask, "that Christ has actually taken flesh, that He has died on an actual cross? Can He, the pure spiritual Being, have come into direct contact and conflict with the defilements of our world?" "Oh! surely not," they replied: "it must have been only an apparent flesh He wore; it was only an apparent death He died." This was enough for some. Others must have a new theory to explain this. No doubt the Evangelists attributed plain, simple, earthly acts to their Lord and Master. So they might. *Jesus* of Nazareth did, no doubt, perform those acts. But the *Christ*, the spiritual Being, must not be identified with Him. Was it not said that the Spirit descended upon Him at His baptism? The Christ is He who is anointed with the Spirit. Why might not the Christ descend into Jesus then, and desert Him again before His passion?

Those who had arrived at this point, were already on the same ground with those in Persia or elsewhere, who spoke of divine helpers and redeemers, coming from the world of light into the world of darkness. There was nothing in what they called Gospel, which essentially differed from this old belief. For it had ceased to be a Gospel. It was no longer a message to mankind about One who had been actually born into this world, that He might claim them and it for His Father and their Father. It was a scheme about the descent of a certain divine essence into the body of a mere man. Such essences might have dwelt in other bodies before; or they might have moved about without any bodies. Might they not, as the Persians said, have come from the stars; the world of light which the

Lect. I.

Christ's body apparent, not real.

Jesus separated from the Christ.

Seeming advancement, real retrogression.

Astrology mingled with Christian Theology.

LECT. I.

Saturninus.

His opinions, how far local, how far human.

good Creator had formed? Must not they have appeared here, to rescue certain holy souls from the evil Creator? Might not all the acts of Christ, as well as His relation to those who had dwelt on earth and been helpers to man before Him, be explained on this hypothesis?

The name of *Saturninus* is connected in the Church of Antioch with doctrines of this kind. They seemed to him and to his followers far more profound than those which had been taught in the Church before. The simpler men in the Church were scandalized by them as startling denials of what was most precious to them. Later times have wondered how opinions, which, when they are brought together, seem so strange and incoherent, could have ever arisen in the mind of one man, or been adopted by others. I apprehend that there was the most profound meaning in the thoughts of those Persian sages, who had asked what this world is, and what other and better world there is than this. But if the news that Jesus Christ had taken flesh and redeemed mankind, was the only possible answer to this question, Saturninus and his friends were not finding out a new and deeper satisfaction of men's difficulties, but setting aside one which had been given. The *form* which their opinions took, was determined by the circumstances in which they lived, or in which they were educated. The temptation to the opinions lay in their desire to be different from other men; in not liking to acknowledge a common Lord, and common Deliverer. It is not safe merely to dwell on their extravagances. It is necessary to remember that these formed themselves by degrees most naturally, and that, if we are in no danger of falling into their particular habits of thought, we are just as much in danger as they were, of accepting the principle, which gave these habits of thought all their mischief and malignity. If we do, the practical results will be the same; we shall not really believe that Christ has come in the flesh more than they did.

May be repeated.

I shall say nothing more about the Church of Antioch in the second century, except that one of its bishops, Theophilus, wrote a defence of the Christian faith, which is still extant; and that we have a fragment by another, Serapion, in reference to a Gospel, passing under the name of St. Peter, which inculcated, he affirms, many false doctrines. On both these subjects I may have to speak to you, when I turn from particular Churches to the Church as forming one Society.

Theophilus, circa A.D. 170.

Serapion, A.D. 181.

LECTURE II.

THE SAME SUBJECT CONTINUED.

CHURCHES IN ASIA MINOR.

<small>LECT. II.
Asia Minor.</small>   I SHALL now pass to the Churches in Asia Minor. One of the Epistles of Ignatius, as I told you, is addressed to the Church of Ephesus. As it is greatly reduced in the Syriac version, I will draw no conclusions from it respecting the character of those to whom it was addressed. But the name Onesimus occurs in both versions. If we may assume,—as most ecclesiastical
<small>*Onesimus at Ephesus.*</small> historians have assumed,—that this Onesimus was he about whom St. Paul wrote to Philemon, a society in one of the wealthiest cities of the Roman empire must have looked up to a runaway slave as its spiritual overseer and father. There is no reason to doubt the tradition. Even the existence of it shows how certain it was that a Gospel which was preached by fishermen, and confessed One who was called the Carpenter's Son as the Son of God, would break the chains of the captive, and establish a much more wonderful equality at the root of society than destroyers of ranks, than the most sweeping revolutions, have been ever able to create.

<small>*Sardis.*</small>   The Church at Sardis, you will remember, was in a very unpromising state when it was addressed by St. John. We may hope that it had recovered its

ground before the middle of the second century; for at that time we find it under the government of a man who was, at all events, a voluminous and painstaking writer. None of his books remain to us, but you shall have the titles of them; because they will tell you what people were thinking about at this time. He wrote on Easter; on Polity; on Prophets; on the Church; on the Lord's Day; on the Nature of Man; on Creation; on the Obedience of Faith; on the Objects of Sense; on the Soul and Body, or the Higher Mind; on Baptism; on the Origin and Birth of Christ; on Prophecy; on Hospitality;—a book called The Key; on the Devil; on the Apocalypse; on the Incarnate God; and a book addressed to the Emperor Antoninus. You will not understand, at present, the occasions which led him to touch upon some of these topics. I shall tell you immediately about one of them.

Lect. II.
Meliton flourished under Marcus Aurelius.
Subjects of his books.

The Overseer of the Church of Smyrna during a great part of this century was Polycarp, who is represented, on good evidence, as having been the friend and disciple of St. John. I call him by this name, *Overseer,* which is a good and venerable name. Yet it describes the office more than the man. If we speak of him as a Father, we shall be much nearer the impression which he made on his contemporaries. If his letter to the Philippians is genuine, as it is generally held to be in England, it shows us what the secret of his influence must have been. There are no discussions in it of such subjects as Meliton handled, —not the least speculation of any kind. It consists

Smyrna.

His Letter.

mainly of extracts from the Canonical Epistles,—not on questions of debate or doctrine, but on purity, and righteousness, and the love of money. If he wrote to an European Church, it indicates a communion which one likes to think may have existed consciously as well as in the spirit, between those which were at a distance from each other. One who knew and revered him, certainly, became a teacher in Gaul.

Sphere of his influence. Still the influence of Polycarp must have mainly been in the regions of Asia Minor. These Churches clung with great tenacity to the customs which *Weight of St. John's authority.* they believed that St. John had observed. I have tried to show how earnestly he laboured that the Jewish calling should not be forgotten in the Gentile world,—that the new commandment should be felt as the real expansion and interpretation of the old. In this spirit, he may have kept up till his dying day something like an observation of the Jewish Paschal feast, while he taught his disciples how Christ had translated it into a higher, — the festival of an accomplished redemption and of a *The Passover and Easter Day.* divine life. There would have been nothing inconsistent in his following the maxims of his youth, as to times and seasons, while he was most possessed with the meaning and power of the Resurrection, as fulfilling all that the Passover had shadowed out. The more the Churches felt the ground on which they were standing, the more wonderful the day of Resurrection appeared to them; the more they hailed it as the new birth-day of the world, which, for the sake of the world, as much as for the sake of their own unity, they were to proclaim by their acts as well as their words. The Apostles had been sent forth to testify of the Resurrection; what had the Church to testify of, that was so glorious a Gospel to mankind, concerning their true King,—concerning the deliverance He had wrought out,—concerning the union He had established between the seen and the unseen world? The connexion of Easter with the Passover was, no doubt, close; but as Christians began to be more separate from the synagogue, they were more disposed to dwell on the difference than the resemblance between the two dispensations. The Christians in the West eagerly insisted that Easter Day must be kept on the first day of the week; that all other celebrations must regulate themselves by this. With those of Asia Minor St. John's example was mightier than any arguments. The day which they had seen, or supposed him to observe, must be the right one. No authority on earth should induce them to change it. Polycarp seems thoroughly to have shared this feeling. We are told that he made a journey to Rome, and argued the question with Anicetus, who was the Overseer of that Church. They could come to no agreement about the subject in controversy; but they parted with a sense of inward communion, which was stronger than any diversity of customs could break. It was not, we shall find, to be so always.

Polycarp belongs to the same class of men with Ignatius; but there are marked individual differences between them. In the scanty records we have of

Lect. II.

Differences in the Churches.

Polycarp and Anicetus. Eusebius, book iv. c. 14.

their lives, these differences are less conspicuous. They come out clearly in the accounts of their deaths. Polycarp survived Ignatius full fifty years. He lived till the reign of Marcus Aurelius. In that reign the Church of Smyrna was sorely persecuted. A letter was written in its name, when it had gained a little rest, which tells of others who fought and fell, but especially how its dear and venerable father endured to the end. From this letter it is evident that the eager longing to suffer which had characterized Ignatius, had been imitated by men with very little of his faith. One Quintus is especially named, who came out of Phrygia, expressly that he might offer himself as a victim for the faith, but who, when he saw the wild beasts, was affrighted, and made the sacrifices and took the oaths which the Proconsul prescribed. Polycarp gave a different example to his flock. A cry went up from the multitude, "Away with the atheists; let Polycarp be sought for." Thereupon, though wishing to remain in the city, he consented to withdraw to a place in the country, where with a few friends he spent his time night and day praying for all men, and for the Churches throughout the world, as was his wont. While he was praying, it is said, he beheld a vision, which assured him that he must be burnt alive. Still his Master's precept to fly, seemed to him binding; he sought another hiding place. It was discovered. Late in the evening, horsemen arrived at the house in which he was concealed. When he heard that they were come, he went down from the upper chamber to meet them.

Marginalia:

LECT. II.

Τῆς Σμυρναίων ἐκκλησίας περὶ μαρτυρίου τοῦ ἁγίου Πολυκάρπου. *A somewhat abridged version in Eusebius, book iv. c. 14.*

Polycarp retreating from persecution.

He is discovered.

They wondered at his quietness and his dignity, and at the pains they had been taking to apprehend so old a man. He desired his attendants to bring forth food and drink for them. He himself asked an hour for uninterrupted prayer. For two hours, it is said, he continued his supplications, remembering all with whom he had ever conversed, little and great, illustrious and insignificant, and the whole Catholic Church throughout the world. Then they placed him upon an ass and brought him into the city, the day being the Sabbath immediately preceding the Easter festival. The Irenarch asked him what harm there was in saying Lord Cæsar, and in offering sacrifice, and what else was required of him. At first he did not answer them. Then, when they continued, he said, "I am not going to do what you advise me to do."[1] As he entered into the arena, says the writer of the letter, a voice from Heaven was heard saying to him, "Be strong, and be a man, Polycarp." That such a voice, or one imparting still higher strength than this, reached his inward ear, we cannot doubt, from what followed—though the by-standers may have only dreamed that they caught the echo of it. When he was brought before the Proconsul, he was asked whether he was Polycarp. On his confessing to the name,—"Have compassion on thy age," said the Proconsul; "swear by the fortune of Cæsar; abandon thy error; cry aloud, Away with the Atheists." Then

His Prayer.

The Voice.

Polycarp and the Proconsul

---

[1] The unhappy Latin translator substitutes for this famous answer, the following piece of rant :—Ad hoc se nunquam perduci non igne, non ferro, non arctorum doloribus vinculorum, non fame, non exsilio, non flagellis."!!

LECT. II.

turning with a firm face to all the people, lifting his hand, and looking up to Heaven, Polycarp said, "Away with the Atheists!" "Take the oath, and renounce Christ," said the Proconsul, "and I will release thee." Polycarp answered, "Eighty and six years have I served Him, and He hath done me no wrong; and how can I speak evil of my King, my Saviour?" "Swear by the fortune of Cæsar," said the Proconsul. "If from mere idleness," answered Polycarp, "thou requirest that I should swear by the fortune of Cæsar, pretending that thou dost not know who I am, hear me. I am a Christian. But if thou wishest to know the Christian doctrine, give me a day, and hear." The Proconsul said, "Persuade the people." (Probably to save him, the Roman really wishing to do so, if the mob could have been satisfied.) Polycarp said, "Thee I have counted worthy to hear our doctrine; for we are bidden to pay all seemly reverence, such as is not destructive of us, to the powers and authorities that are ordained by God. But these I count not worthy that I should make my apology to them." The Proconsul said to him, "I have wild beasts: to these I may cast you, if you change not your mind." "It is good," he answered, "to change from the worse to the better, not from the better to the worse." The other replied to him, "If you care nothing for wild beasts, I can cause you to be consumed with fire." Polycarp said, "Thou threatenest the fire that burns for an hour and speedily is quenched. Thou knowest not the fire of the coming judgment, and of eternal punishment that

The oath.

The mob.

is kept for the ungodly. But why tarriest thou? Order whichever thou pleasest." Then, it is said, the countenance of Polycarp was filled with exceeding courage and joy; and the Proconsul sent a herald into the midst of the arena, proclaiming, "Polycarp hath confessed himself to be a Christian." Thereupon the multitude of the Jews and Gentiles that dwelt in Smyrna cried aloud, "This is the teacher of impiety, —the Father of the Christians, who teacheth multitudes not to sacrifice, nor to worship the gods." So speaking, they urged the Asiarch,—an officer who had the care of the games, uniting in himself some civil with some sacerdotal functions,—that he would let loose a lion upon him. The person appealed to, refused, seeing that his office had expired. Then they cried out, "That he should be burnt alive,"— according to the intimation, his biographer adds, that he had received in his vision. The multitude ran eagerly to fetch the wood and what else was needful, for the burning; the Jews, as was their custom, being specially busy in this work. Then, when they were about to fasten him with fetters, he said, "Leave me so. For He who has given me power to endure the fire, will give me power, without your securities, to remain unmoved at the stake." Then, when they had bound his arms, he prayed: "Lord God Omnipotent, the Father of Thy beloved and blessed Son, Jesus Christ, through whom we have received the knowledge of Thee, the God of angels and principalities, and of all the creation, and of all the generation of the righteous, who live before Thee; I bless Thee

Lect. II.
The beasts.
The fire.
Prayer at the stake.

LECT. II. that Thou hast counted me worthy of this day and of this hour, that I should have part in the number of Thy witnesses, in the cup of Thy Christ, so to attain to the resurrection of eternal life of soul and of body, through the incorruptibleness of the Holy Spirit. Among these (witnesses) may I be received before Thee to-day for an acceptable offering, according as Thou hast prepared me, and hast manifested beforehand Thy will, and hast accomplished it, who art the faithful and true God. For this and for all things, I praise Thee, I bless Thee, I glorify Thee, with the eternal and heavenly Jesus Christ, Thy beloved Son; with whom to Thee and the Holy Spirit be glory, now, and in the ages to come. Amen." As he finished the prayer, the men who were waiting for that intent kindled the fire.

The remainder of the Letter. What follows is not worthy of Polycarp's words and prayer, seeing that it chiefly refers to the impression on the by-standers, who were liable in that exciting time to various fancies, which seemed more wonderful and divine to them than facts, but which cannot seem so to us, if our minds are in a right state. The historian complains, that through the craft of the devil, the disciples of Polycarp were prevented at first from obtaining any relic of his *Search for remains.* body. He attributes the attempt to rob them of this privilege to the representations of Jews, that they intended to turn the bones into objects of worship. He protests, evidently with the greatest sincerity, against the notion that it was possible for them who acknowledged Christ as the Lord of all, to commit such an offence, however they might desire to reverence those upon whom God had put the highest honour. The Church meant what it said. But it had not yet learnt that the devil's arts might be employed in other ways than to save them from a great temptation; they had not yet learnt that the Jew might be an unconscious instrument in God's hands to warn those who had inherited the stewardship of his fathers against falling into the sins of his fathers.

Such, and so beautiful, are the records of the Church in Smyrna; so accurately did it bear out in the second century, the description which St. John had given in the first of the struggles it would undergo, and the class of enemies it would have to encounter.

We have not similar records of the Church in the particular cities in Asia Minor; but there are two or three of its provinces which offer facts that are very deserving of our notice. You have heard of Trajan's personal conflict with Ignatius in Syria. Several years before his coming there, he had received a letter from his able friend and minister, Caius Plinius, who was Proconsul in Bithynia, asking for his judgment about the treatment of the Christians there. The authenticity of the letter has been doubted; but I think that scholars in general accept it. There is nothing in the tone of it to make it suspicious. If there are some passages which a Christian likes to dwell upon, there are others which show how little the early times were free from the inconstancy and false profession of the later. Pliny assumes that the Christians in his province are to be treated as offenders;

Bithynia.

Pliny went to Bithynia, A.D. 103.

Letters, book x. ep. 96.

that had evidently been the practice before he came to it. But he was not clear about the amount of punishment that was to be awarded to them,—whether it was to be the same for young and old, strong and weak,—whether they were to be pardoned if they retracted,—whether the mere name of Christian, without any evidence of further offences, was to suffice for their condemnation. His course hitherto, he says, had been to ask them whether they were Christians; the second time to threaten punishment. Inflexible obstinacy he assumed to be a crime, though there were no other. Some he sent to Rome, because they were Roman citizens. Many anonymous charges were conveyed to him against different persons: some of these denied that they had ever been Christians; some admitted that they had been three years or more before; one or two had renounced the profession full twenty years. All these submitted to the tests which Pliny imposed. They invoked the gods; offered supplications, with wine and frankincense, to the image of the Emperor, and reviled Christ. These he dismissed. Those who were, indeed, Christians would do none of these things. The recanters told Pliny that the height of their crime or error had consisted in the habit of meeting on a fixed day before it was light; in singing hymns to Christ as to a God; in binding themselves by an oath, to abstain from thefts and adulteries;—not to violate their faith; not to withhold deposits when called to give them up. Then they were wont to depart, and to meet again for the purpose of eating bread. The meal, it appeared, was harmless and "general:" but it was abandoned when the Proconsul published the Emperor's command against secret assemblies. The Proconsul says that he examined two maid-servants by torture, but that he could extract no further testimony from them than this. It was a depraved and extravagant superstition. But he needed the Emperor's directions; for many of all orders, and both sexes, were involved in the charge. The contagion of this superstition had spread not only into cities, but in the villages and country districts. Still, he trusted it might be stopped. There was evidence that the temples which had been almost deserted were beginning to be frequented again, and that sacred solemnities, which had been long intermitted, were renewed. It seemed, therefore, wise to try what might be done by holding out encouragement to a change of mind. Trajan, in his answer, approves the policy of Pliny. He does not wish to lay down general rules, which might not be applicable to all places and circumstances. He would not have Christians sought for; he would have them punished whenever they were accused and convicted;—if they would give some manifest proof of repentance, such as offering to the gods, they should be pardoned. He did not like anonymous accusations: the precedent was bad, and unsuitable to his time.

Lect. II.

Promiscuum is Pliny's word; "common to high and low."

The spread of the Doctrine, and the checks to it.

The Emperor's answer.

What these letters tell us about the general policy of the Roman Empire, and the nature of its conflict with the Church, I shall consider hereafter. I introduce them here, because they throw light upon the

Inference from these Letters.

ON CHURCH HISTORY.

Lect. II.

Of whom the Bithynian Church probably consisted.

condition of a particular province of Asia, at the commencement of the second century. Pliny, it seems to me, does not describe to us an organised Christian society. He does not speak of any one whom he could look upon as the responsible representative and father of the Christian flock, in any of the cities under his government. Possibly Bithynian Jews, who had been led by St. Peter, and other Apostles of the Circumcision, to understand that Jesus was their King, and who felt that they were to testify of Him, by abstaining from surrounding corruption, and by shining as lights in the world—but who still felt themselves too much part of the old Jewish polity to seek for any new social order—formed the bulk of those who gave Pliny so much trouble. Their witness was evidently a very powerful one; it shook the heathenism of Asia, which was already tottering. But the desertions seem to have been numerous. And it is clear from the conclusion of Pliny's letter, that

Heathenism reviving from a shock.

there was a reaction in favour of the old heathenism, the indifference for it being changed into zeal, either by the mere fact of opposition to it, or by the feebleness and inconsistencies of the opposers.

Paphlagonia.

In Paphlagonia, on the borders of the Pontus Euxinus, stood the city of Sinope. Here, about the middle of the second century, we have a glimpse of a Christian Church, and of a Christian bishop. But he only comes before us as the father of a man who is denounced as the introducer of a new and blasphemous doctrine by his contemporaries, and whom some

Marcion apparently went to

in later times have been disposed to represent as a

THE SECOND CENTURY. 197

reformer and champion of truth. This is Marcion. According to the statements we have respecting him, he was the disciple of one Cerdo, a Syrian, who gave the first hint of the opinions which he elaborated. The good God,—so he is said to have taught,—was not the God whom the Jews worshipped. Their God, the God of Abraham, was, he said, a mere Creator or Demiurgus. To deliver men from his oppressive yoke, Christ came into the world. He revealed the benevolent and loving God: He declared the Kingdom of Heaven, into which men might enter, if they renounced this world, and the service of the tyrant. These propositions Marcion is said to have maintained in a book, called Antitheses, wherein he contrasted Judaism and Christianity. He rejected the Gospels of Matthew and Mark as Jewish; he adopted an expurgated and altered version of St. Luke as the only safe narrative of our Lord's life on earth.

LECT. IF.
Rome between A.D. 140 & 150, and studied under Cerdo there.
The good God and the Jewish Demiurgus.
Writings of Marcion.

Those who defend Marcion say, that no trust can be placed in these reports; that they are the misrepresentations of men, who either did not understand what he was aiming at, or who deliberately embraced a false system, against which he was protesting. They think they can perceive very clearly that he was vindicating the Christian liberty which St. Paul preached—the spiritual Gospel, which he had such a hard fight to maintain, against the Judaisers of his days—from the attacks of men, who were trying to impose the same fetters on the Church of the second century. I tell you of this diversity of opinions, because it might startle you if you met with it for the

His defenders.

LECT. II.
How to deal with opposing statements of this kind.

first time in some book. You might fancy there was no security for any records that bear upon human opinions. And no doubt it is true that we cannot arrive at certainty about the faith of Marcion or of any other man. There is another judge than we are; and Christ has forbidden us to take His office. We should never forget that; if we do not, these very oppositions about particular men, will help us rather than hinder us. If we are not in a hurry to form our opinion, or to take a side, we shall be perhaps led so to weigh the evidence, and compare it with what we have known of others and of ourselves, that we shall learn more from the history through the seemingly contradictory interpreters of it, than we could from either separately.

Probability that he desired to defend St. Paul's truth.

I quite believe with Marcion's admirers, that he may have been scandalized by the statements of a Judaical party, which was perhaps predominant among the Christians of his neighbourhood; and that he fled to the Epistles of St. Paul, as a refuge from their hard teaching, and a continual testimony against it. I can quite understand that he may have been strongly and deeply possessed by the New Testament divinity which he found in St. Paul, and that he may have burned to deliver the Church from that which he supposed to be a relapse into an older condition. I can imagine that his faith on these points met with no response from the men who had most influence in Paphlagonia, that some eager disciples clung to him, that he was misunderstood and harshly opposed. But I do not on this account distrust the statements which have come down to us respecting the opinions which he ultimately adopted. It seems to me that such opinions were very likely indeed to grow up in the mind of a man in that age, and that with some modifications they might appear in our own age. At that time it was not possible that men could talk merely of Judaism or Christianity. The one question was, "What God do you worship, what God have you to proclaim to men?" If once a man acquired a violent conviction that the Old Testament was opposed to the New, he could not stop short of the assertion, that the God of the Old Testament was different from the God of the New. And if he looked upon Christ's Gospel as the good news of a redemption, and a redemption from a spiritual oppression, he would begin to argue, that the author of that oppression was the being whom he had previously learnt to contrast with the Father of our Lord Jesus Christ. Having adopted this theory as *the* Christian theory, he would be obliged to practise violence upon facts and documents, in order to bring them into consent with it. Those that were utterly unmanageable he would cast aside; the others he would persuade himself might, by subtractions and additions, become his allies instead of his opponents. To think that the additions and subtractions were most natural, that they restored the true and consistent text, is the next and a most easy process. I am sure I am giving you no history which is at all singular or improbable. If you or I should think that we might not go through it in our own minds, we should be in great danger; for he that

LECT. II.

The old opinion about him not to be rejected.

Processes of mind.

Documents shaped to a purpose.

LECT. II.

The result.

thinketh he standeth, is the man who has most need to take heed lest he fall. I do not say that Marcion was a dishonest or a bad man; but it seems to me most probable, that he arrived at a conclusion which I do consider exceedingly bad,—one that separates the past from the present and the future,—the visible world from the invisible,—the kingdom of earth from the kingdom of heaven,—the Creator from the Father. It has been my great object in former lectures, to show you how essential the Old Testament revelation was to the New Testament; what a riddle the Old would be without the New to explain it. I have told you we should meet with various attempts to tear them asunder. The Ebionite who set up the Old Testament against the New, is one; the Marcionite who glorified the New to the contempt of the Old, is another.

Phrygia.

Hierapolis, in Phrygia, is spoken of as the dwelling-place of Philip the Deacon, during his latter years, with those daughters who are described as prophetesses in the Acts of the Apostles. Our information about him is derived from a man upon whose reports we cannot place much dependence; though he boasts that he did not give heed to the crowd, but sought for the truth from the lips of those who had heard the Apostles. There is something necessary besides the opportunity of hearing wise teachers,—the faculty of apprehending what they teach; and this, Papias does not seem to have possessed. Idle traditions about miraculous cures, and fancies of an outward throne, on which Christ should sit, bodily and visibly,

Papias.
Eusebius,
book iii.
c. 39.

seem to have taken possession of his mind, and to have hindered him from entering into the true mysteries of the Kingdom of Heaven.

The Phrygian temper (the Phrygians, you will remember, were neighbours of those Galatians who were at one time ready to pluck out their eyes to give them St. Paul, and then were tempted by false apostles to think that he had deceived them), seems to have greatly inclined to fanaticism and superstition. That doctrine of an earthly Christ and an outward throne, which had such attractions for Papias, reappeared in another form in the latter part of this century. It was proclaimed at first in a small village of Phrygia. A man named Montanus, who is said to have been originally a priest of Cybele, and two females, Priscilla and Maximilla, affirmed themselves to be possessed by a divine Spirit, which forced them to break through all ordinary rules. "They began to speak in the Church," says an eye-witness, "and to utter strange voices, prophesying contrary to the usage of the Church, and the order that had been received from its commencement." Some conceived that a diabolical spirit had overmastered them, and sought to rebuke it and cast it out. Some were shocked at such efforts to control what they believed to be the Divine Voice. At length the prophets began to denounce the Church generally, as rejecters of the Divine Spirit; to foretel instant and approaching judgments; and to declare that a city in Phrygia was to be the seat of the New Jerusalem. The doctrine spread widely. Apollinarius of Hierapolis,

Montanus, about A.D. 170.

Ἑτεροφωνεῖν, *to speak in strange tongues. See letter in Eusebius, book* v. c. 16.

Pepuza the New Jerusalem.

LECT. II. and many others, girded themselves to encounter it. Montanus and his followers were excommunicated. But he affirmed himself to be the Paraclete, whom our Lord had promised. He had been sent to fill up what had been left imperfect in the teaching of the Apostles,—to restore what had decayed. A more ascetical discipline was needed; the Church had become psychical or carnal. Montanus laid down the rules to which a true Church ought to conform. Only those who adhered to these rules were spiritual men.

In what sense Montanus called himself the Paraclete.

We are not to suppose, because Montanus used this language, that he believed himself to be the Holy Spirit. We may hope he would have shrunk from such blasphemy. He began, probably, with the feeling that the Church was forgetting the Divine Teacher, whom its Lord had promised and had sent.

Sense of want.

He brooded over the thought till he began to suppose that some token of His presence must be vouchsafed, to convince those who had sunk into sloth and indifference. What that token *must be,* he did not, perhaps, very earnestly or reverently inquire. The more startling it was,—the more disorderly,—the better he would be pleased. St. Paul had already warned the Corinthians of their tendency to suppose that the Spirit of Order, of Truth, of Unity, is a Spirit of Confusion, of Self-exaltation, of Division. He had told them that the spirits of true prophets are subject to the prophets. The words had no effect on Montanus. Once yielding to his own impulses, and mistaking them for the power which was to guide them, the words of Scripture were mere carnal fetters

Craving for signs, and rejection of warnings.

THE SECOND CENTURY.

in his eyes, which it was a glory to break. Thus he himself, the possessed, oracular man, became more and more the object of his admiration. The idea of a Spirit, from which he started, was almost entirely obscured. He could think only of an outward Teacher. All Christ's promises seemed to be fulfilled in such a gift. And *he* is the Teacher. *He* is to remould the Church; to lay down its laws; to build the Divine City. Do not forget the lesson. The Cataphrygian doctrine is one which we shall meet with again and again. It lies very near to us all.

Self-idolatry.

But there is another lesson which we have to learn from Phrygia in the second century, before we take leave of it. The teachers of the Churches were very eager to encounter Montanism, and to overthrow it. It was easily shown how much arrogance there was in its prophets; what extravagances they committed; what divisions they were causing. But it was not easy to escape the temptation of setting up an opposite doctrine, for the sake of refuting theirs, and of denying the truths which were hidden under all their errors. Many in Phrygia seem to have concluded that the safest way of escaping from the doctrine about a visible kingdom, was to reject the Apocalypse. Some seem to have persuaded themselves that St. John's Gospel, concerning the Word and the Comforter, was itself the cause of Montanism, and that its testimony should be silenced. The extreme form of this opinion may have been confined to a few, who, in later days, were called *Alogi*, or deniers of the Word. But it was adopted, in a modified form, by a man of

Treatment of Montanus.

The reaction against his doctrine.

The Alogi.

LECT. II.

*Monarch-
ists.
Praxeas
was in
Rome about
A.D. 192.*

eminence in the Phrygian Church, who had been a faithful confessor during some of its persecutions. *Praxeas* appears to have so set his mind on the mischiefs of Montanism, that every doctrine which was hostile to it looked well in his eyes. Was it safe to talk—so he seems to have asked himself—of a Divine Teacher who was distinct from the Eternal Father? Did not such a belief interfere with that witness which the Christian Church was appointed to bear before the Heathen for the Oneness of God? Could not the phrases about the Word be explained to mean only some principle that dwelt in the Father, as a man's thought dwells in him? This is the hint of a theory of which you will hear much in the third century, and in subsequent centuries. We shall meet with it again in the second. I wish you to see how it sprung up in the mind of a Phrygian who had been scandalized by Montanus, and who saw no better way of hindering the progress of his opinions, than by striking at the strong and earnest convictions out of which they grew.

LECTURE III.

THE SAME SUBJECT CONTINUED.

CHURCHES IN GREECE AND EGYPT.

I HAVE nothing special to tell you about the Churches in Macedonia which St. Paul established. You remember that we hear nothing in the Acts of the Apostles of a Church in Athens, though St. Paul's discourse there is one of the most memorable in all Scripture, and the great text and guide for all Missionaries to philosophical Heathens. The single male convert who is mentioned by St. Luke, Dionysius the Areopagite, has been the hero of a multitude of legends. The Churches in Gaul fancied that they owed their origin to him. Books for a long time passed under his name, written probably in the fourth century, which exercised no slight influence upon the thoughts of men in the Middle Ages. We know however, upon what must be considered good authority, that of a Bishop of Corinth, his namesake, in the middle of this century, that he presided over the Christian society in Athens. After him, Publius is mentioned by the same authority as ruling in the Church, and as dying a Martyr. Quadratus, he says, followed, through whose diligence the Church

Athens.

Dionysius the Areopagite.

Eusebius, book iv. c. 23.

was increased, and its faith enkindled. After that he speaks of a decay in faith and Christian fellowship, and of a tendency to apostasy.

The name of Quadratus is of some importance in the history of the Church. He and Aristides addressed *Apologies* to the Emperor Hadrian. This word *Apologies* is a new one. Ignatius and Polycarp wrote *letters* as St. Paul had written letters; they adopted the form of writing of which Scripture had given them examples. The apology is borrowed from another example. Socrates, when he was accused before the tribunal of Athens of introducing new Gods and corrupting the minds of the youth, made a defence or apology. His two disciples, Xenophon and Plato, gave their report of what he had said, or of what they thought he should have said. Their works were familiar to all Athenians. It was most natural that an Athenian should borrow the expression, seeing that he and his friends were charged with the very crimes with which Socrates had been charged in their city. Sometimes they were called Atheists as he was, because they worshipped no visible image; sometimes they were said to be bringing in new dæmons, because they spoke of Christ as the divine King, the Son of God. The charge of drawing away people, and especially the young, from the worship of their country, was common to them with him. The Emperor Hadrian was a great affecter of Greek habits and accomplishments; he was fonder of Athens than of Rome, and had more of the Athenian than of the Roman character. It was likely enough that Quadratus and Aristides should wish to make him acquainted with their actual belief, and that they should use those forms of language with which he and their countrymen were familiar.

The commencement of this *apologetic* literature is an important era in Christian history. It marks a new kind of thought which was springing up in the Church, and a new class of men who were assuming a prominent place in it. I may have to tell you hereafter more of what I think were the effects of this movement for good or for evil. I wish you now to notice where it took its rise, and how it was connected with Greece and with the Roman Empire, because these circumstances are very helpful in enabling us to understand the character of the writings themselves. We have only a very short fragment of the first Apologist; but it is one which gives us a clear hint of the form which the Apologies were likely to take. We feel at once as we read it, that we are no longer listening to a *Gospel*, but to an *argument*. Quadratus, though so far as we can judge in a simple and manly style, still sets about *proving* that our Lord wrought certain miracles. He does not, like the Evangelists, produce his acts of power and healing as if they were the proper and natural acts of the King and Deliverer of the world. The difference is remarkable; the further we proceed the more we shall feel its importance.

You will remember that I spoke to you of a man named Justin, who was born in a village of Samaria.

Lect. III.

Tendencies of this new literature.

Fragment beginning Τοῦ δὲ Σωτῆρος ἡμῶν τὰ ἔργα ἀεὶ παρῆν. *Eusebius ubi supra.*

Justin.

LECT. III. I wished to make you aware of that fact, for I think it has much to do with the after life of Justin; but I said I could not go on with his story because it was not there that his mind received its chief or permanent direction. It is not possible to assign *His culture.* him to any one distinct Church or city; but he certainly owed more of his culture to Greece than to any other country, though he had a semi-Hebrew origin, and though he probably died at Rome. It is in place to speak of him here, as I have just introduced you to the earliest Apologists, and as the defence which he addressed either to Antoninus Pius or Marcus Aurelius is the first which has been preserved to us. But I am still more concerned with another book of his which has always been supposed to contain his own biography, and which throws much light upon this whole period, especially upon the way in which the Jewish and the Greek influences were working together upon the Christian Church.

Jews in the Second Century. The Jew of the second century, after Hadrian had changed the name of his city, and the last effort for the restoration of his nation had been crushed, was a very homeless being. He went about seeking rest and finding none. If he had no higher ambition than to make money, he might gratify his passion in the commercial cities of the empire quite as well now as when he dreamed of a Son of David. If his tastes were more intellectual, he might frequent the different *Their craving for occupation.* schools of Greece or of Egypt, debating all manner of questions about God and man listlessly and ingeniously, because he had ceased to care about them or to hope for any satisfaction upon them, but yet wanted some occupation for his head as well as his hands. Generally the teaching of his childhood, though it produced little effect upon his character, coloured all his thoughts and gave him a certain sense of his own consequence, after the excuses for it had disappeared. At all events, no converse which he had with other men made him hate the Christians less, for they pretended that they had succeeded to the privileges of the children of Abraham, and spoke of a revelation, while he was only a guesser.

A man of this class, named Trypho, is the chief person in the Dialogue of Justin to which I alluded. It is an argument between a Christian and a Jew, but between a Christian and a Jew who both call themselves philosophers. They are supposed to meet on a walk near one of the Greek cities. Justin's cloak led Trypho at once to accost him as a philosopher, and to question him about the sect to which he belonged. Justin demurs to the question, maintaining that philosophy is one, that it is a high gift of God, and that it is not to be denoted by the name of this or that teacher. He expresses his wonder that Trypho should not have learnt more from his own lawgiver and prophets than he could find in the Greek schools; then he proceeds to tell him his own experience. He had tried nearly every Greek sect. One after another had failed to tell him the secret he was in search of. At last he fell in with an old Christian teacher, who persuaded him that Christ had made those things known which others were only

His hatred of the Christians permanent.

Dialogue with Trypho.

The Jew and Christian meeting as Philosophers.

Justin's experience.

disputing and discoursing about. "This," he says, "I found at last to be the safe and profitable philosophy." The confession is received as we might expect; Trypho tells him that it would have been far better for him to have adhered to the philosophy of Plato, or of any other teacher, cultivating fortitude and self-restraint and modesty, than to have been deceived with lying words, and to follow men who were good for nothing. As long as he continued in his earlier course and lived blamelessly, there was hope of his finding a better portion; but when he left God and hoped in a Man, what salvation was left for him? In all friendship, Trypho would advise him first to be circumcised, then to keep the Sabbath and the festivals as Moses had appointed, and generally all things that were written in the law; then he might have some hope of mercy from God. If Christ had been indeed born at all, He was still in obscurity; nor did He know himself, nor had He any power, till Elias came and anointed Him, and made Him manifest to all. "Meanwhile," he says, "you having accepted a vain and idle rumour, are inventing a Christ for yourselves, and are heedlessly throwing away all present blessings for the sake of Him." Justin declares that he has not followed a cunningly devised fable, and that he is willing to give a reason of the hope that is in him. He alludes to some monstrous opinions that were current about Christians, that they were cannibals and held the most horrible orgies. These popular stories Trypho acknowledges that he entirely disbelieves. But he thinks that the

Lect. III.

Trypho's counsel.

Χριστὸς δὲ εἰ καὶ γεγένηται καὶ ἔστι ποῦ, ἄγνωστος ἔστι. κ.τ.λ.

Popular charges against Christians.

commands in the Gospels, which he has taken some pains to acquaint himself with, are such as no one can keep. On the other hand, he is astonished that while the Nazarenes pretend to be pious men and to believe in the prophets, they yet cast aside all those institutions which the law and the prophets had enjoined, and that they placed their hope in a crucified Man. This introduces the substantial part of the controversy. Justin maintains that all the law and the prophets are speaking of a final law and a perfect covenant, which it was needful that all men, and not merely Jews, should keep, who aspired to the divine inheritance. "Christ Himself," he says, "has been given to us as the eternal and final law and the faithful covenant; after which there is no law, nor precept, nor commandment." These words might have led Trypho to suppose that his opponent was setting aside the great principles of the law, and was leaving an opening to all licentiousness. Justin therefore goes on to show that the Christian was asserting the real moral power which the Jew is denying. "There is need," he says, "of another circumcision, and you are boasting of the circumcision in the flesh. The new law wishes us to be *always* keeping sabbath, and you fancy that you are holy if you are idle for one day, not knowing why that day was appointed you. And if you eat unleavened bread, you think you have fulfilled the will of God. Not in these things is the Lord our God well pleased. But if there is any false swearer among you, or thief, let him cease; if there is any

LECT. III.

The perfect Covenant.

Αἰώνιός τε ἡμῖν νόμος καὶ τελευταῖος ὁ Χριστὸς ἐδόθη καὶ ἡ διαθήκη πιστή, μεθ' ἣν οὐ νόμος οὐ πρόσταγμα οὐκ ἐντολή. *Circumcision and Sabbaths.*

P 2

adulterer, let him repent; so the wholesome and true sabbaths of God are kept. If any one has not clean hands, let him wash them, and he is clean. For verily Isaiah did not send you to the bath to wash away murder and other sins, which the whole water of the sea could not cleanse. But, as is reasonable, this was of old that saving spring which followed the penitents, who were cleansed, not with the blood of goats or sheep or the ashes of an heifer, but by faith, through the blood of Christ and His death, who has died for this very end, as Isaiah testifies, saying, The Lord will reveal His holy arm, &c. Through the laver of repentance then," he continues, "and of the knowledge of God which hath been prepared for the transgression of the people of God, we have believed; and we declare that this is indeed that baptism which He proclaimed, the only one which is able to cleanse those who have repented. This is the water of life; whereas you have dug out for yourselves cisterns that are broken, and that can avail you nothing. For what availeth that baptism which cleanseth the flesh and the body only? Baptize the soul from wrath and from covetousness, from envy, from hatred, and, behold, the body is clean too. This is the significance of the unleavened bread, that ye should not do the old works of the bad leaven. But you look upon all things carnally, and count it piety, if while doing such things your souls are filled with deceit and all wickedness."

I do not purpose to make any more extracts from this Dialogue. My object has been to give you some hints about its character, that you may know the writer of it better. He had felt the powerlessness of Judaism and of heathen philosophy to make him be the man which he wanted to be. The outside practices of the synagogue,—the mere talk of the schools,—had offended him equally, and had proved equally ineffectual for his needs. He wanted a power which could make him another man,—which could enable him to do the things which the law prescribed, and know what the philosophers reasoned about. He desired to be both a real philosopher and a Jew in the highest sense of the word. One respects him for trying to meet men on their own ground, and to show that Christ can speak to each man in the tongue wherein he was born, according to the habits of thought in which he was educated. But there seems to have been a little affectation in his continuing to wear the philosophical cloak; and I do not know that he was more just to the Greek philosophers because he assumed to be one of another kind himself. Justin belongs, in some measure, to the new argumentative class of the Apologists. But he mixed with their tendency much of true simplicity. The Gospel had been a deliverance to him out of wearisome disputations. He was not so much disposed, as many of his contemporaries, to make it a theme and an excuse for fresh disputations.

I said that the Apology of Quadratus was addressed to Hadrian, an affecter of Greek fashions, and the introducer of one of the most shameful forms of new idolatry into the empire. His two successors were

Lect. III.

Strength of Justin.

Weakness.

Justin's Apology. The worship of Antinous referred to by Justin, Apol.i.p.71. Ed. Paris.

LECT. III. of a far nobler temper. Antoninus Pius acquired his
The just and name from his old Roman habit of mind; especially
the philosophical Emperor. from his reverence for his parents. Marcus Aurelius
united to Roman justice the best form of Greek
wisdom. It is not easy to determine in which of the
two reigns Justin's Apology was written; there is much
in the opening of it which might incline us to think
Character first of one, then of the other. He appeals to the
of the Emperor as acknowledging principles of righteousness
Apology determined and truth, by which all his acts should be regulated.
by the characters of He appeals to him also expressly as a philosopher. In
the Emperors. the former character he invites him to a severe examination of the conduct of the Christians, who ought to
be condemned if they are found guilty of any crime
against their fellow-citizens, or any offence against the
state; who ought not to be condemned for a mere name.
In the latter character, he invites him to an examination
of the actual faith of the Christians, reminding him
that Socrates had been charged with Atheism precisely for the same reason as they were, because he
protested against the acknowledging of visible and
High moral corrupt divinities. There is a brave and healthy tone
tone of about this part of the Apology, an assertion of the
Justin. Righteousness of God and of the Righteousness that
He demands of rulers, which is to me infinitely more
delightful than any of the mere reasonings of Justin,
or of his brother Apologists. There was peril even
here; since it is always dangerous for men to be
making out a case for themselves. But it is a peril
which must sometimes be incurred; and Justin
shows that he cared far more to justify the ways

of God to men than to justify the class to which he belonged. *Lect. III.*

He had, too, a genuine faith in the Emperor to whom he writes; a belief that there was that in him which could respond to the truth he was asserting. It was not a false confidence, though it appeared to be belied by the result. Marcus Aurelius had sympathies with what is pure and just and good. His philosophy was no mere fashion or pretence. He sought to be right and to do right. Nevertheless, his philosophy itself and the very piety he tried to cultivate, made him hostile to Christians. Justin died at Rome, probably by order of this very emperor, who was instigated against him, it is said, by Crescens, one of the philosophers of his court.[1] *Faith in M. Aurelius.* *Justin's death.*

[1] As Tatian calls himself an Assyrian, I have no right to notice him in this division of the subject. But, as he was a pupil of Justin, and as his chief book is an Oration against the Greeks, I do not know where I could refer to the melancholy but useful moral which his work and life suggest, better than here. All that is most offensive in the Apologetic literature comes out in him. How his Oration can have won the praise of "excellent" from so fair and reasonable a judge as Du Pin, I cannot conceive. It appears to me, in spite of occasional flashes of eloquence, which prove Tatian to have been a very able man, morally offensive and mischievous. He starts with the purpose of proving that the Greeks derived their wisdom from the Barbarians, whom they despised,—not a very important thesis for a Christian writer to maintain, and which is established by the most unsatisfactory evidence. Then he gathers together the miserable gossip of Greek anecdote-mongers, to convict the best Greek writers and thinkers of the foulest crimes. The moral contrast between Tatian and his master we could never have lost sight of, if we had not fallen into a way of thinking that all arguments for Christianity ought to be commended, even when they have been the means of leading many to reject it, and more to disgrace it. Tatian ended with becoming an Encratite—that is to say, he pronounced marriage unholy, as being an indulgence of the flesh, which was essentially evil. A fit and almost necessary result for a man who did not think of things pure and lovely—who rejoiced in iniquity, not in the truth.

216 ON CHURCH HISTORY.

LECT. III.

Athenagoras.
His Apology is referred to the year A.D. 177.

Treatise on the Resurrection.

Dionysius of Corinth belongs to the age of the Antonines.

Eusebius, book iv. c. 23.

Athenagoras was a cotemporary of Justin. He is usually spoken of as an Athenian, though some recent scholars would place him in Alexandria. He fell, as much as any of the Apologists, into the fashion of calling himself a philosopher and Christianity a philosophy. I do not find as much to sympathise with in Athenagoras as in Justin; he writes more like a professional arguer and sophist, less like one to whom the Gospel has given a new life. His books are more mere books than Justin's, and tell us much less of the man. He wrote a treatise on the Resurrection, which, I own, seems to me very clever, cold, and unsatisfactory. The few words, " Christ has risen, and become the first-fruits of them that slept," are worth all the elaborate arguments and theories which Athenagoras has deduced from a mixture of old Greek notions about the soul and the body with his Christian lore.

It is a relief to turn from this learned and accomplished reasoner to a genuine pastor of a flock. Such *Dionysius of Corinth* seems to have been. He is a letter-writer, not an apologist. We have only some fragments of him in Eusebius, but they are very valuable as exhibitions of his own character, and as hints respecting the condition of the Churches. I have quoted already from his Epistle to the Athenians. Eusebius mentions another to the Lacedemonians, "instructing them in right doctrine, and exhorting them to faith and unity;" another to the Church in Nicomedia, in which he contends against the doctrine of Marcion. A third, he says, was addressed to Gortyna and the other Churches in Crete, wherein he makes mention of their overseer Philip, and of the Church under him, as being memorable for many worthy deeds. He speaks of another to Gnossus in Crete, alluding to some maxims respecting virginity which the Bishop Pinytus had encouraged or enjoined, and which Dionysius conjures him to relax. Pinytus in his answer complained of the tenderness of Dionysius, and maintained that he gave only milk, not the meat which strong Christians required.

Subjects of the Letters.

In a letter to the Churches of Pontus, Dionysius appears to have " commented on the Scriptures, and to have discoursed of marriage and purity." His most memorable and agreeable testimony is in a letter to the Church of Rome, which I shall have to extract when I speak of that Church. In the course of the letter he alludes to the Epistle of Clemens, the Roman Bishop, to the Corinthians, and observes that they had been reading it in Corinth on that very day, being the holy day of the Lord, and that they should always keep it to read for their admonition, as well as the former, which he had written to them. But he makes a remark about his own letters, which discloses one of the characteristically evil tendencies of this time. They had been mangled and interpolated; and he adds that it is no wonder ordinary writings received such treatment, when the Scriptures were exposed to it, when the words of Apostles were altered and perverted to suit the convenience of those who were introducing false doctrines.

Mutilation of documents.

These fragments of Dionysius are more important for what they suggest than for what they contain;

LECT. III. one aspect of the Church militant, in the second century, is faithfully presented in them. But it has need to be compared and connected with others, of which I have spoken and am about to speak, before the image of it can come out clearly and fairly before us.

Alexandria. The Church in Alexandria is said to have been founded by St. Mark. There is no strong evidence which should induce us to dispute the tradition or to affirm it. The after condition of the Church was little affected by its supposed origin; it was very much affected by other circumstances, which existed in Alexandria before the Gospel was preached there.

Reference to the character of the Jewish teachers there. To some of these I referred when I was speaking of St. John's Gospel: I told you how much the Alexandrian Jews had dwelt upon the Divine Word or Wisdom, of whom the Jewish Scriptures testify so continually; how while they had believed that the Word had chosen their own countrymen to be the witnesses of the invisible God to the world, they had acknowledged that the wisdom of Gentile sages must also have come from Him; how, in their impatience of those who merely adhered to the dry letter of Scripture, and saw no spiritual sense in it, they had changed its plain and beautiful histories into fantastical, often jejune allegories. I told you how St. John had claimed their truths, when he affirmed that the Word was with God and the Word was God; and that all light is from Him, and that the Light lighteneth all who come into the world, and that all things are made by Him; how he separated

THE SECOND CENTURY. 219

these truths from mere symbols, and established them on the facts of our Lord's life on earth; how he connected all the doctrines of our Lord's life before the worlds were, with the assertion that He was made flesh, and manifested forth the glory of the Father, in humiliation and suffering. LECT. III.

You must bear these facts in mind, when you hear what I have to tell you respecting the Church in Alexandria. Eusebius gives us a list of the overseers who ruled over it in the second century; but they are mere names; we know nothing that they did or spoke. On the other hand, we have full records of a number of teachers who arose in this Church, and who propagated doctrines in it which were very memorable in that age, and which are very important for all Ecclesiastical history. I must mention a few of them. *Effect of this teaching in the Church.*

Basileides belongs to the reigns of Hadrian and Antoninus Pius: that his mind was formed in Egypt there can be no doubt, though he may have been born in Syria. He used to speak of Glaucus, a scribe, or interpreter of St. Peter, as the teacher from whom he had received his wisdom; his followers boasted that St. Matthias was the head of their school. Any disciple, or any Apostle, may have awakened the thoughts in the mind of Basileides, out of which he fashioned his system, for they were true and divine thoughts. He believed that the knowledge of God is the highest blessing which man can attain; that those who are received into the new Covenant are meant to enter into that *Basileides.* *His alleged teachers.* *His convictions.*

fulness of knowledge which kings and prophets had sighed for; that the manifestation of the fulness of the Godhead is in some way connected with the manifestation of the Divine Word or Wisdom. Moreover, if he took the words of the Gospels in their plain signification, he must suppose that a Kingdom of Heaven—a spiritual world—had been opened to men, and that they might enter into the mysteries of it. Was not man himself a part of this spiritual world? Was not the wonderful Reason with which God had endowed him—the power of knowing invisible things—were not even all the subordinate faculties of his soul—proofs that he too was a spirit, that he had a divine and heavenly birth, that he was a fellow with the Angels?

Is not this high and scriptural doctrine? If any one denies it, must he not deny the lessons which St. Paul and St. John are labouring to communicate? Starting, then, from this point, Basileides proceeded to connect together the different ideas, each of which had such a justification in the language of the Scripture, such a witness of their truth in his own heart. He began to construct a theory or system,—about the way in which man may ascend to the knowledge of God; about the way in which it was possible that the infinite fulness of God should be brought near to the perceptions and faculties of man; about the relation between these perceptions and faculties, and the spiritual powers or beings which may or may not have partaken of man's fall—which may be drawing him to good or tempting him to evil. Do you wonder that any man should undertake such a task as this;—to organise and construct, not merely this universe in which we dwell, but all and every possible universe, past, present, and to come; to show how they have begun to exist; under what laws they exist, what beings dwell in them? Are you startled and overwhelmed with the thought that the creature, in his eagerness to assert and glorify the fulness of the Godhead, should actually reduce it under his own terms and definitions? Wonder if you will, but do not deal hardly with Basileides. The temptation to do all this is one, not only into which it is easy to fall, but which it is exceedingly hard for thoughtful, even for devout men to avoid. Each step seems to follow so closely, so naturally, upon the one that went before—there is such delight in linking our conceptions together— there is such a wonderful satisfaction in gazing at the Babylons which we have built, that it is only men very ignorant of themselves, who can be without sorrow and fellow feeling for those who have fashioned what seem to us the most unsightly, and what have proved to be the most unsafe, of these intellectual worlds.

Merits of Basileides. Clemens of Alexandria has preserved to us a number of separate thoughts and sayings of Basileides, from which much is to be learnt; in which there are clear indications that he had a desire to assert the goodness of God; that he had perceptions of the relations which exist between different qualities in men; that he felt what a battle men have to fight

LECT. III. with their own propensities, and with evil powers; that he had a skill in definition. But when once a man begins to build a system, the very gifts and qualities which might serve in the investigation of truth, become the greatest hindrances to it. He must make the different parts of the scheme fit into each other; his dexterity is shown, not in detecting facts, but in cutting them square. The great *object* of Basileides, to lead men upwards to the knowledge of God, was defeated by his system, for the God whom he desired to contemplate as above all, the ground and root of all things, was included in the system, was merely one portion of it. The great *principle* from which he started, that the Word or Wisdom of God is the means whereby man rises to the knowledge of God, was overturned by the system; for this Word only became one of a number of powers and agents who were acting upon men and drawing their life from God, or one of the faculties by which man apprehends God. The faith in God which Basileides certainly wished to cherish became identical with the knowledge which was to be the result of it, and the knowledge at last terminated in itself. It is a great thing to know—what? Basileides, who was, I should think, far better than his system,[1] might have found an answer by falling on his knees,—careless what became of his beautiful logic, provided he could be saved from being an Atheist. With those who accepted

How they were turned to mischief.

Results.

---

[1] His respect for marriage is one of the redeeming points in his character, and marks a very decided difference between him and many other Gnostics.

his system it was not so. His son Isidorus indeed seems to have striven, with honest filial reverence, to vindicate what he had learnt of him from some of its worse consequences. The after teachers completed the theory and excluded the glimpses of air and sunshine that had broken in through the creaks which the caution or piety of their master had left in it.

It is wonderful how easily words are arranged in a scheme when the life is gone out of them, and therefore they can offer no resistance. The Basilidean sect could put Reason, and Wisdom, and Logos, and Power, one after the other; they could speak of the heavens which these had created, and of others that corresponded to them. They could make perfect arrangements of numbers, and explain accurately how all that they saw and could not see, came into being. They were not merely, as you might fancy, talking at random. Their thoughts about the connexion of the different powers and faculties in men were often founded upon a subtle observation, and may suggest valuable hints. But when an earnest man, who had received the Gospel as an announcement that God had really sought after His creatures, and delivered them from their enemies, and claimed them as His children, looked into their doctrine, he found, indeed, most of the words and phrases with which he was familiar; he heard high promises of emancipation, and light, and discovery; but all that he had believed in and hoped for was gone. Christ was lost amidst a multitude of powers and energies that were whirling dizzily in mysterious abysses. The Cross to which

Lect. III.
Isidorus.
The School.

The completed scheme.

Effect on simple Christians.

he had clung as the one witness that God was reconciled to the world, and that Death and Hell were not his masters, was declared to be a fiction or superstition which elect and elevated souls could cast beneath them. God Himself, who was to be the end of all their search, had become a vague abstraction. And though we may believe there is exaggeration in the statements we have received respecting the morals of those who embraced this system,—though such statements are always to be listened to with the greatest caution, because the better men who make them often take them from much worse men, mere gossips and praters, who rejoice in evil, and not in the truth,—and though we may joyfully acknowledge the innocence of the first teacher,—yet we are warranted in thinking that those who lived in this cloud-world could not have found any very definite laws or principles to regulate them in their converse with the actual world of men and women.

Valentinus lived somewhat later than Basileides. He was an Egyptian by birth and by the whole habit of his mind. Clemens has preserved some passages from letters and homilies of his, which show that he was a man of much reflection. He had observed attentively and seriously one of the most important facts in our human life. "God has set one thing over against another," says Solomon; that is to say, each thing in our universe seems as if there were something else that corresponded to it, and was necessary to complete it. "The man is not without the woman," says St. Paul, "nor the woman without the man, in the Lord." Valentinus, I say, had observed this truth and had meditated upon it, as we all should. He traced it through nature, and through the relations of man with man, and of man with his Maker. The union between Christ and the Church corresponded, as St. Paul had pointed out, to the union between the man and the wife; one sustained the other. The more mysterious union still of the Father and the divine Word was beneath this, as St. John's Gospel had so fully declared. Fresh unities or *Syzygies*, as Valentinus called them, presented themselves at every turn; what could be more delightful than to note them, and so to see the harmony of the divine works and the divine principles, in the lowest things and the highest; in the most external and the most inward?

Nothing; if only we continue to watch, and wait and receive new light; and so to admire more and adore more. But oh! the craving for systems, how insatiable it is! how restless the man is till he can get the Universe into his own hands and can settle and complete it, so that no room shall be left for wonder and for fresh discovery! Oh how feverish he is till he can put a centre into the divine order!—yes; till he can become the centre of it himself. So it happened with Valentinus; so did his beautiful observations prove his snares; so did the glorious Syzygies of God's world turn themselves into webs and chains, which bound his own spirit all the while that he was talking of emancipation, and bound Him who would have emancipated it! Basilides had spoken of a

Pleroma or Fulness; Valentinus spoke of a Bythos or Abyss. The first was a good word to express the Perfection of Him of whom are all things and by whom are all things. The second was as good a word to denote that man cannot sound the depths of Godhead,—that he must sink and be lost in it. But how poor are such phrases when they stood in place of the very Being whose nature they sought to describe!—when they actually limited the Fulness and paved the Abyss; when you had a Pleroma for a Father, and the proposition "God is an Abyss" for St. John's "God is Love."

So Basilides had talked of Dynameis or Powers; Valentinus spoke of Æons, or spiritual substances, as distinguished from forms that are clothed with matter. Such powers there must be; it is impossible to contemplate the world without acknowledging them; those who try to resolve all things into the effects of mere mechanism are bewildered every moment, and fall into countless superstitions. We cannot speak of Righteousness, or Wisdom, or Truth, as the Apostles and Prophets speak of them, without feeling that they are spiritual substances; that they are realities which lie beneath our thoughts, not notions which our thoughts create. But when Valentinus undertook to settle the genealogy of these substances— to show how one was derived out of another; or when and by what means they came into contact with human beings—he emptied them of their substance; he turned them into notions of his understanding; and instead of their having any power to work any good for human beings, their only effect was to hide the one great Head of Principalities and Powers—Him in whom and for whom all Angels and Æons are created—to make His work, His redemption, His victory over death and the grave, dreams and fantasies.

LECT. III.

The fact that all things in the universe are in pairs struck Valentinus, and seems to lie at the root of his system. *Carpocrates*, on the other hand, was impressed by the existence of a law or principle of equality in God's dealings with His creatures. The sun shineth upon the good and the evil, upon the just and the unjust. Every creature, man and woman, or sheep, fowl, insect, is equally an object of divine care. From truths of this kind, the worth of which cannot be overrated, Carpocrates proceeded to deduce the doctrine that Law, seeing it distinguishes between good and evil, is to be cast aside; that Property, the creature of Law, partakes of the falsehood of its parent; that marriage, as apportioning God's creatures and interfering with common rights, is equally incompatible with the divine kingdom, the true Society. It has been supposed that he derived this notion from Plato's Republic; but you will hear of its re-appearance, hereafter, among people who had never heard of Plato. It is a scheme into which men are at all times and places exceedingly likely to fall, and none so likely as those who are impressed with the excellence of the Christian Church in that it binds men together, and treats them as all upon a level before God; and

Carpocrates.

Equality.

Law decried.

Communism. Plausibility of it.

228   ON CHURCH HISTORY.

LECT. III.   who think that all the previous discipline by which
God prepared men to feel the eternal difference of
right and wrong, the beauty of family life, the preciousness of national distinctions, is good for nothing, or became obsolete when the universal fellowship in Christ was made known. Depend upon it, if you once fall into this habit of thinking, you may become as

Cure of Communism.   strong communists as Carpocrates was. The cure for the delusion lies in the discovery that instead of obtaining the equality we seek by these methods, we are certain to be opening a way to the most grovelling tyranny. The son of Carpocrates is said to have been worshipped as a god in Cephalonia; the disciples

Effects of it.   of Carpocrates, who were called emphatically *the Gnostics*, because they, more than others, set up speculation in opposition to practice, seem to have consistently followed out their doctrine, that man is not to assert his superiority over the swine.

The Ophites.   By various symbols, sometimes by strange cabalistical words, the old Egyptians had shown their sense of a Wisdom which they could not measure or define, which could not be revealed to the world, but which the initiated priest might hold converse with. One and another of these symbols and strange words were adopted into the systems which I have described, the object of them all being to explain the appearing

The false and true wisdom.   or manifestation of the Divine Word in the world without adopting the doctrine that the Word was made flesh. But all men had been aware—these Gnostics could not be ignorant—that there has been a corrupt and depraving wisdom as well as a purifying and elevating one. Much of their thought was employed on this subject. They were continually trying to explain how the evil wisdom had grown out of the good; how far they were opposed, how far they were identical. The confusion reached its highest point in the teaching of the *Ophites*. The serpent had been an object of worship to many tribes of the earth. Sometimes it was an object of mere horror, as the source of the subtlest mischief; sometimes an object of reverence, as a symbol of the Divine knowledge which men wish for, and feel must be in some way intended for them. The Ophites, blending together these old conceptions with the records in the book of Genesis respecting the Fall and with the Christian doctrine of the Divine Word, seem some of them to have regarded all wisdom as detestable and dangerous, derived from the poison of the Serpent; some of them to have actually identified the Serpent with the Teacher from whom comes the wisdom that is pure, gentle, easy to be intreated. You must not expect to harmonize the different accounts we have of this sect; the contradictions in it show us, more than anything else could, what were the difficulties, not of one of the Gnostical schools, but of all.

It was long, probably, before the Church of Alexandria became aware of the nature of this confusion or of the divine remedy for it; but, at length, the light began very clearly to dawn upon some of its teachers; and if a great portion of the second century only contains a record of opinions that look very

Lect. III.

Confusion of them.

The new School.

monstrous, and of systems that were bewildering and mischievous in proportion to the ingenuity that was exhibited in the construction of them, the latter years of the century disclose as beautiful a history as, I think, we can find anywhere, of the method by which God leads his faithful servants to turn the difficulties in their own hearts, and in the society around them, into instruments for glorifying His Name, for learning and diffusing His Truth.

Eusebius, book v. c. 11. Pantænus.

Pantænus is spoken of by Eusebius as a man of rich cultivation, and of great zeal. He was brought up a Stoic; when he became a Christian, he was so eager to tell heathens of the Gospel, that he went as a missionary to Arabia Felix, possibly even to India. You see the man; he did not live to speculate like Basilides or Valentinus; he had a message for mankind—he had something which he could and must proclaim. But you are not on that account to conclude that Pantænus was indifferent to the lore which he had received from his Stoical teachers, or to that which he found in his own city. He returned thither,

The first Catechist.

and he became the first catechist of the Alexandrian school. I shall have much to say of this school; I wish, therefore, I could tell you more of its founder; but his books are gone, only the savour of his name remains; or it would be more right to say, he lives in the noble pupil whose mind he was permitted in some measure to form.

Clemens.

I have often referred, in this Lecture, to Titus Flavius Clemens. My reports of the different Gnostical teachers have been taken chiefly from him; for though there are other authorities respecting them—I shall refer to one when I speak of the Western Churches— he is immeasurably the best. He lived in their city; he had breathed the atmosphere which they breathed; he could understand them, and he is just to them. He quotes their sentiments respectfully, sometimes with sympathy; he seldom uses disparaging words about the individual men; he evidently wishes us to know what they thought, as much as what he thought about them. Clemens speaks of his own dear master, Pantænus, as a Gnostic; he claims the name for himself; yet there was no man who did so much to undermine the Gnostical systems as he did. I will endeavour to show you in what way. I ought to let you know that much of the work of Clemens falls into the third century. But as the foundations of his teaching were laid, and, probably, his books were written in this time, and as I shall have enough to do in speaking of the successors he left behind him when I come to the next period, I shall introduce him here.

The true Gnostic.

Gnosticism, as I have exhibited it to you in these different Alexandrian teachers, is the search for a knowledge of God. A great and glorious search Clemens thought it was; worth the labour of a life, or of many lives. He had pursued it as a Heathen in the schools of Greece; he eagerly sought the helps which Jewish or Heathen sages could afford him in Egypt. But when he received the doctrine of the Cross, another and wonderful truth flashed upon his mind. God knew him. The words of the 139th

The man seeking to know God.

Lect. III.
God knowing us.

Psalm were livingly true; there was a depth of truth in them which was appalling. "*Thou hast searched me and known me; Thou knowest my downsitting and my uprising; Thou understandest my thoughts long before.*" This was no new discovery; it was a very old one. If any one had spoken of it to Basilides or Carpocrates, he would have smiled at the ignorance and simplicity which could dwell on such a truism. But that truism may become the very centre of a man's thoughts and hopes; it may change the positions and relations of all objects to him. It may at first revolutionize his being; ultimately it may set in order all that had been disturbed and inverted there. So I think it was with Clemens; he could perceive how St. Paul speaks of the γνῶσις or πρόγνωσις of God—of our ἐπίγνωσις of Him; the one answers to the other. He apprehends us that we may apprehend Him. It is in His light that we must see light.

The πρόγνωσις and ἐπίγνωσις.

This must have been the lesson which Clemens had been taught by Pantænus, on account of which he regarded him as the true Gnostic: but if he had it first from him, he had to learn it again for himself. He had another teacher than Pantænus, and it was on the recognition of this Teacher that the Alexandrian catechetical school stood; it existed for the purpose of declaring Him to the Jew, the Greek, the barbarian, the wise and the unwise.

The Teacher.

You must think of Clemens as a lecturer, surrounded by scholars of all ages, who had had the most various kinds of discipline previously; who had

Pupils of the School.

most of them heard a multitude of notions and theo- LECT. III.
ries on every possible subject; who, whether they
were Heathen or Jews, or baptized or preparing
for baptism, had been bred in an exceedingly corrupt city; who had speculated on morality as on
every thing else, but had only now and then heard
that they must practise it. You must recollect that
all of these were familiar with the names WISDOM and
WORD; that these had become customary phrases
of the schools—I had almost said of the market-
place. You will then be able to estimate a little the
books which Clemens has bequeathed to us—books
which, though they are often censured as being
learned and philosophical and mystical, were, I am
convinced, written with a more distinctly practical
purpose, and produced a more practical effect, than
any which we have received from this or almost from
any century.

There are three complete Treatises of Clemens *The Trea-*
Alexandrinus, and some very important fragments *tises of Clemens.*
which are commonly attributed to him. The prin- *Principle*
ciple of all his books is the same. It is not the *of them.*
creatures only who are seeking God; He is seeking
them. In the Heathen Fables, and in the Heathen
Philosophies also, one perceives how men's conceptions of God have darkened His nature—how
they have changed Him into their likeness. But in
these very fables, still more in these philosophies, there
is a witness how God has been withdrawing his
creatures from their own fancies and falsehoods, how
He has been speaking to their hearts of something

true and eternal and substantial—of Himself; how He had been stirring them to feel after Him if haply they might find Him. In all then — even the strangest, the most distorted, apprehensions of God among human beings—in all their apprehensions concerning themselves, of what they were, of what they were to do, and of what they were to leave undone—there was a proof at once of man's impotence, and of the gracious will which was working towards him; at once the proof that God had not left those whom He had formed without a knowledge of Himself, and a pledge that He would reveal Himself more perfectly; that He would lead them to that which they were blindly seeking after. Such, if I understand it right, is the burthen of the first Treatise, the Λόγος Προτρεπτικὸς, which is especially addressed to the Gentiles. It is in strict harmony with the second, which I would recommend any one to read earnestly who wishes to understand Clemens and to know what was the office of his school. I wish you might some of you be persuaded to grapple with the original book, in which you will find difficulties now and then, but which will repay the trouble of mastering them. If you will not do that, you may get a good notion of it from the Analysis of Dr. Kaye, the Bishop of Lincoln.

This Treatise, the Παιδαγωγὸς, develops fully that idea of the Teacher to which I have alluded already, in which lay, I believe, the great counteraction of the false Gnosticism which had been, and was then, so rife in Alexandria. The divine Logos or Word, in this book of Clemens, is no high Power or Æon about whose relation to other Powers or Æons men are to form a system. He is the Son of the Father, the Lover of man, who has undertaken to discipline and educate his spirit, to purge it of its follies and corruptions, to lead it upwards to the knowledge of Him in whose image it was created. That He may accomplish this gracious design, that He may fully reveal the Father, may fully enter into sympathies with the creature, may redeem them from the slavery into which they have fallen, may bring them back to their right condition; the Word must take flesh, must actually die, actually rise again. These acts, which were such scandals to the ordinary Gnostic, which he must invent such a number of subtle devices to get out of his way, seem to Clemens the necessary expression of the divine philanthropy—the only possible means of our deliverance. It follows, from this way of contemplating the subject, that the Word never can be thought of as an abstraction, or as merely a superior Reason in Man. He comes from God; he rules and orders and fashions the hearts to which he comes. He curbs their restlessness, fetches them back when they wander, trains them to submission. All their knowledge comes through acknowledgment of their ignorance; they are not free till they have entirely yielded to His government. *LECT. III.* *Purpose of the Treatise.* *The Word becoming Incarnate.*

The Scriptures, as the full exposition of the government which the Divine Word exercised before His Incarnation, while walking with His disciples on *The Scriptures.*

LECT. III.

Difficulty of understanding them simply.

Saxon culture.

Asceticism of Clemens.

earth, after He ascended, are of course most dear to Clemens. They are his lesson-books; he has no desire to alter, or abridge, or add to them; he would merely desire to know what they are. In studying to find out the sense of them, he was liable to many of the same temptations as Philo, and as those who had succeeded him among the Jews and Christians of Alexandria. It was impossible to breathe the free air of the Mesopotamian plains, on which Abraham fed his flocks—of the hills on which David saw the sun rise—in the lecture-room of a philosophised Greek city. The simple records of family and national life, in which the mystery of God's teaching and of man's learning is contained, were almost sure to be turned into spiritual allegories by men who were formed under the Roman despotism, and had just begun to look for a city that has foundations, whose Builder and Maker is God. Oh! we cannot be thankful enough for our Saxon training—for the reverence of marriage and of all homely morality, with which that has inspired us, —for the glorious privilege of belonging to a nation. This it is which God has used for the interpretation of His Old Testament. This has restored to us the books of the Law and the Prophets in their simple letter. You must not expect Clemens to understand that. But there is much which he did understand that we have forgotten, and which we may be content to sit at his feet, or at the feet of the Teacher to whom he refers all his own wisdom, that we may learn.

As the great object of this teacher is to separate

the flesh or carnal appetites from the spirit in man, much of his book is devoted to methods of discipline. I do not say that these are all of them applicable to us; I do not say that they are all right methods in themselves. Clemens was as likely as any one else to make mistakes in this matter. The same causes which led him often to misunderstand the teaching of Scripture about the things of earth, may have led him to adopt notions and rules which would rather be a bondage than a deliverance to men. Still, his great object is to set them free—to break the chains of sense, of sin, of selfishness, of idolatry, that were binding them. A man who has this end continually before him will not lead us far wrong. If he suggests means which are not helpful generally, or not helpful for us, God will show us some better means. We shall not be the less grateful to the kind friend who has told us what we want, because we do not find him infallible, and are driven, as he would have us driven, to put our trust in a surer Guide.

LECT. III.

The Gnostics, of whom I have spoken to you in this lecture, had two opposite temptations. Sometimes they were inclined to speak of the wisdom or knowledge of God as attainable only by a choice initiated circle. They utterly scorned the vulgar herd of men. Sometimes—as you have seen in the case of Carpocrates—they broke down all distinctions. The righteous and the wicked, the seeker of God and the servant of the devil, were all alike. Clemens, by exhibiting the Divine Word as the Lover of man—of the poor, the ignorant, and the helpless—cast down

The two dangers.

How Clemens sought to avoid them.

the barriers which they had raised. By exhibiting the Divine Word as the great distinguisher between the spirit in man which looks upwards after good, and the flesh which looks downwards to the earth, he vindicated the eternal distinctions which they were abolishing. But here, too, he had his infirmity. Sailing between Scylla and Charybdis, he was sure to be nearer the one rock than the other. He was more afraid of being too general than of being too exclusive; more afraid of profaning the mysteries of the Gospel than of hiding them from those whom they were meant to bless. He had such a sense of God's love to men, and loved them so much himself, that the evil was counteracted in him, and only showed itself now and then. But it was there. He had the notion of a circle of refined and devoted men, to whom truths might be known which the vulgar could not reach. The thought was akin to reverence; but we may find hereafter, that it was akin also to that superstition which is most fatal to reverence. When men seek to put a veil upon that face which God in His Son has made open, they set up their wisdom against His; they lead men to fear something else than Him.

The third treatise of Clemens is the one from which I have taken my extracts respecting Basilides, Valentinus, and Carpocrates. It is a treasure-house of information respecting the opinions of men in the Church and in the world; a gathering together of the information which Clemens had been accumulating since he was a youth. But it is no mere magazine of opinions. They are arranged and harmonized by a man who has entered into them, and feels how they are connected with human life, and who never loses sight of the purpose to which his life was devoted. He does not fashion these opinions into a great system; he does not attach himself to one school of opinion, or bring the doctrines of all schools into consent with his own. He believes that God is leading men through the maze of notions and opinions—of their own crude thoughts and fancies—into the clear day. He is ready and desirous to go down into the mines where they have been toiling, that he may rescue whatever treasures they have found, and that he may show them the open heaven and the bright sun, which he thinks God means them as well as him to enjoy. *Their object and value.*

On the whole, I do not know where we shall look for a purer or a truer man than this Clemens of Alexandria. I should like to be able to tell you something of his countenance and of his manner, as well as to give you more particulars of his history. But the facts are few and unimportant which his modesty has made known to us, or which his successors have preserved. We must be content to make his acquaintance through the words which he has spoken. Judging from them, he seems to me that one of the old Fathers whom we should all have reverenced most as a teacher, and loved best as a friend. *Conclusion.*

LECTURE IV.

THE SAME SUBJECT CONTINUED.

THE CHURCHES IN ITALY AND GAUL.

<small>LECT. IV.
St. Paul.</small>   ST. PAUL did not go to Rome to establish a Church, but to dwell in a prison. He had already addressed his letter to the Christians there whilst he was still working in Greece: when he arrived, we are told that he gathered the Jews about him to explain the reason of his coming; we do not hear of any other interview with the members of the Church than that which took place when some of them met him on his way at Appii Forum.

<small>*Origin of the Roman Church unknown.*</small>   How this Church was formed is altogether obscure; but so it is with most of the Churches we shall hear of. It is only now and then we can connect them with great names of Apostles or Evangelists. If we are not content to believe that the Spirit of God binds men together and teaches them of the meaning and mystery of their fellowship—if we have not accepted that testimony of the Divine record—if it seems to us unsatisfactory, we must, in general, do without information, or invent it for ourselves. For my own part, I think the darkness is better than the torchlight which we kindle. I would rather believe that

God founded a Church to which I belonged, than LECT. IV.
guess what St. Peter or St. Paul may have had to do
with the foundation of it..

St. Peter. The members of the Church I am speaking of
have been rather uneasy in their ignorance on this
and many other topics. If they cannot distinctly
say when the name of Christ was first heard and
confessed among them, they think they can at least
discover who first presided over them, who gave them
the form and consistency of a society. They claim
St. Peter as that person; they believe that he was
the first Overseer of their Church, because they believe also that he was the first of the Apostles,—
the one to whom the keys of the Kingdom of Heaven
were committed; the one whose name denotes the
rock on which the whole Church stands.

I am not the least anxious to dispute the tradition, *Probability or improbability of the traditions respecting him.*
evidently a very old one, that St. Peter went to Rome
and suffered there. It is a question for antiquarians
to settle according to the evidence. I would earnestly entreat you to believe that we have not the
least interest in wishing it settled one way or the
other. Nor have we any interest in proving that he
did not occupy the position which has been assigned
him in the Roman Church. For a reason I have
given you already, it seems to me that we have no
ground for supposing that either at Antioch or Rome
he held the kind of office which belonged to St. James
at Jerusalem. In both cities, of course, his authority
will have been greatly reverenced; but I do not see
why he should be supposed to have fixed himself

R

in any one place, or to have exercised more than a general oversight over those whom he visited voluntarily, or among whom he was brought by necessity.

In what way they are instructive.

Much, however, is to be learnt from these traditions respecting St. Peter; and from the fact that they are connected so closely with the Roman Church. The love of order, of organisation, was, as I have pointed out already, the characteristic of the Roman mind, that which had been expressed in all Roman history. Almost from the moment we get any glimpses of the Church in the capital, we perceive that it has inherited the qualities of the nation; that in these will lie its strength and its temptations.

Roman character.

The impatience of any doubt respecting the person to whom it can refer its existence as a society— the impossibility of feeling that it is one till it has a man's name to give it unity—these are signs which may come out more clearly before us hereafter, but which we may notice at once. We are not to notice

Special tendencies of the faith of Roman Christians.

them only as signs of that which is evil. There was good in them as well as evil, just as there was good mixed with the evil in the party tendencies of the Greeks and in the Gnostical tendencies of the Alexandrians. If the Roman Christians felt that God was setting up a Kingdom which would, in a most real and practical sense, break in pieces the kingdom of the Cæsars, they believed a truth which history has established. And it was the truth which they, more than the inhabitants of other cities, had need to apprehend,—the only one which could sustain them against the pomps of the imperial palace as well as

THE SECOND CENTURY. 243

against its persecutions. If they thought that this kingdom could not be limited to their city, but was to spread further than the empire of which it was the centre had extended, they proved that they believed the words of the Prophets, and believed that Christ had come to fulfil them. If they thought that St. Peter had really opened the doors of this Kingdom when he preached of Christ's resurrection to the Jews at the Pentecost and to the Gentiles who were gathered round Cornelius, they put an honest and simple construction upon the language of Scripture. If they believed that the Apostle of the circumcision—he who had testified that the Jewish calling had been a holy one from the first, and that its meaning had not ceased, but had been deepened and expanded by the manifestation of the Son of David— was bearing that witness to the Latin world, as he had borne it to his own country,—or that the Latins were to feel that the blessings and obligations of the inheritance were theirs, God, and not man, taught them the lesson. How man might pervert what God had taught, we may discover by-and-by.

Its substantial truth.

Though the members of this Church are very certain that St. Peter was its first Overseer or Bishop, they are not agreed who was his successor. Jerome says that the greater part of the Latins regarded Clemens as second after Peter, though many put Linus and Anacletus between them. Clemens is identified by Eusebius and Jerome with the person of whom St. Paul speaks in the Epistle to the Philippians. There is no decisive evidence in favour

Clemens Romanus.

244 ON CHURCH HISTORY.

LECT. IV.

Date of the letter.

Hieronymus, Lib. de Viris illustribus, c. 16; and see the notes in Dr. Jacobson's edition of the Apostolical Fathers, vol. i. p. 8, De Vitâ et Scriptis S. Clementis.

The Epistle.

of this opinion, though there is nothing in the age of Clemens to contradict it. He certainly lived in the first century. Some suppose that his Letter, from which all our real knowledge of him is derived, was written before the destruction of Jerusalem in the year 68; some place it in the reign of Domitian, in 97. Jerome fixes his death in the third year of Trajan. He is therefore the earliest of the Teachers of the Church of whom I have yet spoken to you, one whom I am hardly entitled in strictness to connect with this century. Clemens Romanus, more closely than any other man, connects the apostolical time with the time that followed it. Many of the early Churches seem to have been inclined to receive his letter as an apostolical one; Jerome thinks that he traces in it resemblances to the Epistle to the Hebrews. As to words and phrases, there may be ground for the observation; but if one looks into the substance and character of the Epistles, I cannot conceive any two which were ever written in the world, more entirely unlike.

The letter of Clemens is addressed to the Corinthians. It speaks of the love and order and harmony which had existed for a long time among them, but which had recently been broken up by men who were exciting feuds and factions. To this state of things the writer addresses himself. That same pastoral patriarchal spirit which we discovered in Ignatius and Polycarp, breathes through the whole of it. There is no attempt to grapple with difficult questions, to meet the arguments of Jews or Gentiles, to show how a new world was rising out of the old. It is an exhortation, full of childlike beauty and tenderness, to avoid the spirit of ambition and rivalship which had been the curse of all societies; against which the Scriptures of the Old Testament were so full of warnings; freedom from which had been the great blessing and glory of every saint. At first when you read it you may think that Clemens is uttering a set of moral truisms; you may compare him with his namesake at Alexandria, and be surprised how much less thought and variety there is in the earlier Teacher than in the later, in the Italian than in the Egyptian. But the admirable man of whom we were hearing in the last Lecture would have been the last to invite or sanction the comparison. Nor is it a sound and true one. There is a weight and solemnity in the words of the Roman pastor which we shall feel more and more as we know ourselves and study history. The texts which he quotes so simply, the instances of divisions produced by rivalry, and of the men whom God made great by making them humble, will be read by us as the most solemn prophecies, written at the very commencement of the Church's life, of the blight which was to destroy its blossoms, of the canker which would feed upon its root; prophecies which those to whom Clemens wrote, and those in whose name he wrote, might have done well to lay to heart; but which we shall do well if we think are quite as applicable to ourselves as ever they were to any men in the world.

<small>Lect. IV.</small>
<small>*Its character.*</small>

<small>*Compared with Clemens of Alexandria.*</small>

LECT. IV.

Extract, Epistle, c. 19 and 20. Humility the ground of Peace.

I will give you one extract from Clemens, that you may see he is not the less eloquent because he is simple. "It was the humility of mind, the subjection which was wrought through obedience in those whom I have spoken of, and in all who have received the like testimony, which hath elevated not only us but the generations before us, and all who have received God's oracles in fear and truth. Having then become inheritors of their great and glorious deeds, let us run onwards after that prize of peace which has from the beginning been held forth to us, and let us stretch our eyes to the Father and Creator of the whole universe, and be knit firmly together by those His glorious and unspeakable gifts and benefits of peace; and let us contemplate Him in our spirits, and dwell with the eyes of our soul upon His long-suffering will, and consider how free He is from anger towards all His creation. The heavens, moving by His ordinance, are subject to Him in peace. Day and night accomplish their accustomed course at His bidding, never clashing with each other. Sun and moon and the choirs of stars at His command fulfil the spheres that have been marked out for them, in concord, without any transgression. The pregnant earth at His will in its appointed seasons brings forth the abundant nourishment for men and beasts, and for all the creatures that are upon it, not disputing or changing any of His decrees. The inaccessible abysses and the unknown dispositions of the worlds below are held together by his appointments. The waves of the immeasurable sea gathered into heaps at

Peace throughout the physical universe.

His decree, pass not over the boundaries that have been erected for them, but do, as He has given commandment, for He hath said, "Thus far shalt thou come, and no further." The ocean that has been untrodden by men, and the worlds that are beyond it, are kept even by the same decrees of the great Master. The seasons of spring and summer, and autumn and winter, in peace succeed to each other. The winds in their stations in their own seasons perform their ministries without reluctance. The ever-springing fountains that have been ordained for enjoyment and health, with no failures offer their breasts that men may draw life from them. The very meanest of living beings hold their meetings together in peace and harmony. All these things the great Master and Ruler of all hath ordained to be in peace and harmony, doing good to all, but to us more abundantly who have fled to His mercies through our Lord Jesus Christ, to whom be glory and honour for ever and ever. Amen."

<small>LECT. IV.</small>

This belief in the sacredness and divinity of peace must have been closely connected in the mind of Clemens, and of every member of the Roman Church, with the idea of government. Obedience was to him the secret of blessedness. Nevertheless, there are no distinct indications, I think, in the letter of Clemens, of that complete order in the Church which seems to have grown up in Asia Minor under the eye of St. John, and which in the second century spread itself through the Church generally. If the earlier, even if the later, date

<small>*The letter does not indicate a developed Christian polity.*</small>

assigned to the letter of Clemens be the true one, this is what we should expect. There are passages in his epistle which seem clearly to show that he recognised the priesthood of the Jews as not altogether passed away. Till it had passed away he was not likely, whether he was under the instruction of St. Peter or not, to speak of the Church polity as providing any substitute for it.

The Clementines and Recognitions.

There are certain books connected with the name of Clemens, "the *Clementines*," and "the *Recognitions*," with which he had nothing to do, but which must belong, even in their earliest form, to a late period of the second century. These books, though unjustly attributed to him, are important for the history of the Church. And though it may be difficult to connect them directly with the Church over which Clemens presided, there must be some reason why his name rather than any other was given to them. They will come again under our notice; but I will tell you here that they are books of an Ebionitic character, and that they set up the name of St. Peter expressly as the Apostle of the circumcision, evidently slighting the Apostle of the Gentiles.

Special dangers of those who ruled in the Roman Church.

The tradition is that Clemens died a martyr. There is no proof that he did. But such reports are more probable about the Fathers of the Roman Church than about any other. They were directly under the eyes of the Emperor; and as we shall find when I come to speak more particularly on that subject, there was no Emperor from the end of the first century who did not look upon the Churches with suspicion, and with the more suspicion the more organized they appeared to be. It is therefore quite possible that the eminent men in the Roman Church may have glorified God by their deaths. This may have been their calling. And thus they may have acquired a peculiar reverence as being foremost in danger, *having their dwelling where the throne of Satan was.* As writers, they were less conspicuous than the members of most Churches. After Clemens, there is no one to whom any books or letters can be honestly referred; though, when we come to the ninth century, we shall find that a whole series of letters have been invented for this time, and the names of Roman Fathers forged to endorse them. *[margin: This Church weak in Literature.]*

The Roman Church had, however, one grace which was probably more serviceable to itself and to the Church generally than the gift of composing books could have been. Clemens dwells much on the duty of hospitality. It was one of the truest pentecostal signs, to dispense treasures to the needy, to entertain strangers, to wash the feet of the brethren. These were better proofs that the Spirit was among them than the speaking with tongues. Dionysius of Corinth, in a letter to Soter, who was Overseer or Father of the Roman Church between 168 and 177, bears witness of this disposition in the sister community. There is scarcely a higher commendation extant respecting any. *[margin: Strong in Hospitality.]*

The demand for this proof of Christian love and fellowship must have been greater in Rome than elsewhere, for thither people resorted from all countries. *[margin: Intercourse between the Roman and the other Churches.]*

LECT. IV.

Probability that there would be such intercourse.

Some doubt has been recently thrown by an ingenious writer upon all the stories and documents which assume an intercourse between the Churches, as if they presumed facilities of communication which could not have existed.[1] But the more one considers what Rome had done by the making of roads to create such facilities, and how certain it was that men instinct with a missionary spirit and a spirit of brotherhood would avail themselves of them, the less weight one attaches to such scepticism—the more easily one believes that there will and must have been a confluence of Christians, as well as of other strangers, at the capital—the more easily one credits the reports which occur, I think, in Eusebius, naturally, (wherever I detected a purpose, I should be as much inclined to suspect him as any writer I know,) concerning men of various opinions, and with various intents, who came up to consult with the Roman Overseers. The habit of regarding Rome as a centre must have passed very early from the Empire to the Church. It must have been strengthened in the hearts of Christians by every new case of men brought from a distance, as Ignatius was, to be ex-

---

[1] See the History of the Church of Rome, by the Rev. E. J. Shepherd, (Longman, 1851,) especially the Proof and Illustration, No. 4, Victor, p. 197. It does not fall within my province to speak, in this book, on the question of the authenticity of Cyprian's letters, which Mr. Shepherd has raised and discussed with so much ingenuity. I hope to examine his arguments more completely hereafter; in the meantime one can express nothing but thanks to him for the courage and freedom from all ecclesiastical bias with which he has entered upon his task. Such criticism must lead to good results ultimately, however one may dissent from some of its first conclusions.

posed in the Amphitheatre. Rome became a sacred place as holding the actual tombs of so many martyrs; the fact affording afterwards the excuse for the fiction, that she had possession of innumerable bones which had been consigned to far distant earths and seas. The consequence was nearly inevitable. There would be acts of assumption on the part of the Roman Fathers; they would call forth resistance. To say that these things were not likely in the second century, because it was a time of unruffled moderation and purity, one in which there *could* not be any claims of dominion resembling in kind those which later periods witnessed, is to trifle with the facts of history. We have found other forms of corruption and impurity, why not this? What do all the warnings and exhortations of Clemens mean, if the human heart was free from this evil in that day?—if favourable circumstances were not sure to call it forth?

Claims of authority to be expected in Rome.

The story then to which I alluded before, of Polycarp coming to Rome in the days of Anicetus and discussing with him the time for keeping Easter, though it has been vehemently questioned, seems to me perfectly reasonable. Polycarp was an old man, certainly, to undertake such a journey; but his age has been a good deal exaggerated, to make him better acquainted with the Apostles than he was; and all accounts represent him as unusually hale in body as well as zealous in spirit. It was an occasion worthy of an unusual effort. It was no trifle for an old Asiatic to give up a practice he had learnt from

The Easter Controversy.

St. John; it was a very serious thing for a Christian to feel that the witness which the Christian family was bearing to the world might be weakened by a difference between Orientals and Occidentals. It is consistent, I think, with experience and with the position of the Roman Father, that he should have refused to abandon his own ground, and should have thought it strange for a man of Smyrna to doubt that a Roman was a better judge of customs that were suitable to the Churches generally, than he was. It is equally natural that he should at last have deferred to the venerable age of his companion, and have felt that he had no right to enforce even the most desirable practice on him if it involved a breach of their fellowship.

The story of Polycarp and Anicetus consistent.

The sadder sequel to this narrative I accept on similar grounds. We are told that Victor, the last Roman Overseer of this century, was engaged in the same controversy with Polycrates of Ephesus; that the latter defended what he supposed was the tradition of St. John even more strongly than Polycarp had done; that Victor gave no heed to his arguments, and entirely cast aside the toleration of his predecessor, deliberately excommunicating all Churches which would not keep Easter according to the Western rule. His decision is said to have been arrested by the mild and excellent counsels of Irenæus, the Bishop of Lyons, though it does not appear to what extent his mediation was successful. It has been argued that such an exercise of power in that age is absolutely incredible; that the documents

Victor and Polycrates, Eusebius, book v. c. 24.

Victor's excommunication.

which represent it must be forgeries of a later time; that if they had not been, we should at least have found in the letter of Irenæus some more vehement protest against such an assumption of authority by the Roman, not a mere attempt to dissuade him from the exercise of it. There is, I suspect, a double fallacy in this plausible reasoning. First, it transfers the notions of the middle ages to the second century, and supposes that the exercise of excommunication necessarily implies some formally recognised superiority and authority in the person or the Church whence it proceeds; whereas a weaker body may refuse to hold communion with a stronger, as well as a stronger with a weaker. Secondly, it underrates one of the moral powers which *was* acting upon the Christians at that time. In the age of Polycarp—the influence of St. John, was a power, and a great—in Asia Minor a paramount—one. In the influence of the capital and its associations was another — a counteracting influence to this;—able in the West to overpower it.

What was implied in it.

Counteracting tendencies.

To the same period of Victor belongs another visit from the East, which, if we may trust our authorities, had serious consequences in the West. Praxeas, of whom I have spoken already, full of the mischiefs which the Montanists were causing in Phrygia, denounced them in the capital. That he came thither for the purpose, we need not suppose; being there, it was not strange that he should dwell on the subject that was nearest his heart. With it he seems to have connected his own doctrine of Monachism, into which

Praxeas at Rome.

he had been led through his hostility to Montanus. Victor accepted his denunciations of his opponents; appears to have overlooked the errors of his own system. Such, at least, was the impression which his conduct made on a presbyter of Carthage, who was in Rome at that time, and who, unlike Victor, had conceived the greatest dread of Praxeas, and (first, perhaps, through that dread) an affection for the supposed Paraclete. Of this presbyter I shall have much to tell you. I introduce him here because the disgust with which Victor inspired him had a great effect upon his after life, and upon his relations to the Church generally.

Minucius Felix belongs to the 3d century.

As I have said that the literature of the Roman Church in this century was comparatively insignificant, I should like to make a memorable exception to the remark, by telling you of Minucius Felix, who was a Roman advocate, and wrote a delightful little book called "Octavius," in defence of the Gospel. But, though very eminent men have placed him in the reign of Marcus Aurelius, there is more ground for the opinion which refers him to about the year 230 or 240. I must, therefore, defer my account of him for the present. I have already told you that the last days of Justin were probably passed in Rome.

Gaul.

How and when the Church in Gaul was founded, we know not. The traditions respecting Dionysius the Areopagite, though baseless in themselves, might lead us to suppose that its first teachers came from Greece Proper; but it is more likely that it had an Asiatic origin. The first clear tidings we have of it are in a letter addressed "by the servants of Christ dwelling in Vienna and Lyons of Gaul, to the brethren in Asia and Phrygia, having the same faith and hope of redemption with us: to whom they wish peace and grace and glory from God and from our Lord Jesus Christ." This letter is one of the noblest archives a Church could have,—worth all the miraculous legends in the world. I hope the members of the French Church duly prize it. It tells of the witness which was borne for the name of God by poor men and weak women in the city of Lyons during the reign of Marcus Aurelius. I do not suppose the persecution there was the direct consequence of any order from him. It was more probably a native movement, which the Roman governor could scarcely have checked if he would, but which he encouraged and legalized, acting, no doubt, in conformity with the wishes of the Emperor. The writer of the letter testifies, "that the wrath of the multitude and the governor and the soldiers was especially directed against Sanctus, a deacon from Vienna; and against Maturus, a newly baptized man, but a gallant warrior; and against Attalus, whose family was from Pergamos, who had been for a long time a pillar and support of those who dwelt there; and against Blandina, through whom Christ made it manifest that the things which are poor and uncomely, and are despised by man, are counted of great glory by God, in virtue of their love to Him, which comes forth in power, and does not glory in appearance." "For when we all feared," he goes on, "and her mistress after the flesh likewise,

Eusebius, book v. c. 1.

The letter respecting the persecution

The witnesses.

Blandina.

who had herself been one of the warriors, lest she should not be able to make her confession boldly, because of the weakness of her body, Blandina was filled with such inward might that those who were by turns torturing her from morn to even were exhausted, and confessed that they had no more that they could do to her, and wondered that she still remained breathing after all that she had undergone, seeing that one form of the torment seemed enough to wear out her life, not to speak of so many and various kinds. But the blessed woman seemed to gather new strength, like a brave athlete, in the confession, and she experienced a revival, and rest, and unconsciousness of that which was befalling her, while she cried, 'I am a Christian, and no evil thing goes on amongst us.' Sanctus, likewise, after enduring all manner of ignominies, and insults, and sufferings, his unrighteous foes hoping that through the greatness of his torments they should hear something from him that was not fitting, so steadfastly withstood their purpose, that he did not even utter forth his own name, or the name of his nation, or of the city whence he came, nor whether he was slave or free, but to all that was asked him answered, in the Latin tongue, 'I am a Christian.' This served him for name, for city, for race; but no other voice did the Gentiles hear from him. . . . In whom Christ suffering accomplished His glory, putting down the adversaries and holding forth an example to those who should come after, that there is nothing to be feared where there is the Father's love, nor painful where there is Christ's glory.

The people of Lyons, though they might have *Thyestean Banquets imputed to the Christians of Lyons.* thought the mere profession of a Christian a sufficient warrant for these punishments, had associated with it all manner of horrible imputations. The Christians were supposed to offer human sacrifices, and in their secret feasts to feed upon the victims. The object was, by torture, to bring them to the confession of these enormities. In not a few cases the experiment was successful; the sufferers denied Christ, and confirmed the charges against His disciples. Some of these, along with those who had remained *The Prison.* faithful, and had survived the torture, were thrown into a dark dungeon,—the bodies which had already suffered so much being bound with heavy chains. Many of the young and vigorous died there of suffocation. Pothinus, the Bishop of Lyons, who was *Pothinus.* ninety years of age, and very weak in body, after bearing a good confession, was thrown again into prison, and at the end of two days breathed out his life. Those who had denied the faith there were as ill treated as those who had confessed it, seeing that they had acknowledged themselves to be murderers, and guilty of all manner of crimes. There was a startling contrast between the looks of the two when they were brought forth,—" the one cheerful, glory and much grace being mixed in their countenances, so that even their bonds hung upon them like goodly and bridal ornaments; the other cowed, and with *The Deniers.* pained countenances, and full of shame—reviled, moreover, by the heathen as unmanly cowards—bearing the disgrace which they had put upon themselves,

LECT. IV. having lost their honourable, and glorious, and life-giving title."

Their restoration.

But the example of the one was not lost upon the other. The writer, though inclined to expect various miraculous succours for the faithful, speaks of this as the greatest miracle which was wrought on their behalf, that "through the living the dead were made alive, and that martyrs conferred blessings on those who were not martyrs; and much joy came to the Virgin-mother (the Church) when those whom she had thrown out as dead, she received back alive. For, by means of the true witnesses, many of those who had denied Christ were begotten again and kindled afresh; and being nerved to the struggle, went to the judgment-seat, encouraged by the voice of Him who desireth not the death of a sinner, but is gracious to penitents, that they might be again questioned by the governor," and suffer what he ordained.

Drowning the corpses to prevent resurrection.

The treatment of the corpses is thus described:—
"The bodies of the martyrs, then, having been exposed and left in the open air for six days, having been afterwards burnt and consumed, were cast into the river Rhone which was flowing near, so that no relic of them might remain on the earth. And these things they did, as if they were able to conquer God, and to take away from His servants their regeneration, and, as they said themselves, that they might have no hope of a resurrection—their confidence in which had led them to introduce a strange and new worship, to despise terrors, and to go with joy to

death. 'Let us see now whether they will rise, and whether their God can assist them, and deliver them out of our hands.'"

Eusebius has preserved some further words of this letter, which ought not to be passed over. "Those," he says, "who had withstood the torture, and had undergone all manner of sufferings, but had survived, were greatly displeased when they were called witnesses or martyrs by their brethren. 'Christ,' they said, 'is the faithful and true Martyr, the First-begotten from the dead, and Prince of the divine life. Those may be called martyrs whom Christ hath raised up in their confession, sealing their witness by their departure from earth. We are but poor and indifferent confessors.' And with tears they besought the brethren that continual prayers might be made for them, that they might be perfected. Nevertheless," adds the writer, "though they refused the name, they showed forth the power of martyrdom in deed, speaking with all boldness to the heathen, making manifest their high birth by their patience and their fearlessness towards men, being filled with the fear of God. They humbled themselves," he adds, "under the mighty hand by which they are now exalted. They pleaded for all, they accused none; they delivered all, they bound none; they prayed for those who inflicted all cruelties upon them; they poured out tears for those who had fallen, to the Father; they asked life of Him, and He gave it to them, which also they shared with those who were about them. Conquerors in all things, they have gone to God, having loved

LECT. IV.

C. 2. The surviving confessors refuse to be called Martyrs.

They lived as Martyrs.

Their love.

LECT. VI. peace always, and endowed us with peace, departing in peace; having left no pangs to the mother who bore them, or strife to the brethren, but joy and peace, and unity and love."

Irenæus. The writer of this letter was probably Irenæus "the Peaceable." You may wonder how he came by such a name, and may suspect that some invention has been at work in the words that are given to him, and the stories that are told of him; but it was probably the new name which he received when he was baptized, and therefore may have been chosen by himself, or by his parents, because it expressed the temper of mind which he most admired, or which was most characteristic of him. If he had been a convert from heathenism, he might have taken it in mature life; but, apparently, he was born of
His letter to Florinus. Eusebius, book v. *c.* 20. Christian parents, for he writes thus to Florinus, a presbyter of the Roman Church, who had adopted some opinions which he thought dangerous:—"I knew thee when I was a boy, in the Lower Asia, when thou wert with Polycarp, when thou wert trying to have a good reputation with him; for I remember those things better than the things that have come
Early recollections. to pass recently. The lessons we get in boyhood, growing up with the soul, become one with it; so that I can describe to you the place in which the
Image of the old man. blessed Polycarp used to sit and talk, his goings out and his comings in, the fashion of his life, his look and figure, the discourses which he made to the multitude; how he told us of his intercourse with John, and of others who had seen the Lord; how he

repeated their words, and what he had heard from them concerning the Lord, concerning His mighty acts, concerning His doctrine; for Polycarp having received them from the eye-witnesses of the Word of Life, gave forth all things in harmony with the Scriptures. These things even then, thanks to the mercy of God that was upon me, I diligently listened to, noting them down, not on paper, but in my heart, and ever, by the grace of God, I feed upon them again and again. And I can testify before God that if that blessed and apostolical old man had heard any such doctrine as that you have put forth, he would have cried, and stopped his ears; and uttering his familiar phrase, 'O good God! to what times hast Thou kept me, that I should bear these things!' he would have fled the place in which, sitting or standing, he had heard such words."

LECT. IV.

From this passage we may conclude that Irenæus grew up in Smyrna, and that he was taught from his youth to revere Polycarp. Under what circumstances he left Asia and came into Gaul we are ignorant; but that he was presbyter in Lyons during the persecutions, and became Overseer, perhaps immediately after the death of Pothinus, seems clear. He speaks of himself "as having not learnt the art of words, or cultivated the power of a writer," and "as living among Celts, and chiefly busied with their barbarous dialect." Still his interest in his old home, and in the affairs of the Church at large, must have been as lively as ever. What he says of Polycarp may explain his feelings respecting the Easter question, even apart from his

Irenæus in Gaul.

Heresies, lib. i. *Proœmium.*
περὶ βάρ-
βαρον διά-
λεκτον τὸ
πλεῖστον
ἀσχολου-
μένων.

ON CHURCH HISTORY.

His sympathy with Asia.

love of peace. He thought the Asiatics entirely wrong on that point; but he had an affectionate sympathy with them, and nothing caused him so painful a wrench as the possibility of a separation in spiritual bonds between the new and the old country.

Irenæus as a writer.

His letter to Florinus explains another part of his life, which you may fancy was inconsistent with the conciliatory disposition which the Paschal dispute called forth in him. The work for which he has become memorable is in five books, written " for the exposure and subversion of Gnosis, falsely so called;" or, as the Latin translator (the greater part exists only in a Latin translation) describes it, "against all heretics." Why should the peace-lover have plunged into such a fierce war as this? Why should the simple man who dwelt among barbarians, and had trained himself so little to subtleties of words, have thought himself called to engage with men who had the command of all subtleties? The words I have quoted contain the answer. Irenæus had been brought up under a teacher who knew nothing of theories and opinions; who was never intended to grapple with them; who regarded them with the natural indignation and impatience of an old man, feeling that he had a hold of a truth which he could not part with; who suspected with good reason that many he knew or heard of were substituting their notions for realities; who left it to younger men to see whether there might be any wheat mixed with the tares. Polycarp, we have seen, had his own prejudices. The customs which he thought St. John

Explanation of his work.

Polycarp's feelings as to new opinions.

probably observed were almost as venerable in his eyes as the principles which St. John had been appointed by God to embody in enduring words; nay, the stories which he had heard from the lips of the Apostle may have seemed to him more dear, more sacred, because they were told to him, than his Gospel itself. Irenæus had loved the simplicity of his master's character. He thought he should preserve that simplicity to the Church if he could bring his authority, and what he recollected of his sayings, into direct conflict with the complicated theories of the Gnostics. He thought, as many have done since, that the best way of encountering an error was to set up that in opposition to it, which was at the furthest imaginable distance from it. *Attempt to confront the old with the new.*

Accordingly, Irenæus undertook in that retreat of his at Lyons, while preaching the Gospel to Celtic barbarians, to confute all the opinions which had grown up in the most polished cities of Syria and Egypt. Having this design, and looking at things from this point of view, we cannot wonder at the method he adopted. The Valentinian system was the most refined, the most elaborate of all the Gnostical systems; it had, as I have explained to you, become still more elaborate in the hands of Valentinians than it was in the hands of Valentinus. Irenæus encounters it first, and encounters it in the most matured period of its growth. Another man might have applied himself first to the demolition of some of the simpler forms of error; then, when he had acquired the free use of his tools, have gone on to *The method.*

those that were more knotted and fibrous. Irenæus deliberately adopts the opposite course; because nothing can so astonish his reader, or make him so long for the older Smyrnæan lore, as to be at once cast among the interminable genealogies of those who had tasked their own native ingenuity most, and had besides imported the greatest variety of Gnostical notions from every religion and philosophy under heaven.

The First Book.

The whole of the first of the five books is occupied with an exposition of the different Gnostical systems, proceeding in that inverted order which I have described, from the most to the least complicated. In this book there is much unquestionably that we cannot find elsewhere, and which it is important that we should know. But I cannot believe that, if we had no other help than that which Irenæus affords us, his account would be intelligible, or therefore of any great practical use to us.

Its great merit.

At the same time, I am far from wishing to deny that the honest and simple reverence which Irenæus showed for the words of the Apostle, whom Polycarp had taught him to reverence above all others, was not often more effectual in confuting the systematisers than the arguments to which a more learned and ingenious man might have resorted. Take the following example. The Valentinians had pretended to deduce their different syzygies from the first chapter of St. John's Gospel. They did this by making the various words in the early part of the chapter announcements of different Æons, which together composed what they called an "Ogdoad." Irenæus replies thus: "Manifest is the fiction of this interpretation: for whereas John proclaims one God Almighty, and one only-begotten Christ Jesus, through whom he says that all things became, and declares Him to be the Son of God, Him to be the Only-Begotten, Him to be the Maker of all things, Him to be the true Light that lighteneth every man, Him to be Maker of the world, Him to have come to His own, Him to have been made flesh, and to have dwelt among us, they, twisting the interpretation according to their devices, would have there to be another Only-Begotten, in virtue of an emission or emanation, whom, forsooth, they call Beginning; another to have become the Saviour; another to be the Word, Son of the Only-Begotten; and another the Christ, thrown forth in order to restore or rectify the Pleroma. And having separated each one of these from the truth, and having abused the different names to their own purpose, they contrive that John should make here no mention of the Lord Jesus Christ. For if he spake of the Father, and Grace, and the Only-Begotten, and Truth, and the Word, and Life, and Man, and Church, then, according to their hypothesis, he spake concerning the first Ogdoad in which Jesus was not yet, nor Christ the Teacher of John. But that the Apostle did not speak concerning their syzygies, but concerning our Lord Jesus Christ, whom also he knew as the Word of God, he has made plain. For, gathering up his doctrine concerning the Word whom he had spoken of in the beginning, he adds, 'And the Word was made flesh,

Lect. IV.
Irenæus, lib. i. c. 9 and 10.

The separation of Names.

The Gospel of the One Word.

and dwelt among us.' But according to them, it was not the Word that was made flesh, as He never came out of the Pleroma; but He that came according to a providential arrangement and dispensation, being younger than the Word, the Saviour. Learn then, foolish ones, that Jesus, He that hath suffered for us, He that hath taken up His dwelling in us, He it is that is the Word of God. For if any other of the Æons had become flesh for our salvation, it would have been reasonable for the Apostle to have spoken of that other; but if the Word of the Father, He that descended, is He also who ascended, the only-begotten Son of the only Father, if He was made flesh according to the good pleasure of the Father for man, John has not made his discourse concerning any other, or concerning an Ogdoad, but concerning the Lord Jesus Christ. For according to them, the Word was not made flesh, but the Saviour put on a psychical body, contrived by an unspeakable Providence to be visible and tangible. But flesh is that ancient formation by God out of the dust which took place in the Adam, which flesh John declares the Word of God truly to have become. So their first and original Ogdoad is broken up. For one and the same Person being declared to be Word, and Only-Begotten, and Light, and Life, and Saviour, and Christ, and Son of God, and this Person having become incarnate for us, the machinery of the Ogdoad is dissolved; and this being dissolved, the whole scheme falls to pieces, which they idly dreaming, impute to the Scriptures, having moulded them anew according to their fashion."

THE SECOND CENTURY. 267

This is a very thorough and masterly exposure of the system-builders. Little can be added to it which would not weaken it; for as I endeavoured to show you before, St. John's Gospel, by setting forth the revelation of a Person, is marvellously contrived to shatter the notions which had been already in his day circulated,—equally contrived to anticipate all future experiments to restore these notions, or to put them into new and more plausible shapes. And here, therefore, it seems to me, Irenæus would have done well to leave the whole matter. He had asserted the great principle which undermined the false Gnosticism. He might have spared a refutation of its particular tenets, which he perhaps did not thoroughly understand, and for which he might often be inclined to substitute tenets of his own, which, if they had not been grounded upon so living and deep-rooted a faith, would not have been much better or safer than those they supplanted. It was a great advantage for him certainly to have known Polycarp. But, if he was inclined to put forth Polycarp as *the* teacher of the Church because he had listened to an Apostle,—yes, if he was inclined to make the Apostle himself *the* teacher,—he was contradicting his own words, he was destroying that principle which St. John lived to assert, and in which, as Irenæus in his brighter moments perceived, must lie the real antidote to all erroneous doctrine. When Irenæus forsook this light, he was weak as another man. Motives to superstition, which existed in his age, his circumstances, his character,

Lect. IV.

The Gospel of John, and the Tradition of Polycarp.

Danger of Irenæus.

prevailed over his better reason. He listened to vain gossip; he fell into childish fantasies, which one would rather not dwell upon when one is speaking of so good, and in many respects of so wise, a man. Let us think of his letter about the martyrs of Lyons, and gladly accept the probable report that he became one of the band of martyrs himself; so we shall not forget that he did a better work, and fought a better fight, than when he was writing his five books against all heresies. And now we must pass from the Church of Gaul to another which will occupy us for some time, though we know it almost entirely through one of its members.

LECTURE V.

THE SAME SUBJECT CONTINUED.

THE AFRICAN CHURCH.

I HAVE spoken to you of one part of the African continent; but I prepared you, in my introductory lectures, to expect that what we heard of Egypt would help us very little in understanding the circumstances of that part of Africa whereof Carthage was the capital. In one most important respect, there was indeed a resemblance between the circumstances of these two countries. Both had received a civilization which was foreign, and not only foreign, but unnatural, to them. One country may owe to another some of its most precious gifts. Gaul would never have been what it is, if it had not been invaded by the Franks of Germany. Our country would never have been what it is, if it had not been subdued by the Saxons and Normans. But the civilization which came to us and to our neighbours in this way was preceded, as I shall hope to show you hereafter, by conflicts which matured the seeds under ground —which caused different, apparently opposing, influences to work together—which removed much that had been merely superficial and external, that what

Lect. V.

Contrast between Alexandria and Carthage.

A foreign civilization common to both.

was deeper and more native might come forth with greater strength. It was not so, I think, in the case of either of the countries I am speaking of now. The old Egyptian character and habits were overlaid, and to a great extent stifled, by the Greek civilization which the Ptolemies introduced. The Punic mind was still more crushed by the Roman conquest. Therefore we must look for great and terrible changes to befal these lands. We must not wonder if the Greek culture of the one, and the Latin culture of the other, should both at last be found feeble and merely outward, and if God in His providence should appoint another, apparently a very severe and tremendous, discipline for these countries, which after long ages may fit them to bring forth fruits of which before they were incapable. I say this, not only to prepare you for portions of our history that otherwise might seem very startling and incredible, but also that you may understand better the circumstances of the Christian Churches as they present themselves to us in the second century. You have seen how much of good there was in the Alexandrian Church—how much there was in it that was not good, but artificial and fantastical — nay, what a leaven there was of this even in its noblest and truest men. The same observation will come out, I think, more strongly in reference to the Church in the province of Africa. You will find there a Church which has exerted as great an influence upon the whole of Christendom as any that could be named. You will find one unlike in almost every respect to the Church in Alexandria—unlike in its virtues and in its failings, in the thoughts and habits of its guides, and of those who revolted from their guidance—almost opposed in the effects it has produced upon the world. But you will see also, I think, some signs that the Church had not struck its roots deeply into one land or into the other; that it had not taken hold of those who were the proper inhabitants of the soil; that in the one country it was far too purely Greek, in the other far too exclusively Latin. My meaning must be explained by the history. Part of it you will not understand till a later time; part, I think, will be evident from the account I am about to give you of the man to whom I referred at the close of my last lecture. *Its artificial character.*

The Church of Carthage may have been established early in this century; but we know nothing of its doings till we stumble at once upon the writings of Q. Septimius Florens Tertullianus. It might be a question in his case, as in the case of Clemens, whether he should be more properly referred to the second century or to the third. Some of his books must have been composed before the reign of S. Severus, but the greater part fall within his reign; some may possibly belong to that of Caracalla. But I have no hesitation about reckoning him in the second century, to which Severus himself most strictly belongs. His mind was formed in this age; he had already given the impression of his mind to Carthage, or if not, had exhibited what were its tendencies, within the period which these lectures embrace. *Age of Tertullian.*

Passage of Eusebius relating to Tertullian.

Eusebius scarcely mentions Tertullian in his history; one sentence contains the notice which he gives of him; it is, I conceive, an important one. "Tertullian," he says, "was a man profoundly acquainted with the Roman laws, and in other respects conspicuous and very illustrious at Rome." Eusebius was apparently ignorant of Tertullian's real country; perhaps he had not read his books. In his own "Apology," he calls Africa "our country." Again and again he assumes it to be so. Eusebius might therefore only mean that he was a Latin; but he might also have heard that he exercised the function of an advocate in Rome. Everything in Tertullian's writings confirms the opinion that he had been carefully educated in Roman law, still more carefully in Roman rhetoric.

A Jurisconsult. A Rhetorician. An Advocate.

There were abundant opportunities for studying rhetoric in the schools of Carthage, but for the exercise of his profession he more probably went to the capital. It was the great age of Roman lawyers and jurisconsults; Papinianus, the most eminent of them, was the counsellor of Severus. Tertullian may have ceased to be a lawyer when he became a Christian, (he speaks of himself as originally a Pagan,) but he certainly brought with him to his new faith the fruits of his former discipline. It is disputed whether he was ever ordained a presbyter, (Jerome says confidently that he was, and he is probably right,) but it is certain that whatever other functions he exercised, and whatever changes his mind underwent, he continued an advocate and a rhetorician to the last.

A Presbyter.

He was a consummate advocate, and a splendid

THE SECOND CENTURY. 273

rhetorician. He has never the least difficulty in maintaining an argument upon any topic; he can always crush an opponent, if he cannot convince him. There are passages of striking declamation in his writings which can scarcely be paralleled in any author of ancient or modern times. Though his style is laboured, often very obscure, full of strange phrases, arising, Niebuhr says, from an affectation of antiquity which belonged to his time[1] and country, it is always forcible and imposing. More is to be learnt from his books than, perhaps, from those of any other Father, about the practices of the early Church; there are no books that contain so many hints and anticipations of opinions and practices which were to be developed in after times.

LECT. V.
His intellectual qualities.

I have told you some of Tertullian's intellectual merits; I am sure he had also great moral virtues. He was thoroughly earnest in his belief. People speak of his African vehemence; but if God calls a man into existence in a particular country, He

His moral qualities.

[1] The strangeness of his style has been attributed by some ingenious writers to the pressure of Christian ideas, under which the classical Latin gave way. But I have yet to discover that Minucius Felix, Cyprian, Lactantius, Augustin, who did not adopt his extraordinary phraseology, who could write ordinary and intelligible Latin of the iron age, were less possessed with Christian ideas than he was. Any one who will be at the pains to look into any "Clavis Tertulliana," (*e.g.* the one which is affixed to Semler's edition,) may judge for himself how many of his difficult and uncouth forms of expression have anything to do with the special doctrines of the Gospel. I do not say—it is hard to say in any case—how far they were genuine representations of the mind of the man; how far they were merely fantastic; but I do contend that Christianity is not in the least responsible for them, except that he desired to make it technical, and to separate it from the common sympathies.

T

means him surely to have the qualities of that country, not of some other. Vehemence is not an evil thing in itself, but a good. It has its temptations, as the opposite habit of feeling has, but I do not know that the temptations are greater; at all events, they can be resisted, and the hot blood may glorify God and be serviceable to mankind as much as the cold. We may hope that Tertullian was aware of the dangers to which his peculiar character made him liable; nobody, certainly, was more alive to the dangers which assaulted himself and his countrymen from without; no one was more eager for plans of discipline to ward

His temper. them off. If he does not seem to have been always equally on his guard against the internal provocations to anger and bitterness, we are not judges what his conflicts with himself may have been. We have no right to suppose that he imposed a less strict rule upon himself than upon his brethren; and, therefore, as he dwelt continually on the necessity of penitence for them, we may assume that it followed his own falls.

Tertullian the Lawyer. I confess that I find less fault with the passionate temper which Tertullian is supposed to have derived from his country, than with the skill in supporting a cause, which he owed to his Roman education. A man who is betrayed into hard words against an opponent may be ashamed of himself, and may make amends by greater generosity afterwards; but Tertullian is systematically hard and overbearing with those he is attacking. To use our English expression, he feels that he is *retained* against them, and that he should be unjust to his client if he did not exhibit the opposite side in the worst possible light. You will say, perhaps, that his client was Christianity, and that a man might be well afraid of betraying such a cause. I fully believe that that was Tertullian's feeling: let him have all the benefit of the admission. But it seems to me an utterly wrong feeling. Think of a poor earth-born man taking Christianity under his patronage. It was precisely the mistake of the Carthaginian to do this, as it has been the mistake of thousands of others. They have thought that the Gospel was *their* cause, which *they* had to manage, to defend by their wit and chicanery. The truth was not something above them to be adored, sought after, lived for, died for; it was something which they had grasped and comprehended, which was precious because it belonged to them, and which they were to defend against all invaders by fair means or foul.

Tertullian the patron of Christianity.

In the ordinary accounts which are given of Tertullian and of his works, especially by writers of the Romish communion, you will find a line drawn between two periods of his life. "No one," it is said, "was so strictly orthodox and catholic for a long term of years; afterwards he conceived a disgust for the Romish Bishop Victor, partly from his supposed encouragement of Praxeas; then he threw himself vehemently into Montanism, acknowledged Montanus as the Paraclete, and used the same terms which he used in denouncing the great body of the Church." No doubt there are books of Tertullian's which seem to be clear from all taint of the doctrine which he subsequently adopted; no doubt there are others which distinctly

Ordinary division of Tertullian's life and writings.

avow it. But the task of arranging his books in reference to this change has been a difficult one, and to some who have engaged in it must have been a very painful one; for the works which they would most like to claim as maintaining the true faith, and as confuting heretics, were confessedly written after the time in which he became a heretic himself. To this class, for instance, Du Pin, a most reasonable critic, himself a Romanist, refers the book "On the Prescriptions of Heretics," which is often quoted as containing the most perfect and satisfactory rule for distinguishing false opinions from the true. Five long books against Marcion, one against Hermogenes, one against Praxeas, one against the Jews, one on the Soul, one on the Resurrection of the Flesh, one on the Flesh of Jesus Christ, are placed by this equitable judge in the same list. Others on Modesty, on Fasts, on Flight in Persecution, were written expressly for the Montanists, and in opposition to the great body of the Church. There remain a book on Baptism, on Prayer, on Penitence, his Apology for the Christian Religion, some books on Patience, which are supposed to belong to the first stage of his life, and a few others which fall into a transition period between his Orthodoxy and his Montanism.

Another difficulty has troubled some of Tertullian's critics, connected with his domestic life. There are two books addressed to his wife; the object of them is to persuade her to remain single after his death,—not, he solemnly assures her, because he has any jealousy of her falling into the hands of another man, but because he is thoroughly convinced that she would lose in spiritual life by again entering into wedlock. It is quite clear from the whole tenor of the book, that Tertullian undervalued marriage, looking upon it as a necessity for many men, but as involving the sacrifice of a nobler moral condition which might be attained. He comments in the usual style upon the seventh chapter of the First Epistle to the Corinthians, and, like a judicious advocate, does not touch at all upon the Epistle to the Ephesians. These books would have been, therefore, very acceptable to those who exclude the priesthood from marriage, if they did not suggest the question, how Tertullian himself came to be married. Jerome affirms that he was a priest; Tertullian's authority as a Church Doctor would be diminished if he was not one. But if he was a presbyter when he wrote this treatise, presbyters must at that time have been permitted to have wives. I state the case nearly as it is put by Du Pin. On the general subject I may have to speak by-and-by; I am interested in it now only as it illustrates the life and thoughts of Tertullian.

The marriage of a Priest.

The tone of feeling which comes out in these two books was characteristic of all which Tertullian wrote on similar subjects. Some persons must read these books; they are necessary to our understanding of the growth of opinions in the Church—necessary to the interpretation of many of its greatest puzzles and conflicts. But I dare not say that they are purifying or elevating books; I dare not say that they give me

Tertullian, books De Habitu Mulierum, De Pudicitia, &c.

LECT. V.

Book De Præscriptionibus Hæreticorum.

Application.

a gratifying impression of the mind of the man who wrote them. That he was a religious man I do not doubt, one who aimed at the cultivation of a high religious sentiment; but if by a religious sentiment is meant a sentiment in accordance with the mind and spirit of either the Old or the New Testament, we must look for it elsewhere than here.

The book to which I have alluded, "On the Prescriptions of Heretics," explains the statement of Eusebius respecting Tertullian, and shows how much his mind was cast in a legal mould. According to the Roman law, which we have imitated in our English law, a man whom an adverse claimant sought to disturb in the possession of his property, might plead that he had had possession of it for a given number of years. This was his *prescription*, which made it unnecessary that he should establish his original title to it by any further evidence. What a satisfactory method this would be, thought Tertullian, to use against those who would disturb us in our spiritual possessions! Why need we trouble ourselves to prove, by arguments from Scripture, our title to them? Why cannot we turn round and say, "We have held these doctrines without dispute since the time of the Apostles: what business have you to pretend that any others can be truer than they?" There was a wonderful charm in this thought to a person of Tertullian's disposition. He was delighted to seize a maxim with which he had been familiar; he was delighted with his own ingenuity in bringing it to bear on a new subject; and he was delighted, because he looked upon the Christian faith very much as a property of his, which he was to maintain against those who would intrude upon it. If another Roman lawyer had been allowed to speak, he might have said, "But, after all, do you find it easier to prove this uninterrupted possession, than to defend the title itself? Is there no difficulty in bringing evidence on that point as well as on the other? May not the difficulty be increased for your successors?" A heathen disputant might have said, "If you rest all upon prescription, cannot we plead a prescription for our idolatries? And if you say that your prescription starts from Apostles, must not you explain how these Apostles acquired their original right? and does not that involve the very necessity you seek to get rid of?" Christian objectors did actually say, "Our Lord commanded us to ask that we might receive, to seek that we might find, to knock that it might be opened." Whatever answer Tertullian had ready for the other objectors, these he could silence with a dashing, peremptory interpretation of our Lord's words. Asking, seeking, and knocking, are very well for those to whom the truth has not been made known; to us it *has* been made known; therefore, for us such acts are unnecessary. I find it hard to stifle my indignation at such trifling with the Divine precept. And yet this treatise, the leading maxim of which could not be sustained, as its clever author knew, without that outrage, has been a text-book among those who reverence the words of their Divine Master!

I have told you that the man who had this receipt

Lect. V.

Objections to the method from different quarters.

Asking not necessary to those who have.

for extinguishing heretics was himself a heretic at the time he composed it. But if he was so, he could make up for his own departures from the faith of the Church at large by the most unscrupulous language respecting all others. He begins his treatise against Marcion with a description of the inhospitable character of the Pontus Euxinus near which he dwelt, and the ferocity of those who inhabited its coasts. "But," he goes on, "nothing in Pontus is so barbarous and dark as this, that it is the birth-place of Marcion, who is wilder than the Scythian, more unstable than the Hamaxobian, more inhuman than the Massagetæ, more audacious than the Amazon, darker than the clouds, colder than the winter, more fragile than the ice, more deceitful than the Danube, more precipitous than the Caucasus." Having named the Caucasus, he goes on to compare him with Prometheus, and then with different animals, especially with the mice of that region.

I have said that I did not complain of the passion into which Tertullian is sometimes betrayed; but this is not passion at all,—it is the vulgar vituperation of a professional advocate. However little he might have cared to spare Marcion, a man who had a real sense of the awful question that was involved in the dispute between them would not have indulged in this frantic abuse. The very issue upon which Tertullian puts it, whether there were two Gods, or one living and true God, would have taught him the impertinence and profaneness of such an introduction to so grave and dreadful a controversy.

THE SECOND CENTURY.

New heretics, however, were not more scorned and hated by Tertullian than old philosophers. Because the heretics had borrowed from the philosophers, he thought the first step to extinguish the one was to destroy the reputation of the other. In his Prescriptions, he pours forth his rich vocabulary of vituperation upon Aristotle; his treatise On the Soul is introduced by sneers at the prison discourse of Socrates on immortality. His insinuations against the man are heartless and mean; but it is far worse when he proceeds to deal with the question itself, which Socrates so solemnly and earnestly brought before his disciples. Tertullian avers broadly, that since nothing could be known on such a subject but what it pleased God to reveal, it was wrong to think about the matter, and that Socrates was, in fact, more devil-inspired than ordinary heathens.[1] There is no other sense to be put upon his words than this; and they may well make us inquire by what process a man could have worked himself into a conviction, which startles and outrages the conscience of every one who hears it. The process

LECT. V.

His treatment of Philosophers. Book De Animâ, c. 1 and 2.

Socrates, according to Tertullian.

---

[1] De Animâ, c. 1. Adeo omnis illa tunc sapientia Socratis de industriâ venerat consultæ æquanimitatis, non de fiduciâ compertæ veritatis. Cui enim veritas comperta sine Deo? cui Deus cognitus sine Christo? cui Christus exploratus sine Spiritu Sancto? cui Spiritus Sanctus accommodatus sine fidei sacramento? Sane Socrates facilius diverso spiritu agebatur. Si quidem aiunt dæmonium illi a puero adhæsisse, pessimum revera pædogogum, etsi post deos et cum diis dæmonia deputantur per philosophos et poetas. Nondum enim Christianæ potestatis documenta processerant quæ vim istam perniciosissimam, nec unquam bonam, antiqui erroris artificem, omnis veritatis avocatricem, sola traducit. Quod si idcirco sapientissimus Socrates secundum Pythii quoque dæmonis suffragium *scilicet negotium navantis* socio suo, &c.

Tertullian's religion.

is this: Tertullian believed that he had been taught a religion which he was to maintain against all other religions. It was good for nothing in his eyes, unless he could show that it set aside all that honest men had been thinking of, and feeling after, before it was proclaimed. That was the proof that it came from God; that was the only comfortable evidence Tertullian could have, that the inheritance which had been left him was safe against invaders. I believe that his doctrine was far more fatal to that which he defended than to that which he opposed; nay, that it has been the doctrine which, more than any other, has hid the glory of Christ's Gospel from men, and has been the cause of its becoming blended with the heathenism from which Tertullian professed to separate it.

His flattery of Christians.

There is a part of this passage, at the opening of the treatise On the Soul, which is very characteristic of Tertullian, and is, I think, intensely mischievous. In order to throw contempt upon Socrates, he contrasts his prison scene, and his drinking the hemlock, with the constancy of the Christian martyrs, who "did not bring in new demons, but drove out old ones; who did not corrupt the minds of the youth, but informed them with all modesty; who did not sustain the unjust sentence of one city, but of the whole world, for the sake of a truth more hateful because more full; who did not swallow the cup with a sort of luxurious enjoyment, but endured to be burnt alive," &c.: a sentence exhibiting all the cleverness of Tertullian, but, it seems to me, most immoral, most corrupting to the minds of Christians, because inflating them with a sense of their own superiority, teaching them to regard themselves as righteous, and to despise others.

And this is to me so much the effect of nearly all Tertullian's ingenious arguments and splendid oratory, that I often feel tempted to wish they had been used against the Gospel; I think then I could have done them greater justice. But that is a wrong desire; they would not be such warnings to us as they are, if we will use them aright, of the dangers into which Christians may fall—they would not be such prophecies of the evils into which the Church has fallen, if they had been turned in a different direction. What I do most fervently beseech of you, what I would ask of God for you, is that you may be preserved from admiration of that kind of wit and intellectual power, which does not humble itself to be the servant and soldier of the Gospel, for the glory of God and the good of mankind, but assumes to be the champion and protector of the Gospel, and so turns it to the denial of God's goodness and truth, and to the injury of those for whom Christ died. If I thought less of Tertullian's gifts than I do; if I did not see from the history of the Church how much power he had exercised over it; if all that seems to me most wrong and dangerous in him, was not extremely likely to recommend itself as right and safe, I should speak less strongly. As it is, I must think that no man has lived in the Church whom God

Effects of his writings.

intends less as an example, and more as a beacon, to the members of it.

Tertullian the Apologist.

Tertullian's Apology is far from being his most important work, yet it has become more associated than any other with his name. And this is not wonderful. Tertullian may almost be called the Apologist; every book he has written is an Apology. He would not have liked to be told so, for the word suggests philosophy and Socrates; but it was the misfortune and retribution of his habit of mind, that he was compelled to imitate those whom he trampled upon; to entangle himself in subtle reasoning while he denounced reasoning; to be superstitious while he raved against superstition; to fall into heresy while he could speak of nothing but destruction to heretics. There are passages in his books, worthy to be remembered and written in one's heart, in which he draws the most beautiful distinctions; others where he seems in love with what is natural and simple; presently you find the distinctions have entrapped you into propositions utterly subversive of the premises from which they are deduced, that the admiration of simplicity obliges you to some most artificial conceit. His treatise On the Veiling of Virgins (you must not suppose that it has anything to do with nuns and convents, of which this age knew nothing; it only treats about the proper dress of unmarried women) opens with a noble contrast between Truth and Custom, one which was often quoted in the ecclesiastical discussions of the middle ages, and

Book De Velandis Virginibus.

THE SECOND CENTURY. 285

cannot be dwelt upon too much by any of us. But this very contrast is the plea for erecting a certain practice, which was probably desirable in Africa at that time, into a principle; for though there are passages in the treatise which seem to allow the liberty of Churches to judge what is best for themselves in such cases, the whole effect of it is to make an external rule part of the moral and spiritual code. The treatise On Baptism begins with a vindication, just and eloquent, of the ordinance, as an illustration of the simplicity of God's operations, and with a complaint, well founded though surlily expressed, of those who despise it for that reason. But he straightway enters into a series of refined speculations about the nature, and properties, and uses of water; some of them reasonable and suggestive, all of them ingenious; but surely most inapplicable, when the object was to set forth the character of a sacrament, which was to be received by the poor and ignorant no less than the wise, as a testimony of what God was, and of what He had done for them. Even when Tertullian appeals, as he does in the book On the Testimony of the Soul, to the witness which men bear for God, and against their own idolatrous notions of Him, by their common, unconscious language,—a fertile and most interesting subject, and one upon which the writer entered with good-will, because it enabled him to throw out an insinuation against some of his brethren who had appealed to the wisdom of heathen sages, when they ought to have appealed to the sense of mankind,—even then you see how much

LECT. V.

Book De Baptismo.

Book De Testimonio Animæ.

Lect. V. the practised rhetorician is mixing his own skilful and far-fetched fancies with the plain popular convictions which were most alien from them.

Neander. The Anti-Gnosticus.

A very eminent historian and thinker of our day, dissatisfied with the ordinary attempts to divide Tertullian into two men,—the adherent to the Church, and the adherent to Montanism,—perceiving that he is essentially the same person in both his periods, has endeavoured to explain the end and upshot of his whole life by calling him "The Anti-Gnostic." No doubt a horror of Gnosticism was a prominent characteristic in the mind of this distinguished African. If the offence which was given him respecting Praxeas was the immediate *occasion* of his aversion to Montanism, the secret *cause* of it may have been a feeling that the Montanists were more opposed to all the Alexandrian speculators, and offered a better protection against them, than the Church at large. But one requires to understand upon what ground he adopted that opinion, and why a Phrygian theory should have been so much more palatable to him than an Egyptian one. Much, I think,

Montanism a resting-place for a restless man.

may be attributed to the discontent and impatience into which a man falls who regards Christianity as I have told you that Tertullian did. The spirit requires something to rest in, which is not what it is always defending and protecting; that which it claims as a property does not offer it a home. In hours of weariness it will cry out for something new to be given it; it will embrace the new thing all the more readily, if it comes without any pomp of argument and demonstration. It will bow down to a teacher who claims divine inspiration, that it may be delivered from the burden of its own dreary subtleties—that it may throw off, if possible, its own intellectual haughtiness. At whose feet the oblation is made, signifies comparatively little.

I think, too, that while Tertullian was always speaking of spiritual things and a spiritual world, he must have been conscious that the Spirit which our Lord promised—the Spirit which was to unite, the Spirit of meekness and charity, and which was to guide into all truth—had not yet received his entire homage, had not subdued his strong passions to itself, or driven out the proud demon of self. If he could obtain this blessing by a voluntary abdication of his own judgment,—by laying himself low before some outward Paraclete,—he might hope that the One whom he could not see would reign more triumphantly in his heart.

Some of the passages which I have quoted from his writings, after he became a Montanist, do not afford much ground for thinking that the expectation was fulfilled. At all events they are not *less* presumptuous—they do not show *less* reliance upon his own powers—than his earlier writings. He had only found a larger field for censure,—more men whom he could denounce as earthly and sensual. Montanism, however, could still afford him consolation, such as it was. It was not merely an escape from the Gnostical speculations; it was a new religion. This was what Tertullian had all along craved for. He did not really want a

LECT. V.

It was a submission of the intellect.

It held out the hope of a more spiritual state of mind.

This blessing apparently not attained.

Tertullian desired a religion of his own.

Lect. V.

Humility may have been the ultimate effect of his struggles and disappointments.

Church—a great divine and human fellowship—in which he was one member; he wished for a religion well-compacted, severe, exclusive, according to which he might shape his life, which he might support against all who rejected it, which might separate him from the mass of mankind. His biography, so far as we know it, is the great test and experiment whether this is really the one thing needful,—the good thing which God has prepared for those that love Him. I believe and trust that there is another part of that biography which we do not know: if the veil were withdrawn from that, we should find that the great Apologist became once more the little child, content to give up himself, and to be one of that family in heaven and earth which is named with the name of Christ, not of Montanus or of Tertullian.

LECTURE VI.

THE CHURCH AND THE GODS.

I HAVE now finished what I had to tell you about the separate Churches. I must try to bring before you something like a picture of the whole Church. Much of what I say will be grounded upon what you have already heard about particular places and particular men: some facts must be added which could not be brought under any of the previous heads. My main business will be—what I announced before—to show you how the Church fulfilled the calling which she had received from God; how far she failed of fulfilling.

We talk familiarly, in an off-hand way, of the Church and the world. Oftentimes we attach to the world the notion of a society which is pursuing secular objects and neglecting religion; we think of the Church, as a society which is despised for being too religious—because it cares chiefly for divine exercises — because it exaggerates the sacredness of public services — because it cultivates in its interior circle a transcendent morality and purity. If you apply these maxims to the second century, you will make a very great mistake indeed. The people in Antioch and Alexandria were sensual and corrupt enough; they pursued secular objects, money and pleasure, as men do here—more systematically, perhaps, with far fewer restraints of opinion—but they were not irreligious. Religion formed one of their regular formal occupations; it entered into all their occupations; it was connected with most of their amusements; it blended with every part of their local polity. Each city had its own peculiar gods, priests, sacrifices, festivals, which it had inherited from former days, and to which it clung as its most proper and native characteristic; the sign that it was a city of the past, though its civil freedom was gone, and though it was merged in the great empire. Then every part of the imperial system was religious. The Jupiter of the Capitol was still acknowledged as the power which held the state together. The Pantheon, with him as its centre, was capable of a continual expansion; it did actually expand to meet every new emergency, to take in each new form of worship that had prevailed in any of the conquered tribes. But the Roman gods still retained their own ascendency; they were incorporated into the history of the land. The institution of their priests—the reasons for the sacrifices that were offered to them—formed a principal element in the narratives which reminded the people of their greatness, and in what way their forefathers achieved it. The life of the particular families which composed the state, and whose deeds had made it illustrious, were associated with traditions of the gods; the images of the great men, which their descendants

Lect. VI.
Not an irreligious world.

The religion of particular places.

The religion of the Empire.

Roman religion specifically.

National.

preserved and contemplated, could not be separated from the images of the household deities. The more you read, the more you will perceive how auguries, divinations, and sacrifices, were worked into the whole tissue of social life at that time. It is true that the faith of the people at large had grown weaker; they were not the least sure whether the gods heard them, or even whether there were gods to hear. But they did not forego their devotions for this scepticism. Their actual sorrows, individual and political, were not less than they had been; the stings of conscience were not less. Something must be done to obtain comfort and relief, even if it was done in desperation. It was judicious therefore, they thought, as well as natural, to adhere to the old rites. They were performed more in fear than before, more to avert the anger of evil powers; but they were performed. And if the nature of other powers that were worshipped was uncertain, the power of the emperor was indisputable. The gods had assuredly delegated their authority to him; his name must be sworn by; to his image must sacrifices, with all fear and observance, be presented; not to do so was to violate the duty of a citizen, which in this, as in all things else, was dependent upon religion, and could in no way be disengaged from it.

Nor must you forget the fact to which I have so often alluded, that besides the vast religious *machinery* of the Roman world, there were flying about in all directions men who made light of mere machinery, and appealed to the sense in our hearts of hidden

What they professed to do.

powers, which may act upon us suddenly for good or for mischief, which may affect our souls or our bodies, which may restore health or throw us into sickness, which may give us marvellous intimations of terrible or fortunate events that have befallen or are to befal individuals or states. If you leave the enchanters, auguries, prophets, of Jewish or heathen origin, out of your calculation, when you are trying to understand the *world* of the second century, you

Their freedom from rules.

will have a very imperfect conception of it. These men had all the influence which those possess in all ages who are supposed not to be bound by the rules and terms of an organized community—to have a secret illumination and divine afflatus; and yet, on

Yet not without system.

the other hand, there was a method in all their madness. Many of them possessed real knowledge; they addressed themselves to undoubted instincts, fears, hopes, in their fellow-creatures; and having shaken off to a great extent the sense of moral obligation, they could turn these to account fearlessly. The speculators and gold-seekers of the age had long discovered that inspirations might be made a regular and profitable branch of trade.

The Church accused of Atheism.

And if this was the world, what was the Church? In the eyes of their heathen neighbours, its members were an utterly godless race. The name which the people of Smyrna gave them, when they called for vengeance on Polycarp, was the name they bore everywhere. They were the Atheists. A people without images, who frequented no temples, who offered no sacrifices—what could it mean? Yet a people who

evidently had a fellowship—a strong, close organiza- *Lect. VI.*
tion—who were intimately bound together with each
other in each city, who held evidently some strange
bond of intimacy with those in distant cities! What
could go on in those private meetings of theirs?
It was impossible that they should not have some
sacrifices. Words had been heard from them which
seemed to signify that they thought much of sacrifice—nay, of a human sacrifice. Horrors, no doubt, *Suspected of*
not to be spoken of, were enacted in their late *fearful crimes.*
and early assemblies. Some affirmed that they de-
voured human victims. What a small step was it
from that charge, to suppose that those victims were
their own children! Intelligent men, like Trypho,
might not attach much weight to these reports;
men with great opportunities of information, like
Pliny, might almost know that they were groundless.
But Trypho was as much scandalized as any one *Why Trypho*
could be, by what seemed to be the Christians' neglect *denounced them.*
of all the ceremonies, which, if they believed the
Jewish Scriptures, they ought to practise. However
harmless the meetings before sunrise might be, which
Pliny heard of from the tortured servants, the "super- *Why Pliny*
stition," nevertheless, seemed to him *exitiabilis;* for *denounced them.*
it was secret—it had the signs of a conspiracy—it was
like no other; it undermined the religion of the
empire. However paltry might be its exercises, or its
apparent instruments, it had a power which could
not be overlooked, which was affecting all classes and
conditions of Trajan's subjects.

How was this power put forth? How did it make

itself felt? I can only answer the question by referring to the name into which those who seemed Atheists to the Polytheists of the world around them were baptized. Their baptism declared that they confessed a *Father*. The name was no new one to the population in the midst of which they were dwelling. It was familiar to Greeks. Homer had spoken continually of the Father of gods and men. Romans, who had adopted Greek poetry and mythology, had yet deeper associations with the name than they had. It was connected with their domestic hearth, with a multitude of old thoughts,—sadly worn out, but never lost,—of which that hearth had been the centre; with the polity which had been based on the reverence for fathers. Think of such words as these ringing in the ears of Greeks and Romans: "The Father of all has spoken to us. His name is not a mere name. He has emancipated us from our slavery to visible things; He has actually claimed and adopted us as His children." Think, I say, of such words uttered in the ears of men who were crushed under a weight of religious rites and observances, who felt they had no hold on any living being in heaven or earth, or under the earth, yet who felt that there was some God, to whom all other gods owed obedience, and before whom men were to tremble. But, then, add that these were not mere words—that all the language and institutions of those who spoke them had this name of Father at their basis—and you will understand something of the charm with which they worked. If you ask me how they made their point good—how they proved to people that they had a right to call themselves children of God—I can give you a very poor answer, and I am not sure that theirs would have been much better. Their attempts at proofs and evidences were very numerous, sometimes very ingenious; they could fetch them from Scripture and from nature, from types and from plain history. There were precious grains of wheat in their arguments, but I am forced to express my conviction that there was also much chaff; and I feel confident that it was not the best arguments or the worst which influenced the hearts of heathens or of Jews. It was the Gospel—"There is such a Father for you," speaking to those who had need of one, and were craving for one—which was immeasurably mightier than all the authorities by which it was supported, and which imparted its own momentum to those that had least force of their own. Those argued best who were most conscious of this truth; those who could not argue at all, broke down strong-holds more effectually by their lives and their deaths.

LECT. VI.
The arguments of the Christians did not help them much.

Here, then, was the first great engine that undermined that vast polytheistic world which I have described to you. The Jews, who protested against the Christians as deserters to a Nazarene impostor, asked why they could not stop here? Was not the declaration of a One God the all-sufficient protest against many gods? If that was all that the Church had said, no doubt it had merely repeated what the synagogue had been saying for so long, and saying

Why could they not be content with preaching Monotheism?

LECT. VI. not altogether in vain—for its testimony had been one of the great powers which had shaken the faith of heathenism,—but certainly without establishing a faith, or effecting any great moral change in the condition of the world. To speak of a Father was not the same thing as to speak of a One God; heathens as much as Christians felt that it was not. The difference is the turning point of the most perplexing questions of the second century. To understand those questions, you must fix your minds resolutely upon it—still more, to understand the effect

The Creator. which the Church actually produced. The simplest and bravest men lifted up their voices to proclaim a Creator of heaven and earth. Only so far as they made that proclamation, could they rescue men from the worship of things in heaven and earth. When they made it thoroughly and boldly, they were able to look upon nature with clear and joyful eyes; to speak of its peace and harmony as the Roman Clemens does in that extract I read to you,—an extract which is a specimen of a number of passages that

Admiration of Nature. occur in the writers of this century. Their eyes were often opened to see a beauty and order in the world, which had been hidden even from the most graceful and accomplished thinkers of the old time. But this illumination came from their belief: " *Our Father* is the Creator of heaven and earth. We are not a part of these things which we look upon; we are above them. We belong to another economy; we are citizens of His kingdom, members of His family."

And, therefore, it was inevitable that the Church should utter the second Name in its baptismal formula, if there was to be any meaning and power in the first. Was it enough for them to say, "We have a Father, for a great Prophet and Teacher has come down from heaven to teach us?" By speaking thus, would they have broken the chains which bound the necks of the heathens around them? would they have brought about any fellowship among those who were divided by places and traditions? The people about them believed in a multitude of dæmons, demigods, sons of the gods—beings who connected together earth and heaven—rulers of cities, who were also rulers of sun, or of moon, or of stars. They believed in intellectual powers and moral virtues, as well as in powers of darkness and evil, which they clothed with forms. What teacher or prophet could rise above all this complicated machinery? what exchange would he have been for all these messengers and mediators? The thought of them was a burden upon the spirit; they were masses of clouds which darkened the heaven, and hid the face of God; but they had grown up out of the wants of the human heart, and however feeble, and unsatisfactory, and burdensome they were, the heart must cling to them till it found a substitute for them. When the members of the Church spoke of an only-begotten Son of God—of a living Word, who was the Lord of men's spirits and the Lord of angels, in whom the mind and will of the Father uttered itself to His creatures, in whom He acknowledged them as His children—this substitute

Lect. VI.
The Son or Word.

Dæmons, Demigods, Sons of Gods, Virtues, Powers.

The only substitute for them.

was provided. This news shook not earth only, but also heaven. It did not encounter one of the popular schemes of worship, but all of them. It encountered them, not by taking away anything from the heart on which it had rested, but by showing it what it had to rest upon; how it had been seeking at a distance for that which was at home; how it had been building castles and prisons from fragments of the Rock upon which God had built His universe.

The second great puzzle of this century.

But how was this Divine Son, this eternal Word, connected with the poor, miserable, sinful creatures to whom He was proclaimed? This, as you have seen, was the second of the great puzzles by which the minds of men in the second century were perplexed. All the great questions and controversies of the time were involved in the question, whether they might really identify this Divine Word with Jesus, the Man of sorrows, who had died upon the cross. We have seen how some of the debates on this subject were conducted; we shall have to return to them again. What I am speaking of now is the power which the Church exercised on the surrounding world; and this power, I conceive, was greater or smaller in proportion to the strength or weakness with which she asserted

Jesus of Nazareth, the Word made flesh.

the position that the Son of God had actually taken human flesh, and suffered under Pontius Pilate, and been crucified, dead, and buried. Where that message was proclaimed broadly and nakedly, all the schemes by which men had sought to make their way from earth to heaven—to bring the gods into peace and reconciliation with men, to avoid the penalties of evil, to escape from the conscience of it—were supplanted by the one great doctrine and fact, that a reconciliation had been made between God and His creatures, that He had made peace with them. The condition of humanity was placed upon a new ground, for a Son of man had been revealed. Whatever might have been its condition, He was now declared to be its centre and its root.

The reconciliation accomplished.

But this testimony of reconciliation, mighty as it was, would have been utterly ineffectual without that one which the Apostles had borne at first, which they were sent forth to bear, which was the characteristically Christian testimony. "Christ is risen!" was the altogether amazing and monstrous proclamation which sounded in the ears of a scoffing, exhausted, lazy generation,—tired of miracles, hopeless of any blessing to themselves or the world,—from an insignificant body who were believed to be Atheists, and to eat the flesh of children. And yet, if the previous message were listened to, this must be received; not the authority of the teacher, but the conscience of the disciple, demanded that it should. The words of the Apostle, "It is not *possible* that He should be holden of death," were the natural, necessary sequel to the announcement of the living Word, in whom all power dwelt, and yet who had humbled Himself, and submitted to the death of the cross. And so, amidst the multitudes who confessed dæmons to be great, and the emperor to be in some sense greater than the dæmons, but who positively knew that death was greater than the emperor, and was the tyrant of each of them, there

The Resurrection of Christ.

Power of this message.

went forth the actual news of a Conqueror of death, news which, if at first it was incredible, almost ridiculous, yet spoke to hearts that had been craving for it ever since they began to beat, and had an assurance within that it must be true, unless the whole universe was a lie. Their assurance of immortality had come to them in a thousand ways before. Every Tartarian and Elysian story bore as authentic tidings of it to the popular mind, as the inquiries of the most serious thinkers did to theirs. But the Church preached not of immortality, but of resurrection—not of the surviving of some particle of our nature, but of the resurrection of man—not of the resurrection of a man, but of the Son of man, of the Lover of men, of Him who had borne death for man. And yet if these acts done for men—this condescension to their misery—had been all, the perpetual longing in men to send up their thoughts and prayers to One above them would have been unsatisfied; the belief in a heaven, which had been the strongest, the most helpful to them of all—with whatever confusions it had been mingled, however it had cut them off from their gods—would have been extinguished. He is gone up on high to His Father—He lives to make intercession for us—was the great sequel to the message of resurrection. All who heard it felt that the first part of it would have been unmeaning without the second.

With these thoughts of immortality had been inseparably associated the witness of a separation between the right and the wrong doer; the dreams

Tartarus and Elysium.

Ascension. Intercession.

of Æacus and Rhadamanthus; the dim, hazy vision of fields in which the blessed wandered; the vision that rose not more distinctly, but far more frequently and naturally, before the conscious criminal, of a dark river, and groans, and solitude. How utterly ineffectual these anticipations were to produce morality, or to check crime, the open atrocities of the Roman world, which the sword of the magistrate, not the terrors of the priests, kept from being utterly destructive,—not to speak of the stench of its more inward and secret corruptions, may sufficiently attest. The message of resurrection went forth in the second century, as it had done from St. Paul's lips at Athens and before Felix, joined with the message of judgment. The Divine Word, the Lord of the hearts and reins of men, He who had come into the world to redeem them from their evil, knew what that evil was. He would bring it to light; whatever was done or spoken in darkness, would come out into the broad day. His voice would be heard by the whole creation; the dead as much as the quick would own it. To connect judgment with a Person—with an actual Discerner of thoughts and intents—with a Deliverer,—what a change was this from that old, worn-out apprehension of a world after death, which was so inoperative for morality, but upon which the religious scheme of the empire had by degrees established itself! When this trumpet was blown, the walls of the great Roman Jericho shook more than at almost any other sound. Had it been blown more strongly, they might have fallen

Lect. VI.

Visions of Judgment.

Christ the Judge.

down at once; for though such a prophecy of judgment was so new, it awakened the oldest and deepest convictions that had been slumbering in the spirits of men.

The Holy Spirit.

But the Gospel of a resurrection and of a judgment would have been unintelligible,—it would not have been a Gospel, because it would have come with no pledge of a new and higher life,—if the third name in the Christian covenant had been separated from the other two. You have heard how the news of a Spirit coming down to dwell among men was interwoven with all that our Lord did upon earth, with all that He spoke of a kingdom of heaven which was at hand. You have heard how the preaching of the resurrection, on the day of Pentecost, interpreted the sound of the rushing and mighty wind, and the cloven tongues of fire that sat upon the Apostles. You have heard how the gift of this Spirit created the Christian society out of the chaos of Jewish sects, changed the ministers and members of it from ignorant cowards into brave and wise men. But to understand the real power of the announcement that such a Spirit of truth, and unity, and power had come, you must think of it in connexion with that lying spirit by which the diviners and enchanters of the Roman world were possessed. I use that language deliberately. The teachers of the second century talked of evil spirits and diabolical possession. We often abuse their words to a superstitious meaning; it may often have had that meaning in their mouths. But the more one considers the horror

The Spirit of Truth in opposition to the Spirit of Falsehood.

of lying,—the more one considers that those lies which connect themselves with the name of God are the most inward, essential, radical of all lies, that they are those which enter into the spirit of a man, and corrupt and destroy him, and that all outward lies of act and word are their progeny; the more one is compelled to talk of a spirit of lies, to talk of it as penetrating the habits and temper of an age, as coming forth in innumerable forms, but as concentrated in the religious impostors, in those who abuse spiritual influences and terrors to fleshly and earthly purposes. And the more simply one adheres to the language of Scripture in saying that the Spirit of truth, the Spirit of the Father, the Spirit with which Christ was anointed, is given to men to renew them in the spirit of their minds, to deliver them from the spirit of lies, to cast him out; the more we understand how it is possible that a man or a world should be regenerated. To oppose the Holy Spirit, the one uniting Spirit, to the unholy and dividing spirit which they saw working its portents all around them, was assuredly one chief part of the mission of the Church in this century—one which all its higher members understood that they were to fulfil. *Lect. VI. Overthrow of the Magicians.*

But the Holy Spirit did not merely exorcise that which was unholy. He testified to those who yielded to Him, that they were members of a holy body. There could be no limits assigned to this body; it stood in Christ the eternal Word; the fetters of time and space had been broken down for it. The Christians knew inwardly that they were united to *The Holy Body.*

LECT. VI.
Universal.

The perplexity: Separate and yet universal, saints and yet men.

Communion essential to Christian life.

those who were separated from them by lands, and seas, and death. In so far as they were partakers of God's love, they had fellowship with all the creatures over whom that love extended.

But here the third great difficulty forced itself upon them. The Spirit separated them from the corrupt world by which they were hemmed in; He made them saints. They seemed brought into a narrower, smaller circle than other men—actually brought into it by the suspicions and hatred of Jews and heathens—spiritually and inwardly brought into it, in proportion as they acquired a disgust for the practices in which when Jews and heathens they took delight. And yet the effect of their union with Christ, of the power and indwelling of His divine Spirit, was to enlarge their hearts, to give them sympathies which they never had before—sympathies with that which is human—sympathies with the publicans and sinners, with whom their Lord conversed on earth, and for whom He died. Were they to be more exclusive than others, or wider, broader, more catholic?

Whether individuals could answer this question or not, the Church, so far as it carried on a successful war against heathenism, found the answer. That which undermined the divided, exclusive fellowships into which heathen worshippers were necessarily broken up—as worshippers of natural idols, as servants of local gods, as devoted to mere objects of sense—was the *communion* of saints. The discovery that this apparently narrow and separating body was really able to embrace all within its circle,—that it could not contract itself, without being false to its profession. The Church was feared so far as its members were united; so far as they held themselves separate from all contact with idols; so far as they were ready to embrace all idolaters. Herein lay the secret of that power which the world around trembled at,—herein the secret of the attraction which was continually bringing men from all quarters into the Christian circle.

Terror of a United Body.

But the force of this magnet would not have been felt by those who were drawing near to different altars, for the sake of getting some relief from the reproaches of conscience, if another had not been joined with it. The Christian Church could say boldly, " God for Christ's sake has forgiven us." It could invite men to lay the burden which was oppressing them before God. It could say, ' This forgiveness is for you. The Spirit of forgiveness, who makes the heart guileless and loving, is for you. When God takes you as His children, He puts away your offences; and He promises that each day you shall receive that cleansing and renewal of heart— that inward restoration which you will more and more feel that you need.' What a blow was this one proclamation to the whole scheme of priestcraft, by which men had aimed at bringing Heaven to overlook the wrongs which they knew they had committed! What an assurance it was, not of ease in the evil, but of deliverance out of it!

Forgiveness of sins.

The great blow to Priestcraft.

Something more was needed still. For with bodies actually bowed down by sickness and anguish, it is

x

Bodily resurrection. not enough to be told of a deliverance that has been effected for their spirits; of a Spirit who unites those spirits to Christ and to each other. It is not enough to hear that Christ, the Son of God, has redeemed His own body from death. They need to be told that those bodies of theirs, which are groaning under a heavy and intolerable burden, shall be rescued from it; that they shall be delivered from disease and death. The power of the Spirit is not complete over the enemies of men, if this news cannot be declared to them. The Church uttered this promise, too, in the ears of men who were subject to this bondage. It said, "If the Spirit of Him who raised up Christ dwell in you, He shall also quicken your mortal bodies." Nay, it spoke words deeper even than these—not perhaps as fully understood, but yet most necessary for those who had confessed death to be their master. It spoke of the Spirit as making men partakers of the eternal life which was with the Father, and which Christ had manifested.

Life eternal.

Origin of the Creed. I have been repeating, as you will have perceived, the principal articles in what we call the Apostles' Creed, because I could not find any other way of telling you so well in what kind of armour it was that the Church in the second century fought, whenever she gained any victories. I do not care to prove that these were just the words or phrases in which she delivered her message. That it was the substance of her message, I think you will be convinced the more you read the different books to which I have referred you in former Lectures, and compare them together. There does occur in several of these books a form of words, very like our "I believe." It is evidently put forth as the baptized man's confession. People in later times were so puzzled to understand how the second century should have got such a creed, and how after centuries should have retained it, that they fell into the strangest fancies to explain the marvel. Some of the Christian writers had called it "an apostolical tradition." Might it not then be asserted, that the Apostles had met together to construct it? that perhaps each Apostle had originated a clause? Might not Polycarp have had it from St. John? Might it not have been given as a deposit to all the Churches to keep? No Evangelist or Apostle, I need scarcely tell you, has given any account of a meeting for this purpose, though St. Luke does speak of two or three of the Apostles meeting to discuss the question of circumcision. A writer of the third century,—the earliest of religious novelists,—a man who feigned the name of Clemens for a book which he called the "Recognitions,"—certainly introduces the twelve Apostles holding a disputation, and reports speeches which each of them made. But this audacious and profane, though far from stupid or ill-meaning romancer, merely used the lips of Apostles as instruments for giving currency to his own sentiments; not one of the honester and wiser Fathers would have either ventured to assert the Apostolical Convocation as a fact, nor to introduce it

Attempts to solve the mystery.

Was it constructed by a Council of Apostles?

The Novelist of the third century. See Recognitions, lib. i. c. 55. St. Peter tells Clemens how the Apostles were summoned before Caiaphas, and answered by turns to different objectors.

LECT. VI.

The Creed naturally developed out of the Baptismal name.

Prayer.

The Lord's Prayer.

into a fiction. The Creed, I think you will see, grew up in a much simpler and more natural manner. The apostolic tradition the Christian Church had: the baptismal formula was that tradition. The Church had the writings of the Apostles, who were sent forth with the commission to preach the name into which they baptized. The Church had the experience of heathen corruptions and heathen needs. And the Spirit of God was promised to them, to make the words which they had received, and all the experiences of others and of themselves, effectual to guide them into truth. If we want more than this, to show how they may have obtained this confession, we have not yet learned what an Ecclesia is, or why such a body has existed in our world.

Do not however suppose that a mere creed, if it were the best in the world, could have expressed divine principles to the members of the Church, or have made them effectual for subverting heathenism. The relations of men to God must utter themselves in prayer and praise. Any other language is imperfect language; it may give us the shell of a belief,—it cannot express the life and essence of it. If there had not been an "Our Father" as well as an "I believe," the Church would have fared very ill in its battles with the world. There, the whole mystery of God's revelation of Himself to His creatures is presumed in their invocation of Him. He has made them His children, therefore they speak to Him. That His Name may be hallowed by them, and known upon the earth, is the end for which He has called them, and for which they exist. But *He* must hallow that Name; they cannot, otherwise than as His instruments. They are sure that He has a kingdom in them, and a kingdom over the whole earth; they desire that His kingdom should come mightily in both. They know that His will is the right will—that there are those who obey it; they desire that their wills and all wills may be subdued to it. He has provided all things that man wants; they desire to bless Him for them, and to receive His gifts each day from His hand, and that all should share them together. They want that forgiveness which comes to them only while they forgive, and, therefore, the Spirit of forgiveness, which includes both blessings. They have a Tempter near them, and God only can keep them from him; there is evil within and without—He only can deliver them from it.

<small>LECT. VI.</small>

That this prayer was the root of all the prayers of the Church in the second century,—that they unfolded themselves out of it,—we have abundant evidence. Each clause in the prayer struck at the heart of some superstition that had enslaved human spirits,—at the great and cardinal superstition of all, that prayer, instead of coming from God, and being the creature's act of sacrifice and submission to Him— its flight to Him from the evil that was oppressing it —was an effort to convert His will, to make Him favourable to avert the evil of which He was the author. This prayer converted everything else into an organ of prayer and thanksgiving. It threw back a light upon the old psalms, explaining the enemies

<small>*This Prayer the centre of the devotions of the early Church.*</small>

<small>*The Psalms.*</small>

with which David was struggling,—his confidence, his confessions, his cries to be judged,—his feeling that when he was praying, all Israel was praying with him; that when he was giving thanks, he was praising the Lord of the whole earth. It turned all the gifts of nature into excuses for praise, because they were not gifts of nature but of God. It found a necessity and encouragement to prayer in dungeons, fires, wild beasts.

Polycarp's universal Prayer.

You have heard how Polycarp prayed, not, as his Latin translator represents, for support to himself in his hour of peril, but for the whole Church and for all mankind. His sympathies expanded and became deeper as that hour approached which most men regard as separating them from others, and as obliging them to fix their thoughts upon themselves. Whence came the difference? I tried to indicate the cause of it when I was speaking of him and of Ignatius; but the subject is so important, and is so involved in the one of which I am speaking now, that I must present it to you from another side.

The Heathen Sacrifice.

I have told you what the heathen world said of the Christians in reference to sacrifice. Sometimes they were thought to neglect sacrifice altogether; sometimes it was suspected that they offered sacrifices of the most monstrous kind. Evidently *this* was the point on which there was most difficulty in understanding them; this, therefore, was the test to which they were always brought: Would they offer sacrifices, or not? would they rather be sacrificed themselves than do it? The answer was distinct:

'We cannot offer your sacrifices; we choose to be sacrifices ourselves. For the great human Sacrifice has been offered; it is upon that we feed in those secret meetings you speculate about. We believe that Sacrifice to have been offered for the whole world; therefore it is our right and privilege to offer ourselves as sacrifices to God.'

<small>LECT. VI.

The Human Sacrifice.</small>

I want you to connect these three things in your mind: the heathen sacrifices which each man was to offer, to make the gods propitious to him; the Christian declaration that the Sacrifice had been offered once for all, and that by it God had reconciled the world to Himself; and the belief of the Christian man, that his own death was a sacrifice which God had prepared, and which He would accept for the sake of His Son. Then, I think, you will understand why Polycarp was not thinking of his own death, but of Christ's death at that time, and, because of Christ's death, therefore, of all everywhere for whom He died. And then, I think, you will further understand what was and must have been the centre of all Christian worship, in order that it might carry out the principle and meaning of the Lord's Prayer. There are many differences of statements about the liturgies of this time; but the most learned antiquarians, and scholars of different nations and different schools, seem to be agreed on this point; the Eucharist was the centre of the worship; everything was referred to that. Thanksgiving and praise for a complete and accepted sacrifice, a sacrifice for the sins of the whole world, was at the root of all devotion

<small>*The connexion between them.*

The death of Christ, not his own death, present to a martyr.

The Eucharist.</small>

LECT. VI.

The apex as well as the base of worship and hope.

and all praise: everything was included and gathered up in that service. There was the highest utterance of praise and thanksgiving, there was the lowliest confession and humiliation; there they sought the power to act and to suffer; there they learnt that to make an oblation of themselves, was not to do a great act in order to win a great prize, but was itself the highest gift and prize that God could bestow on them,—a participation in the life and death of His Son. Therefore, of all the weapons in the Christian armoury with which they shattered the old gods, and those who served them and burnt incense to them, this, I conceive, was the most powerful, at least it was that which explained the purpose and direction of all the rest.

LECTURE VII.

THE SAME SUBJECT CONTINUED.

THE FAILURES OF THE CHURCH IN THE BATTLE WITH THE GODS.

WE have lost the guidance of Scripture as to the facts of our story; we have not lost it at all as to the principle by which we are to judge of the facts. The history of the called people in its earliest stages is the interpretation of its history in the latest. What we are told of Jews after they entered Canaan, may teach when we are to look for victories, when for defeats, to the Church after it had got a footing in the Roman world.

The cases were, indeed, widely different. The Church was to conquer for itself no special land; the one in which the Jewish capital and temple had stood was given up to the heathen world. It was not to expel the old inhabitants of the world into which it came; it had a message of peace and deliverance to them. Its power lay in its weakness; it was to subdue by enduring. But in spite of these differences, —in spite of those other mighty differences between the new Covenant and the old, the revelation by prophets and angels, and the revelation by a Son, which every day of conflict between the Church and the Synagogue

LECT. VII.
The Bible a guide to the history of the second century.

The Jews in Canaan.

Differences and contrasts.

LECT. VII.
Resemblance in principles and dangers.

brought into stronger light,—the underground was the same. If the members of the Church forgot that they were a called body,—called out to do a work, called by God,—they became powerless, just as the members of the Nation became from the same cause. If they did not think that their work was to be a blessing to all the families of the earth, they contracted precisely the habits which had led the Jews to reject the Son of Man, to anathematise the Apostles of the Gentiles, to be rejected and anathematised themselves.

Sympathy with Heathens.

These two evils—the forgetfulness of their calling and covenant, the fancy that they were possessors, not stewards of the blessings they had received—had gone through all periods of the history; sometimes the tendency to idolatry, sometimes the tendency to despise and hate idolaters, being more conspicuous. Each implied the other. They were fain to fall into superstition, if they did not feel they were sent to deliver the earth from it, by fighting for the living and true God. They were sure to contract hardness and exclusiveness, and dislike of mankind, if they ever supposed that Judaism was a special religion which they were to uphold against other religions. In the language of the Psalmist, they forgot God's counsel; they dwelt among the heathen, and learned their works. In the language of the Apostles, they became enemies to God, and contrary to all men.

Hatred of Heathens.

Duty of the Church Historian.

Amidst the noble and beautiful records of the second century, it behoves us, if we would follow the light which Scripture gives us, and not choose a way of our own, to notice these same causes of disappointment, that we may be more thankful for the successes, that we may be less surprised when we see the seeds of evil and of good, the wheat and the tares, multiplying and growing together in after generations. We shall be preserved from a great many blunders, a great many acts of injustice, a great many unfaithful complainings, if we do not frame to ourselves the notion of a golden age in this century or any other; if we believe that the good men of that day deserve to be contemplated, precisely because they were men prone to all the evils to which we are prone, prone to the particular evils of their own age and country, great in God, paltry in themselves; heroic examples, therefore, when they trusted in God and forgot themselves; beacons when they trusted in themselves and forgot God. *How to think of this period.*

Nor is it impossible or over bold, as some would persuade us, to declare when we are to admire them, and when we are to shun them. If that is so, history is a delusion; God has not written it; we are left to crawl before any idols whom our forefathers may have set up, or whom we may set up. We may easily call it reverence to do this, but it is no such thing. It is irreverence towards God; it is unbelief in Him, and in the word He has given us. No doubt we may make a thousand mistakes in interpreting His words and the signs of His providence, as well as in estimating the characters of His servants. But we shall make far fewer mistakes, if we desire earnestly and faithfully to honour whatever is true and honest, and just and *Fear of condemning the acts of good men.*

The cowardly course not the safe one.

LECT. VII.

Necessity of acknowledging a higher wisdom than man's, if we would appreciate them.

The opposite course leads to injustice and insincerity.

lovely, because we are sure that it is of God, and to hate whatever is contrary to this, when it appears in the best man or the worst, in Christian or heathen; we shall make far fewer mistakes if we act upon this principle, hoping for the Spirit of truth to make us see the truth every day more clearly, than if we feign to admire deeds or words which directly contradict and counteract each other, and have evidently produced the most opposite effects, because we are afraid of seeming to condemn what better men than we have done or approved. I do not find that those who profess this principle act upon it. I see them applying it one moment very strictly, when a set of favourites of their own are in peril—deserting it when they are sitting in judgment upon those whom they dislike. I find great censoriousness and harshness mixed with this boast of humility. Therefore I would once for all discard those maxims which it seeks to canonise. If God teaches us to judge ourselves, He will not allow us to judge other men harshly; He will not permit us even to call anything evil, till we have seen and worshipped the good to which it is opposed, or which it is counterfeiting. But He will enable us,—if we desire to be purged of the evil ourselves, and not to be betrayed by the counterfeit,—to see how those whose steps we would follow have yielded to the one, and been led astray by the other. Cultivate love and admiration all you can; the more you cultivate them, the less will you endure falsehood, the more able will you be to detect it. Fear God; and then you will not fear, when His truth demands it, to speak boldly about the ways in which some even of His most faithful servants have thwarted His purposes.

If what I said in the last Lecture is true, the work of the Christian Church in the second century was as wonderful a one as it is possible for us to think or dream of. We use the word to *regenerate* sometimes dogmatically, sometimes carelessly. Now we argue, whether the blessing of regeneration is communicated by God in a certain ordinance to individual men; now we speak, as if we might by some plans of ours regenerate society. If we would meditate a little upon the war of the world and the Church at this time, we might clear our minds on both these topics; we might begin to understand one another better.

Think of any set of men undertaking to reform such a society as the Roman empire! Think of such a set of men undertaking it as those I have described to you,—a handful of people, brought up in the very system they would have to contend with, infected with all its worst notions and corruptions! But think of any one of these men undertaking to reform himself; to get down to the root of his own evil, and to extirpate it! One here and one there makes the experiment. He has done his best, or thinks he has, and he is in despair. Then he hears the message —'God Himself gives you a new and diviner birth; He takes you to be His children.' Supposing a man to believe this news, and to be baptized, and to find himself one of a family which believes

LECT. VII.

Regeneration.

Debates about the word.

Reformation and Regeneration.

LECT VII. the same, he could not but understand that that had been done for him which he had been unable to do for himself. Whereas he had before thought only of *reforming* himself, of making himself a better man, he will now naturally change that word for the other. If he was really radically reformed in the will and purpose of his mind, it was because God had *regenerated* him; the nobler inward state implied a birth from above. He was right because the Right and True Being had recognised him as His; he was right just so long as he stood on that ground—as he renounced every other. But if his baptism thus explained to him his own position,—thus signified to him that he was planted on a deeper root, and was therefore capable of a better life,—did it not show him also what must be the ground of a general and social reformation? What else could renew this carcase of Roman civilization, which the Roman religion was making more putrid every day, but the belief of a living Father, but the news that He had redeemed men in His Son? Might not this Gospel *re-form* the society? would not the reform be a *regeneration?*

The divine and human tasks.
It was a mighty work this for such a set of poor outcasts as the Church was composed of to meditate. Very few of them could meditate it or dream of it; nor was it the least necessary that they should. They had only to speak the truth which had been taught them, to bear witness of that they knew, to testify that they had seen; the rest they must leave to God. To make the mustard-seed shoot forth into a tree,

THE SECOND CENTURY. 319

was His work; to scatter the seed on the ground, and, if it pleased Him, to enrich the ground with their blood, was theirs. And therefore, as I think we have seen already, no teacher of the Church failed through simplicity, or through ignorance of the various and complex opinions of the people among whom he was dwelling. If he said broadly and nakedly the thing he had to say, the word met thoughts and hopes that had been struggling, or that had been stifled. The princess in her thorny bower felt that her lips had been touched, not by any mortal, but by the true Lover; and as she awoke out of her slumber, all the attendants that were torpid and fixed around her awakened also. Whenever there was a true voice really coming out of the heart of a man, there was some heart that responded to it,—some one which said, "I believe, not because of thy saying; I know for myself that He whom you speak of is the Christ, the Son of God."

Simplicity not the cause of failure;

The defect was much more in the absence of this simplicity. You will not misunderstand me to mean that God did not raise up men of various endowments for various occasions; that He did not bring men from the East as well as from the West, from the schools as well as from the seat of custom, or that one set of His servants were less faithful than another; the history of the second century is a confutation of any such notion. Justin and Clemens of Alexandria gave as much proof that they were possessed with the spirit of the Gospel, and were ready to live and die for it, as Ignatius or Polycarp. They would not have been

But the want of simplicity.

LECT. VII.

320   ON CHURCH HISTORY.

LECT. VII. simple and honest men, if they had adopted the
*Different dialect or mode of thinking of Ignatius or Polycarp;
signs of
simplicity.* in them that would not have been natural but
affected, for it had pleased God that they should be
educated differently; it would not have been doing
their own work, but intruding upon one which they
had not been set to do.

The attempt But what I mean is this. It was a most easy thing
*to build up
a Christian* for Christians, who looked round and saw what a
religion.   number of religions there were in the Roman empire,
to fancy that they were the proselytes of a new
religion; one a great deal better than any that had
been before it, one which was to break all others in
pieces, one which would obtain for them much
greater blessings than any other hereafter, though it
might subject them to some penalties here. They
might say, "This Christian religion of ours is to
beat down the heathen religions, to beat down
the old national religions. We have not, indeed,
got swords with which we can do that at present;
our opponents have them, and we must submit
to their violence till our turn comes round. But,
in the meantime, words may do much; we can
argue, and reason, and demolish their conclusions;
we can strengthen our own position; we can draw
the lines about our opinions more definitely and
accurately; we can organize our customs, and habits,
and scheme of worship; we can be always putting
ourselves into an attitude of defence. Sometimes we
can invade the enemy, and carry one or another of his
posts; by degrees our religion will become a really

great and formidable power to the world around us. At the same time we shall become much more secure of the blessings of it ourselves."

Now, what I affirm is that this view of their position was one which Christians were exceedingly likely to take up; that it was one from which the best and truest men could not always free themselves; but that it was one which was fatal to the simplicity of the Christian faith—equally fatal to its effect on Roman Polytheism.

I will endeavour to illustrate what I have said by going over the ground which we have just been travelling. You have seen how the Apostles' Creed unfolded itself out of the name into which the members of the Church were baptized,—how, so unfolding itself, it really expressed a *belief* in a Father, a Son, and a Spirit. But do you not see how easy it was for men to say, "This Creed is what divides us from other men. As Zeus is the god of the Greeks, as Ammon is adored by the Egyptians, as the Romans boast of Mars, so this is the Being whom we Christians worship." When I put the feeling into words, I am sure it will cause a shrinking and revolting in all your minds. That is what I wish—thank God for it! I believe that it would have caused a still greater shock to the mind of any devout man in the second century. Polycarp would have cried out, as Irenæus tells us he did, "What times I have fallen upon, that I should hear such things as these!" He would have been certain, though he might not have been able to say why, that the truth he was believing in had been

Faith in God turning into an opinion about God.

Y

changed into something else,—that the shell remained, but that the substance was gone. But a man who had become an habitual arguer about his faith, would soon become unconscious of this difference. The more he disputed, the more evanescent it would be. At last he would come to think it was not a difference at all. If a man could explain in accurate terms what his opinion was about the Being whom he worshipped; if he could point out why he rejected this or that notion which some other person had put forward concerning the Father, or the Word, or the Spirit; or if he could expose some Greek, or Egyptian, or Roman notion respecting their divinities; or if he could confound the Jews, who supposed that they were confessing the one Jehovah; his mind was satisfied; he had been fighting the Christian fight, —he was a champion of the divine Name. Yes, of one whom he had chosen to be a Father, but not of a Father who had claimed him to be a child; of one whom he had acknowledged as a Son and Word of God, not of a Son or Word of God in whom he had been created and redeemed, and who had chosen him that he should go forth and bear fruit; of a Spirit to whom he could attach great titles, on whom he could bestow high reverence, not of a Spirit who had come down to purify him of his evils, to mould him anew, to unite him to his brethren. Yes, of a Name which he could use for confuting other men, for attacking their errors, for cutting them off; not of a Name which could renew and regenerate the hearts, the faith, the worship, of all nations.

It was impossible there could be this change without another, which affected the ordinance wherein men were sealed with this name. When they received it simply, it was the most beautiful and broad testimony of their adoption,—of their being clean and pure by being grafted upon the true root,—of the new and divine well of life within them. But the heathens had their purifications and lustrations; the Jews had theirs. The earnest and true-hearted Justin perceived, as you will have heard in the extract I gave you from his dialogue with Trypho, how the Christian sacrament resembled these, how it differed from them; that while *they* testified the need of an inward purification, but could only confer an outward one, *it* bore witness that God was commencing His renewal from within, that He was making the tree good that the fruit might be good. But those who would set up a Christianity which should be an anti-heathenism or an anti-judaism, might take either of two apparently opposite courses. They might say, " What have we to do with this water,—this old Jewish or heathen type? what care we for these outward lustrations, if we can be made what we want to be within?" Or they might glorify the act of baptism as being the Christians' great service and ceremony, which contradistinguished them from heathens and Jews, and whereto it had pleased God to attach for their sakes certain unspeakable and miraculous blessings, from which the world at large was excluded. Each of these ways seemed wonderfully right to those who took it. They could not question that they were

Lect. VII.

Effect on the idea of Baptism.

The two notions of the ordinance.

LECT. VII.

The Cainites.

Tertullian's book on Baptism.

He denounces Infant Baptism.

maintaining the high dignity and purity of the Christian religion, and putting down its adversaries. A class of heretics called Cainites set up the first theory; Tertullian's book on Baptism, which was written expressly to answer them, may be looked upon as the earliest and most elaborate exposition of the second. It opens at once with a denunciation of those who rejected baptism; it goes on to speak of the true believers as simple fish who could not be persuaded to leave their water by the anglers on the shore,—a pleasantry which might be looked upon as pardonable if the subject were less serious, or which might be accepted as an innocent *niaiserie* in a simple-minded man; but which must be regarded as an intolerable affectation in a man so cultivated and artificial as the Carthaginian presbyter was. The treatise, in spite of many valuable passages in it, is I think worthy of this commencement, full of refinement, reasoning, disputation, tending to build up a theory about baptism, and to destroy its life. Rightly and consistently Tertullian argues against the administration of it to infants. If it was to be the mere sign of the salvation which God had purposed to give one set of men, and from which He designed to exclude the rest, it was most unreasonable that those who could make no profession of their faith, who could not in any wise prove themselves to be other than Jews or heathens, should be admitted to a participation of it. Tertullian's mind, which was most clear and acute in following out its own conclusions, at once perceived the contradiction. If the

Church had been allowed to follow its own impulses, and draw its own lines about itself, either the Cainite or the Tertullian practice would have prevailed; Baptism would have been rejected, or it would have been limited to the adult professor. But since God designed it for the mark of a communion of saints, which was to be the witness of a redemption for mankind, neither the heretic nor the Church doctor had power to defeat His purpose, though they might succeed in disguising it from the eyes of many, both of those who were to bear and of those who were to receive the testimony.

What I have said has reference especially to the *idea* of baptism, and its connexion with the Divine name. But with this were closely associated certain *practices* which gradually gained ground in the Church, and which might be innocent and useful, or pernicious, according to the principle which was recognised as lying at the root of them. *Exorcism* became connected with baptism in the second century, not habitually or universally, but so frequently and in so many places, as to intimate a feeling in the Church of some close relation between them. The words which I quoted from Ignatius, in his conversation with Trajan, may show you how naturally the thought of this relation would have sprung up. Christians were the enemies of the dæmons; God had delivered them from the powers of evil; God had sent them to do battle with these powers. What truths were here! What a deep practical understanding did they show of the fact that Christ had triumphed

<small>LECT. VII.</small>

<small>Practices connected with Baptism.</small>

<small>Exorcism.</small>

over the Spirit of evil, had denied and broken in pieces his power; and that His disciples, in the faith of that conquest, were to wrestle not chiefly with outward enemies, but with the powers of spiritual wickedness which were trying to claim them as their subjects! What a significant translation into act it seemed of these principles, for the convert to say at baptism, "I renounce the dominion of evil spirits," or for him who administered the rite to say, " I declare thee free from them!"

How it was abused.

But the moment baptism was regarded, not as a witness of God's truth and of Christ's redemption, but of an advantage which a particular set of men had acquired over another set, this formula was sure to acquire a different, almost an opposite sense. It was not any longer a denial of the devil's right over mankind; but rather a vehement assertion of it. The exorcism came to mean, "Other men are his rightful subjects; we claim a special exemption from his yoke." Here was shown the danger of any additions to Christ's ordinance, however pleasing or even profitable they might be for a time and to certain persons. The flesh was sure to turn them to its own uses,—the natural heart would make them excuses for superstition and for exclusion.

The Chrism.

The use of *Chrism*, or of anointing with oil, also seems to have gained ground in this century. It imparted not only to old words of the Scripture, but to old practices of heathenism, a new and living force. The Spirit, it said, is the oil of gladness of which the Psalmist speaks: this was that which fitted kings, and prophets, and priests for their work. In a lower sense, it prepared runners and wrestlers for the combat, after their bodies had been brought down and purged of their grossness by hard and scanty fare. A lesson surely of the greatest worth, and not open, so far as one can see, to the same kind of objection as the last of which I spoke. But there was *this* objection : anointing with oil was a custom most suitable to the East, not equally intelligible to Occidentals. There was danger, therefore, lest a local custom should put itself forward in the character of a universal law; a danger comparatively slight as long as the Church maintained the sense of its divine calling, and was engaged heartily in its divine work, but most serious when it began to think that it was an isolated body which was to fence itself round with a set of habits with which other men had nothing to do. The oil would then be no longer the oil of gladness—it would speak no more of a Spirit given; it would be itself the miserable substitute for that Spirit.

Use and dangers of it.

In connexion with this anointing, I have hinted at the discipline or acts of self-restraint, which the members of the Church in the second century practised in order to fit themselves for the work they had to do, and to bring their bodies into subjection. There was a difficulty about these acts. They felt the necessity of strictly obeying our Lord's command; they were not to appear to men to fast, but to their Father who saw them in secret; and yet there was an almost necessary community in all the doings of a body which had a common Lord to serve, and common sins to confess. There was a still more true

Fasts.

Difficulty.

LECT. VII. and necessary tendency to connect all their acts with the acts of their Lord; to feel that His fasting and temptation must be the foundation and the strength of theirs. So long as they felt that discipline had no virtue of its own,—that it was only a preparation for service, only a sign of submission to God's Spirit, that He might work in them more freely to will and do God's pleasure—a means to the emancipation of body and soul from the sloth and luxury which enfeebled both,—so long these apparent difficulties were sure to right themselves in practice. While that salutary, almost excessive, fear of Judaical practices to which Justin gave utterance, prevailed, the Church was not likely to impose rules upon its members, which might make them think that they were subject to the old covenant of the letter, not to the new covenant of the Spirit. It is clear from many proofs that this feeling was strong in the Church; sometimes it might degenerate into laxity and carelessness. But it is equally clear that the opposite tendency was gaining ground. The Montanist was vehemently desirous that the Christian asceticism should be a match for that of the Pythagorean or the Brahmin. Tertullian, when he became a Montanist, and gave full loose to the desire for building up a great religion which had been always working in him, reviled, denounced, almost anathematised the body of the Church, for the imperfection and irregularity of its observances. While the mild Irenæus was arguing with Victor, that there had always been a variety of customs with reference both

Way out of it.

The opposing tendencies.

Tertullian de Jejuniis.

to the fast and to the festival, and that to draw the lines too close was to endanger the fellowship of the Church, the Carthaginian was finding fault with the same Victor and with his Roman community, for not recognising a sufficiently stringent and unbending rule; was denouncing them and Christians generally, because, as he said, they only spent a few days in mourning the Bridegroom's absence from His Church. His voice, though it was raised at first in denunciation of that which he affirmed to be a current practice, was nevertheless one which was sure to attract a great many listeners then and afterwards. Though it was at variance with some of the tendencies of the natural heart, it was in accordance with others which are quite as strong; it conspired with the pride of soul which had led so many in former days, and was leading so many then, to the contempt of the body; it conspired with that other and subtler pride, which preferred to obtain redemption for itself rather than to receive redemption from God. And therefore, like the other tendencies of which I have spoken, it helped to bring many of the superstitions of heathenism into the Church, while it laboured to make the Church more of a rival to heathenism.

Tertullian's doctrine; to what it appealed.

I have alluded more than once to the experiments which were made to bring the different Churches to an understanding about the great resurrection festival which they were to celebrate, and to the failure of these experiments.[1] Considering the great apparent

The Festival.

---

[1] The dread of "Sabbatising," which Justin so faithfully expressed, and in which he felt so much to be involved, might have made him and

LECT. VII. reasonableness of them, there could scarcely have been a more distinct proof that it was not the will of God that men should settle these questions at once by formal decrees; that they must come to unity by another process; that any attempt to hasten it or force it would tend to the subversion, not to the maintenance, of the true ecclesiastical order. Nevertheless, the sense of the necessity and duty of order and unity, and the conviction that in worship that unity and order must be realized most perfectly, was continually expressing itself in some beautiful attempt to connect days and hours with holy acts, and these with the acts of our Lord's life upon earth. Then when these thoughts had sprung up, as thoughts spring up in the mind of some poet or artist, and had produced forms which were suitable to them, there was a hurry and impatience to get them fixed and stereotyped,—the same diseased craving being everywhere visible that the Church might present a well-

Days, hours, stations.

many others afraid of sanctioning the new Sabbath—the weekly resurrection day—as a fixed ordinance of the Church. But it did not require their sanction. Like all other great institutions, ecclesiastical and civil, that have taken root in the modern world, it established itself without precept or pre-arrangement, by the force of an inward law, which men could not control or fashion according to their pleasure. The day of rest had been asserted once for all by the revelation to the Jews, as one of the permanent laws of humanity, framed in conformity with a divine and eternal principle, to which the divisions of time must at last adapt themselves. The Christian Church could not repeal the enactment. It could only say, "The divine and eternal principle of rest was never fully developed till the resurrection; those who believe in the resurrection *must* make the Lord's-day their Sabbath." And this truth only dawned upon them by degrees. They *found* themselves observing the day; in time they learnt more or less clearly why they observed it.

compacted religious system to the world—the same LECT. VII.
forgetfulness of the danger lest it should become such
another world itself.

The question may sometimes present itself to you, *The sacred books.*
"How did the Christians of the second century know
which books they should reckon divine and authoritative, and what they should reject? Had they any
divine intimation on this subject? Were they not
liable to confusion and mistake?" The answer must
be given simply. They did not always know what
books they should reckon divine and authoritative;
they doubted about some which we include in our
canon; they were disposed to account some as of great
value which we do not esteem at all. They had no
message from heaven, such as Mahometans say that
they have, about their books; they changed their
minds at different periods of their lives respecting
some by which they had set great store. Instead *The helps which men need for a work, provided for them.*
of hiding these facts from you, I wish to bring them
under your notice, because they seem to me in perfect
consistency with all we have heard hitherto, and with
the whole course of God's government and education;
they show more clearly than almost any other facts
what that government and education is. He calls men
to a work; then He teaches them to know what they
need, in order that they may be enabled to do their
work rightly; He shows them how He has provided
for their wants. As long as the members of the *The Church finding the Bible.*
Church in the second century were conscious of their
calling, I do not think that they had the least difficulty in discovering what lesson-books they wanted to

LECT. VII. train them for fulfilling it. They found in the Jewish writings, and in the writings of the Apostles, the history of the manifestation of the Divine Word, their King and Saviour, through different ages—the history of the gradual revelation of the Divine name into which they were baptized. They found the history of God's calling out of a people to witness of His name. They found His Old Testament passing into a New. They found *themselves;* what they were; what they had to do; what divine aid they had and might reckon upon. They might not be able to trace all the steps of the history. They might often jump at conclusions, and mar the truth with their fancies.

And gathering the sense of it according to their need. But, on the whole, there was what they needed to know; there was that which they could learn nowhere except there; there was that which interpreted what they saw and heard elsewhere.

Learning to distinguish. Although, therefore, they could not exactly tell why so good and honest a letter as that of the Roman Clemens should not stand among the apostolical documents, it did not really hold a place among them. It gave useful hints which they were glad to profit by,—but it assumed the existence of a revelation which it could not impart; it practically renounced any extravagant claims that might be put forth in its behalf.

The Shepherd of Hermas. It was not exactly the same with another book, which, if not as early as the letter of Clemens, belongs assuredly to a very early time. This is the "Shepherd of Hermas." We have only a Latin translation of it, and it has probably suffered additions which are more serious than mutilations would have been. It is divided into three parts, *Visions, Precepts,* and *Similitudes.* Good was no doubt to be got out of it by humble minds, which can often derive nourishment from that which is in itself dry, and have a wonderful capacity of rejecting what is mischievous without detecting it. Hermas gave them the hint that there was a living Teacher and Shepherd, and a Church here and in the other world, and that nature is full of images and likenesses of the spiritual kingdom. So far he assured them of what they might have known from a better source. What he added to their knowledge was soon discovered not to be very helpful. When Tertullian became a Montanist, he rejected Hermas on other grounds than his want of apostolical authority; he found in him sentiments which clashed with his own religious scheme.

<small>LECT. VII.

Character of the book, use and feebleness of it.</small>

I wish you to see that the supposed confusion between such books as these, and those that had a higher origin, was not serious so long as the Church was seeking to teach and bless the nations. Even the venerable name of Barnabas did not succeed in procuring for an Epistle which passed under his name, and which, though not his, may possibly have come from his country, and have been written by some disciple of his, more than a doubtful and passing recognition: for the Epistle, from whomsoever it came, was for idlers, not for men of business,—for those who had leisure to play with the phrases, and forms, and analogies of Scripture,—not

<small>*Letter of Barnabas.*

Why it could not stand the trial of fire.</small>

for those who needed its truths to break down strongholds. External criticism did not sever it from the writings of the companion of Barnabas. They separate themselves, as the writers whose name they bear once did, because the difference is so sharp between them that they cannot go to the same work, or carry out the same ends.

When the Bible ceases to be received as a book of life, and as a divine teacher.

But all this was greatly changed when the sense of this work grew feeble, and when that other work of setting up a Christian religion was substituted for it. You do not at first perceive the alteration. Texts are quoted as respectfully, the apostolical authority seems to be as much heeded by the doctors, who are busy in constructing an anti-Pagan or anti-Jewish system, as by those who are declaring a Gospel for the renewal of mankind. But look more closely, and you will observe that the main diligence of the former class is employed in showing that such and such passages of Scriptures confute adverse opinions,—that such and such passages do *not* confute theirs, though they seem to do so. *Now*, a text is a sharp stone which can be hurled at an enemy— 'how can he withstand that?' *Now* it has an inconvenient, awkward edge, which must be smoothed away lest it should do mischief. Every page of Tertullian almost would illustrate what I am saying, and would furnish terrible instances of the irreverent torturing of Scripture to his own purposes, —of a resolute determination that it shall never contradict or weaken any purpose of his—all the while that he professes to take it as his guide and his judge.

But the most serious consequence of this habit of mind,—closely connected with the one to which I have just referred,—was the loss of truthfulness and of the love of truth among those who yielded to it. When it was once supposed that the Spirit of truth had not come to guide men into all truth, but to build up a new scheme, by attaching themselves to which they secured the favour of God and the salvation of their souls, it was scarcely possible that fraud should not be thought as prudent, and as lawful, and as necessary, by Christian teachers, as it was by heathens. When your first thought is, how you may convert a man from darkness to light, fictions are awful and intolerable to you; your only trust is in Him who is true, and in whom is no lie. When your first thought is, how you may get *proselytes*, you will hate facts, you will resort to fictions; you will do things that a plain man of the world will blush at and think shameful, to compass so great an object. And when you have compassed it, remember who told us the result: I dare not use such words if He had not used them. *We make our proselyte two-fold more the child of hell than ourselves.* The seeds of this frightful evil were sown and began to spring up, in the second century.

Habit of lying for God.

How it steals upon Christians.

Many of the heretics found their account in mutilating the Gospels and Epistles, or in forging gospels and epistles to confirm their own opinions. This was a providential circumstance for the Church; it made those who opposed the heretics more conscious of the sinfulness of such acts than they would otherwise

The forgeries of the heretics helped to make the Church less false;

have been; it cultivated in them the power of discriminating between spurious writings and genuine. But I cannot affirm that these practices were confined to the heretics. There were a number of legends put forth respecting our Lord's life on earth, and respecting the deeds of His Apostles, which must have had a different origin. A man who was thoroughly convinced that an opinion which he had adopted on one side or on another was very important, and required to be defended, or that some story would promote piety, might persuade himself, after a little battling with his conscience, that it was no great crime to forge an Apostle's name in support of it. I said that the author of the books which bear the name of Clemens, portions of which at least belong to this century, was not apparently an ill-intentioned man. I do not retract that opinion; yet just listen to one of the wicked statements which this man puts forth, without any indication of shame or remorse. He pretends that the Pharisee Gamaliel had a secret understanding with the Apostles—that he was in fact a Christian convert—but that he agreed with them to suppress his convictions, in order that he might serve their cause more effectually in the Sanhedrim! St. Peter is actually made to communicate this fact as a valuable and interesting secret to Clemens, his young convert. Now, the author of the "Recognitions," though not an orthodox writer, though in many respects an heretical one, is yet a most vehement supporter of some of the maxims which were gaining currency at that time in the Latin Church. St. Peter

THE SECOND CENTURY.   337

is with him the Apostle of the West; St. Peter invests Clemens with his episcopal office at Rome; St. Peter writes to James, whom he recognises as the great Jerusalem Apostle, enclosing certain writings of his which are only to be divulged to persons whom he has tried and found faithful, and which James binds them, under a most tremendous anathema, (quoting at the same time his own opinion against oaths,) to keep as a sacred deposit. There is a temper of mind disclosed in such a work as this which cannot have been confined to a man, which must have been infecting the time, though there may have been great and powerful antidotes, which prevented it from producing all the mischief which it was to produce afterwards. In that story of Gamaliel lies the germ of a doctrine of concealment and suppression of truth which was to take the most various forms, and to put on the most seemly disguises. In that story of the communication of the books, and the curse upon the reading of them, is the hint of the terror which men would in due time conceive of the Scriptures being known to the people, the hint also of a doctrine respecting secret lore, which was already taking hold of better and wiser men than the pseudo Clemens.

Lect. VII.
The Epistle of Peter to James, and the Anathema, belong to the Clementines.

The story of Gamaliel significant of much.

 I told you that even Clemens of Alexandria was not free from a temptation of this kind. His devout mind revolted, no doubt, at much of the talk which he heard concerning divine truths. He felt that they are lying beneath all our thought; and that terrible mischief comes when we project them outside of us, and handle them, play with them, argue about them.

Feelings of the Alexandrian Clemens about reserve.

z

LECT. VII.　He knew the worth of silence and secret communion; he had perceived a force in what the teachers of Alexandria said of principles, which the carnal and vulgar soul cannot apprehend. But how near are precious truths to the falsehoods which are most destructive of them! The reverence for mystery, which in the mind of an earnest and faithful man means the reverence for a truth which he cannot grasp, but on which he can rest, and which is as close to others as it is to him, may become in the worse moments of his own life—will become, when other men catch it from him—the boast of some profound treasure which he and one or two more have got sight of, which is hid in a mine of theirs, of which men in general are to know nothing. Mysteries there had been in all the religions of the world—mysteries there were in nearly all the schools of philosophy; surely Christianity cannot be without its mystery! Might it not be said that the mystery of Christianity was the deepest of all—that it was that depth which was quite unfathomable?

The mysteries.

The mystery of Sacrifice.

Surely this might be said. If there was any meaning in the facts or principles which the Church proclaimed, it must be said. Was not the sacrifice of the Only-Begotten of the Father this mystery of unfathomable love? Was not this something which no words could measure, no images set forth? So the Church believed. The celebration of the Eucharist, as the centre and principle of all its worship, embodied the belief; but it embodied also the belief that a sacrifice had been offered for the sins of the

The Eucharistical mystery.

whole world, a sacrifice which had taken away the sins of the world. It embodied the belief that that unfathomable love of God had been revealed to men, and that the poorest beggar, the most miserable sinner, might enter into it, dwell in it, feed upon it, be penetrated and possessed by it. If one of these convictions drove out the other, what would happen? The celebration of the Eucharist would become indeed a mystery, the Christian counterpart of that which the Egyptian priests gloried in; but it would no longer be a mystery of thanksgiving for a love that had been manifested in a stupendous act. The service would be mysterious, that is to say, it would be kept from the public gaze; it would be reserved for the initiated; but that which it signified would more and more disappear,—it would be lost in the service. Those who had sought for something too inward, too unutterable for words or forms, would find these continually putting themselves forth in place of it. And then, in process of time, there would be a demand that the other side of the truth which had been suppressed should be brought out. The sacrifice which is for men must be made broad, palpable, visible, that men may confess it and adore it. If there is that in it which answers to the heathen mysteries, there must be also that which answers to the open heathen sacrifices. The Eucharist, considered as a bond of peace to all the members of the Church—a testimony of Christ's death to the world—answered to both, for it declared in the simplest form the fulfilment of both by God, the full realization of both by

Opposite errors united.

man. The same Eucharist, reduced into a mere part of a religious system, corresponded now to one, now to the other; it was a new mystery, gathering up into itself all the exclusiveness of the old; it was a new sacrifice, gathering into itself all the superstition of the old. What could it do, when it assumed this shape, to break in pieces the fetters by which men were bound; to testify of the truth which makes free?

The Presbyter celebrating the Eucharist.

There are some who fancy that they can trace up this evil in the second century, and in subsequent centuries, to the growth of a persuasion that the presbyter in the Christian Church corresponded to the old sacrificial priest of the Jew and of the Gentile, and, therefore, that he was the person who could alone administer the Eucharist. I do not myself see how the Church could have avoided feeling that the elder brother of the community was testifying of the great Elder Brother who had gone up to the right hand of God, and, therefore, that the duty of setting forth the finished sacrifice appertained most fittingly to him. I do not suppose that there was any law or decree designating him to the office, any more than there was a law or decree fixing which were the books of Scripture, or that the Sunday should supersede the Saturday as the day of rest. I do not suppose that the Church did adopt this practice at once; it seems to me to have been one of those ordinances which worked themselves out in the called body under the Divine teaching; because it was suitable to its whole character and constitution,—because in no other way could the unity and universality of the sacrifice, and

Reasonableness of the practice.

the fact that Christ had already offered and completed it, have been so perfectly expressed. It is not in the association of the presbyter with the old priest that I find the degradation of the Christian Sacrament, but in the confusion of the one with the other, in the notion that the Christian presbyter was like the Jewish, a witness of that mystery which was not yet revealed, of a Lamb which had not yet been offered and accepted—like the heathen, a witness that the mind of the Father was to be made propitious by the oblations of His creatures. Here is that mystery of iniquity which I believe has ever been working itself out by the side of the mystery of godliness. I have been tracing some of the indications of them both in these last two Lectures; and I wish you to meditate on them well, that you may be able to watch their growth in each subsequent century; still more, that you may be able to distinguish them in your own hearts.

LECT. VII.

The real confusion.

LECTURE VIII.

THE CHURCH AND THE EMPERORS.

<small>Lect. VIII.
The Overseer or Bishop.</small>

WHAT I said about the Presbyter in my last Lecture will have perplexed you, if you have not connected it with some hints which I threw out respecting the constitution of the Church in former Lectures. You will have observed that I have scarcely ever used the word *Bishop* in speaking of the different Christian communities. I have abstained from it, not because I dislike the word, or because I think it does not fitly describe any class of persons in the second century, but because it does not at once suggest the meaning of the Greek word of which it is the rendering. At the risk, therefore, of appearing pedantic, I have talked of the "Overseers" of the Churches whenever I have had occasion to translate the original word. But I have taken one or two opportunities of remarking, that I do not think that even this title expresses fully and satisfactorily the condition of the person who commonly bore it, or the feeling with which the Church regarded him. I believe that not only in that century, but in all subsequent centuries, we should understand the character of the Church better, if we resorted to our own old

<small>*Patriarchal constitution of the Church.*</small>

English phrase of *Fathers in God*. There may be difficulties in the application of that phrase, arising from various circumstances with which you will become more familiar hereafter. In later times, when the Empire and the Church were united, Patriarchs began to be distinguished from Bishops for civil purposes, in a certain sense for ecclesiastical purposes. The Patriarchs or Fathers in the East became associated with certain sees; in the West, the Bishop of a particular see claimed to be the universal Pope or Father. But these very facts, though they cause some embarrassment in the use of the word, make our recollection of it the more necessary. It will give a continuity to all your thoughts of Church history if you fix it on your minds now. Above all, it will be a great help in understanding the subject which I touched upon at the close of the last Lecture, still more in understanding the subject upon which I shall speak to you in the present.

LECT. VIII.

The Jewish nation, I said, was not only called out to bear witness against false gods, but against tyrannical men, against the scheme or system of society which is denoted in Scripture as the Babel or Babylonian system. The huge empires of the East were the great antagonist powers to the Jewish nation. So long as it maintained its own faith in God, its own unity as a nation, so long its very existence bore witness that a kingdom stands on righteousness, and not on force.

Office of the Jewish nation in respect of great empires.

When the Jewish nation was gone, in what way could the Church take up this testimony? We are

Supposed extinction of this function in the Church.

LECT. VIII. apt to think, many of us, that it might be a very effectual protester against paganism, that it might by degrees undermine that; but that it had not much to do with the Roman polity, nay, that it was bound to stand aloof from any interference with that polity. The Christians of Rome were told by the Apostle in the days of Nero, that they were to be subject to the powers that be, nay, that Nero's power itself was ordained of God. Were they to take part in conspiracies against the emperors? If they had, how they would have displayed their weakness as men! how certainly they would have disobeyed God, and have been refused any succour from Him!

The Church declares itself loyal to the emperors.

All this is very true, and all this was most distinctly acknowledged by the teachers of the second century. The apologists professed, without exception, the allegiance and loyalty of the members of their community to the emperors. They challenged their opponents to bring evidence which could convict them of any acts of disloyalty; they denied that they were restrained from them by fear so much as by conscience. To be treasonable to the visible king would be to sin against the invisible one; their sacraments to the one bound them not to violate their obligations to the other.

Its indifference to the proceedings of the world at large.

Not only is this true; but it is true also that the Christians were indifferent to the policy of the Roman empire in a way in which the old Jews never could be indifferent to the policy of the nations which surrounded them. To a great extent Christians in the second century cultivated this indifference. Their citizenship, they said, was in heaven,—their hopes were there; the arrangements of states, the negotiations and battles which other men deemed so important, did not concern them. It was impossible for men who were penetrated with the divine charity to carry out this maxim; the famines, pestilences, wars which afflicted the world, must have had a solemn interest for those who loved Christ. Readers of the Jewish Scriptures could not but perceive that God was represented in them as taking part in mundane events; they could not suppose that these were merely types of some spiritual principle. Yet this was assuredly the inclination of their minds; their circumstances greatly favoured it. So far, therefore, as the Church was under the direction of its teachers, we may readily admit that it would have been perfectly innocent of any interference with the existing conditions of the empire; that it would never have given it that amount of disturbance to which it had been subject from the province of Palestine before the destruction of the Jewish capital.

But the Church was *not* under the direction of the individual men who composed it; they had *not* the power to determine how far they should affect the politics of the earth. We may say boldly, the Church could not have borne that protest which it did bear against paganism, without bearing at the very same moment a protest against the military despotism of Rome: it could not undermine the one without undermining the other. This truth has never been fairly and fully proclaimed either by pagan,

The Church a protester against the empire in spite of itself.

Christian, or infidel writers; but all these have implicitly confessed it. The conviction has been forced upon them, that the rise of the Church was necessarily contemporaneous with the decline and fall of the Roman empire.

The emperors conscious of the fact.

The emperors themselves had a clearer instinct on this subject than the members of the Church. There was not one of them, from Nerva to Commodus, who was not a man of much more than average intelligence and average benevolence; not one, with the exception perhaps of Hadrian, for whom we may not claim positive moral worth. It may be asserted, almost as confidently, that just in proportion to their worth, was their suspicion of the Christian Church. Trajan feared it more than Hadrian; Marcus Aurelius feared it more than Trajan. The fact is undoubted; how is it to be accounted for?

They did not merely punish the Christians for opposing Paganism;

To say that the emperors were interested in the support of paganism is true; what I told you in the last Lecture but one will show you how true it is. The whole social condition of the empire was bound up with the worship of the gods; the hierarchy could not be separated from the imperial system. But this is not all the truth. The emperors evidently felt that the Christian Church, as such, was dangerous to the empire, as such; mighty as the one was, insignificant as the other was, they were antagonists, one of which must perish if the other was to live. And the more you consider the Church in that light in which I have endeavoured to set it before you—as a family or patriarchal society growing up in each city, with

But as a political enemy.

a father as its head, that father being a witness of a common Father in heaven—the more you will perceive how reasonable this apprehension was; how much more formidable such a body was than one which came forward with greater apparent pretensions; which encountered the military power with its own weapons, or which merely exhibited the pattern of a national fellowship, as the Jews had done, in contrast with it.

If you speak of the Church as monarchical, or aristocratical, or democratical, or as combining these elements, you introduce notions with which the Greek and the Roman world were perfectly familiar,—notions that had been tried in different combinations, and had been to all appearance exhausted. A society thus constructed would have led men back to one of those experiments which had been pronounced futile, on the day when the general became the king of kings. But here was an experiment of quite a different kind, thrust upon the notice of all the imperial provinces. It was the simplest, most primitive of all forms of society, older than any of those national forms which the great tyranny had extinguished. And this simplest form of society was also proclaimed to be divine and comprehensive. God was said to be revealing Himself as the Head and Parent of a family, and that family was to spread itself east and west, north and south, to the ends of the earth.

Pliny found the Christians in Bithynia effecting a real and practical, if not a permanent revolution.

Old forms of government worn out.

Pliny's apprehensions respecting the Church well founded.

He was too wise a man not to know that a movement in the heart of a society, affecting its habits, customs, principles, is far more serious than any which disturbs its surface. He had a right to feel and to warn his master, that he should not slight the indications of such a movement, merely because the conduct of those who professed the new superstition was orderly. He had a right to think that a faith of this kind could not be treated, as it was the policy of the empire to treat the religions with which he had up to that time been acquainted. There was a something in it which, as a statesman, he could not but acknowledge had a political, not merely a religious, significance.

His judgment confirmed by Trajan's observations at Antioch.

This conclusion he arrived at upon evidence far less clear and decisive than that which Trajan found out for himself. The venerable appearance of Ignatius made the sort of influence he was exerting more conspicuous. He was not merely the teacher of a doctrine; his disciples reverenced him on some other ground than the words which he spoke. There was an order and government of a very peculiar sort among his people; they were evidently connected, by secret ramifications, with men whom they had never seen or heard of. Secret societies were prohibited by the wisdom of the empire, as freemasons' lodges are in some countries of modern Europe; here was a secret society which might spread underground through Europe and Asia, and which, if not checked, might make itself known by some tremendous explosion.

Such language applied to the fathers of the Church

may seem to us very strange; but we must not evade the force of it by false pleas, which are as inconsistent with our faith as they would be with Trajan's. The real question is, whether the Church was revolutionary or regenerative; whether it had a commission to destroy Roman greatness, or to bring it forth out of the mass of corruption under which it was hidden; whether it was disturbing the laws and principles which bind man to man, or vindicating them and placing them on their true and eternal foundation; whether it was going back to the source of order, and refinement, and civilization, or merely hastening a return to barbarism. This question must, of course, be answered differently, according as we think that the Church was or was not a body called out to be a blessing to mankind. But the conclusions of the emperors corresponded more strictly to the facts which they saw—they have been more confirmed by the experience of the world—than the doctrines of those who pretend that the Church was a harmless fellowship, which would have worked no mischief to the dynasties of the earth, which would have left them as it found them, if they had not rudely endeavoured to crush it. The case is not so. We say of the principles of this society—

False attempts to represent the Church as harmless.

Revolution and regeneration.

"Igneus est ollis vigor et cœlestis origo,"

and its fiery strength was to manifest itself by consuming what was corrupt and insincere; the celestial origin was to make itself good by overcoming that which had a dark and subterranean origin.

Lect. VIII.

The Emperors less persecutors than the Mobs.

I have guarded you already against the supposition that the emperors were the direct or the main instigators of the persecutions which have been reported to us in different Churches. The mobs had far more share in them than the proconsuls; proconsuls were often more responsible for them than the emperors. Eusebius gives us several imperial rescripts (and if not of positive authority, they may at least have a true foundation), which were designed to abate the popular violence, and to give the Christians the advantage of some of the laws which protected the other subjects of the state. Such signs of moderation only make it more obvious that the policy which the best emperors adopted was not the result of cruelty but of conviction; being what they were, they could not act otherwise. As conservators of the state, they must put down those who, with whatever motives, were to all appearance working for the subversion of it.

Nevertheless they were obliged to do their utmost for the extinction of the Church.

Character and designs of Marcus Aurelius.

I cannot doubt that it was the piety of the emperor Marcus Aurelius—his genuine unaffected piety, as well as his desire of upholding the state which had been committed to his care—that led him to feel more strongly, and act more severely against the Christians, than any of his predecessors. No one felt more keenly and bitterly than he did, the decay of moral strength among his people; few saw more clearly that moral strength must be grounded upon faith in the invisible. I wish you and I confessed as sincerely as he seems to have done, the presence of a righteous Judge of his acts and thoughts, or sought as much to impress other men with that conviction. If his subjects had lost so much of their faith in the gods already—so much of their sense of right and wrong,—what a crime it must be to make them more irreligious still! to take from them the sanctions upon which their conduct depended! Were not the Christians doing this? Were not they teaching citizens and even slaves to despise the gods? What a duty must it be for him to do all that in him lay to stop such an infection, to preserve and strengthen the internal life of the empire, as the only means of preserving its external machinery.

So I believe he reasoned, and such reasoning led him to be a persecutor. I should feel it a great sin to pass judgment upon him. We can see so clearly how the subject may have presented itself to his mind; we can tell so little that, in the same circumstances, we might not have acted more harshly, less conscientiously, than he did. He was not a superstitious man; he laboured hard to deliver himself from superstition, and to preserve an awe at once, and an affection, for the divine Power. He thought, as most statesmen and philosophers do, that the common people must be superstitious in order to be moral; that fear of the future must be the chief means of keeping them right; but I do not find that he held that opinion more strongly than many apparently earnest believers in Christ hold it. And, looking at the utterly corrupt and sunken condition of the world in his day, what man had greater excuse for saying, "Only the vulgarest motives can keep these people from the most intolerable crimes"?

His conduct, seen from his point of view, quite justifiable.

352 ON CHURCH HISTORY.

LECT. VIII.

Why Christians were sure that they ought to incur the risk of undermining the Roman religion;

Those who had received the Gospel *knew* that this reasoning, in which it might have been difficult to detect a flaw, was radically and essentially false. They knew what had reclaimed them from evil habits and principles—what alone could reclaim them. Nothing but a message from God, that it was His will to set them free from the secret chains by which they were bound, could, they were sure, have enabled them to cast away those chains; they could not have heartily confessed Him as a Lawgiver and a Judge, unless they had first confessed Him as a Redeemer. They could not therefore be careful to answer the arguments of such men as Marcus Aurelius, though they may often have been staggered by them; they could leave themselves and the world too in God's hands. They were sure that when they refused to offer sacrifice to the image of the emperor, they were refusing to sanction a lie which never could help to make Romans or any

Even though they were undermining it and the empire together.

men righteous or obedient; they were sure that when they were owning Him who made the great sacrifice on the cross to be the King of all kings, they were asserting the truth which had restored them, and which had power to restore the universe. They had nothing more to do, but to offer themselves as sacrifices in that faith. Their cause was with the Lord, and their work with their God. It was His world and not theirs, in which they were dwelling; in his own good time, He might show clearly that the kingdoms of it were the kingdoms of Him and of His Christ.

I can never affect to doubt that this faith of the martyrs was a true faith, and consequently that their preaching and their acts were, as Marcus Aurelius and the emperors generally thought they were, helping to break in pieces the fabric of the world as it then stood—helping to bring about an entirely new social order. But I cannot doubt, also, that there were feelings and notions working at that time in the minds of Christians—to work more mightily afterwards—which were greatly at variance with this faith, which served even in that day to weaken and counteract the effects of it, which have made the blessed issues of that faith in after ages doubtful to many, which have marred and debased them, where their existence is most manifest. Of these I must speak now, as I did in the last Lecture of the causes which made the Christian testimony against Paganism feeble and contradictory.

Lect. VIII. Influences that weakened their testimony on behalf of political justice.

I. The catechetical teachers of Alexandria—admirable and noble men as they were, and great as the service was which they rendered in certain directions to the Gospel—cannot be said to have assisted in giving effect to this part of its witness. By asserting the knowledge of God to be the supreme good, by setting Him forth as willing to give His creatures this knowledge, they struck at the root of Polytheism; but they left the rulers of the earth the only region which they claimed, to use it as they might. I do not call them abstract speculators; I have said that they were practical teachers, helpers of Jews, Gentiles, and Christians, men who brought their knowledge to bear on common difficulties and outward temptations. But they were in no sense

1. The spiritualism of the Alexandrians.

A A

politicians; they scarcely contemplated the Church was a polity; they looked upon it—in the best, not in the party, sense of that word—as a school. Whatever revelations of the Scriptures bore upon spiritual truths, they grasped with a wonderful intuition; whatever revelations bore upon the order and government of earth, they twisted to a spiritual sense. They held out no promise or hope, therefore, of a reformation of human society; the wishes that pointed to such an object had apparently little which answered to them in their hearts. The Apocalypse they were inclined to disbelieve in, because it seemed to speak of a redeemed earth. Here was *their* weakness, and it was the cause of an opposite weakness elsewhere.

II. For there was a very decided reaction in another part of the Church against these spiritualising tendencies—a very strong determination to say, "God has spoken about the things of earth as well as the things of heaven, and we will take His words in their plain and obvious sense." The cardinal illustration of this tendency is to be found in the latter chapters of the fifth book of Irenæus, from the 32d chapter to the end.[1] Some persons see in these chapters nothing but carnal dreams. I confess they are to me exceedingly delightful, not only as protests against the rage for allegorising which was gaining so much ground in the Church—not only as a healthy attempt to maintain that

---

[1] To confound the doctrine of Irenæus with that of Cerinthus is shamefully unjust. If any one will carefully read the chapter to which I have referred, he will find that Irenæus was much further from the sensualists than he was from the allegorisers.

vines and fig-trees are vines and fig-trees in the Bible as they would be elsewhere—but also for the bright and cheerful hopes which they show were dwelling in this good man's heart. He was sure that God had made the fields to bring forth and bud, and that some day the most barren of them would give seed to the sower, and bread to the eater; he was sure that some day there would be righteousness, and not violence, in the dealings of men with each other. There, among his wild Gauls, he was cherishing these visions of what should be after the resurrection of the just: he knew not how much he was doing that they might be fulfilled.

Why, then, do I set down these visions as among the signs that the Church was not fully understanding her work? Because it seems to me that though Irenæus was right to expect that Christ's kingdom should come on the earth,—though it was good and wholesome for him to think that God's will should be done there as well as in heaven—he was not believing the words, which he refused to allegorise, in their full and plain sense, so long as he failed to acknowledge that this kingdom *had* come, that Christ was even then the King of the earth, and that every man who was baptized with water, or who baptized the earth with his blood, was declaring audibly to the emperors and their servants, "This Gaul, and Italy, and Africa, are verily His, and not yours."

But it was partial, because projected into the future.

Irenæus hoped that after the resurrection, the earth would be what God meant it to be. He might have been—must have been—right, that when he joined the assembly of the just made perfect, he should see more

Hopes of what should be after the resurrection.

blessings descending upon the earth than he had seen while he was upon it; perhaps he might be the instrument of bestowing many more upon it than he could win for it here. He might be right that mighty and long battles would have to be fought, and new crimes committed, and new dynasties established and overthrown, before the cross of Christ would thoroughly subdue either Romans or Celts; but he could not be right in postponing to a distant future that supremacy which the Church, by all her acts, by the form of her polity, by her very existence, was asserting for her Master in that day.

The third class; the defenders of the Church as an existing polity.

III. This was a truth to which Christians of another class were strongly alive. They felt that the order of the Church was a real and divine order; that God must have established it; that the preservation of it was as sacred a part of their duty as the preservation of their faith.

Feeling of Clemens and Ignatius.

Supposing all the passages of Ignatius about the authority of the Overseer were struck out of his letters, still there is both in him and in Clemens a sense of the unspeakable necessity of order to the existence of the Church, a demand for a *filial* obedience on the part of its members to those who are set over them, which cannot be got rid of, and which indicated even more than they expressed. Evidently these writers perceived a very close and intimate relation between the divine Name on which the society stood, and its political constitution,—a very strong conviction that any disturbance of its unity, through the insubordination of any of its members, might be fatal to its inward life, as well

THE SECOND CENTURY. 357

as to the effect which it was to produce on the world. LECT.VIII.

And surely they were right. When our Lord laid down the principle, that in His kingdom the chief of all is the servant of all, He proclaimed the great paradox on which all society rests, one which the ruler of states and the chief of hosts must act upon, if subjects and armies are not to be in slavery or in anarchy. But in the Church this law was to be embodied and carried out, that men might see it working there, and confess it to be indeed God's law, and the law of their lives. The restless assertion of rights and powers, in one brother against another, Clemens and Ignatius felt must be destructive of the Church's polity, and therefore of its testimony. In one of the passages in the letters, which is omitted in the modern version, the Overseer is spoken of as the keynote of a symphony. The words may be interpolated; but they indicate a feeling which was more characteristic of Ignatius than of those who, in later times, are likely to have abused his name for the purpose of drawing formal lines about the different offices of the Church. The disposition to do this soon made itself manifest. One can never tell what circumstances may justify the establishment of clear and verbal definitions about the limits of the power which this or that man is to exercise. They may become indispensable, but they presume the existence of something wrong; and if they check the growth of the wrong in one direction, they often promote it in another. In the Church order everything, as we have

Radical principle of the divine kingdom.

Distinctions and definitions.

LECT. VIII. seen, depended upon the acknowledgment of *relations*
Relations between the ministers and members of the Church.
and offices. If this acknowledgment was lost, and they began to
be regarded as mere *officials*, their character was lost;
nor did you restore it by calling them *divine* officials,
by saying that God put them into their places. No
doubt He did; but the places which they claimed
when they began to jostle each other, and to fight
about precedence, were not those which He meant
for them.

This is a point which ought especially to be understood in reading Church history. You will hear
Orders in great discussions about the time when the Orders in
the Church. the Church began to be clearly distinguished from
each other, when the Overseer obtained the full
recognition of his difference from the Presbyter, when
the Presbyter learnt how he stood apart from the
Deacon, when the broad line was drawn between the
Clergy and the people or Laity. You will find much
learning on all sides; you will sometimes be quite
bewildered by the evidence which shows that these
differences were and were not clearly perceived in the
second century. You will hear of a number of offices
besides these, all demanded by the gradually increasing wants of the Church; and you will be asked
how these were distinguished from what we in
England commonly call the three Orders.

A Polity I believe, as I have told you, that the polity of
and a
Hierarchy. the Church is not made up of a set of offices, three
or more; that it has a different and much deeper
ground. But just as men very early began to think

of substituting a Christian religion for the Gospel of Jesus Christ, so I think they very early began to think of substituting a *hierarchy* for a *polity*. There was a hierarchy in the Roman empire—a huge sacerdotal machinery. It had lost its root in anything sacred or divine; but it was a vast scheme of offices which the imperial power was anxious to preserve, hoping to be preserved by it. Weak as the Church was at first, it had promises and pledges of expansion in it. Might it not some day expand into such an hierarchy as this? Rome did not grow in a day. Its walls were once said to have been leaped over by the brother of their founder. Why might not the walls of the Church, if they were well laid and carefully cemented now, rise into as goodly a city? *Earthly dreams of what the Church might be.*

Alas! it was too true a dream. They *might* do this; the Church might become the image of this old hierarchical system. But God had a different work for her; she was sent to remould His world, not to make a world for herself. A number of men in the second century were working for the first end, laboriously and lovingly; there were those who were working chiefly for the other. It cannot be affirmed that the false idea was not mixed with the true in the one, nor the true with the false in the other. We cannot ascertain the amount of right or wrong in any person; but history shows what were the results of the right and the wrong,—that the true Churchman was working out deliverance, that the false was forging fresh chains for mankind. *The divine and human design counteracting each other.*

IV. But there is a fourth aspect of this subject,

which came before us while we were studying the records of the Roman Church. There was not merely a tendency to establish the Church into a hierarchy of offices ; there was a tendency to give that hierarchy a centre. You cannot wonder that such a feeling should have arisen very early indeed in the minds of Churchmen—arisen long before they were aware of it themselves. Their Jewish origin must never be overlooked or forgotten. The sense of succeeding to Jewish privileges and responsibilities was, as I have endeavoured to make you feel, most precious and important to their existence. But Jerusalem had been a centre to the Jewish faith and polity. It had perished through its rejection of the true King. Why might He not be acknowledged in some other great city? Why might He not make that His capital? If this were possible, what must the city be? Must it not be the one to which God had already given the dominion of the world?

It is not a mere fancy that such thoughts were at work in the minds of men at this time. I have referred to the Homilies which bear the name of Clement, and which are worked up into a story in the Recognitions. They must have been written shortly after the second century, probably in it. There we see a very curious process. The Ebionite, the man whose whole faith was in the city where St. James presided, and in him as the teacher of what he took to be the pure original Jewish religion, as reformed by Christ the divine Prophet, transfers his affections to Rome, looks upon St. Peter as holding there the place which St. James held at Jerusalem, and assumes the name of Clemens that he may magnify this new position, and connect it with the old ideas. This seems to be the true meaning of these documents. It has been somewhat lost sight of because the person who wrote them, in conformity with his Ebionitic notions, makes many remarks about Sacrifice which were not in accordance with the after doctrines of the Roman Church, and mixes heretical traditions with his pretended narratives of the apostolical teaching. Nevertheless, he does very distinctly enable us to trace the unfolding of the notion, that St. Peter was to be the primate of a universal society, and was to have Rome for his New Jerusalem. And he does very clearly show that the root of that opinion must lie in a low conception of our Lord's character and work; in the acknowledgment of Him as a great Prophet and Teacher, who delegates His authority to some man, not as the eternal King and Overseer of His Church, not as the living Corner-stone by which alone it is held together. Believing this to be the fact, I cannot help looking upon the stories respecting Victor as additional illustrations of a tendency, which though only beginning to show itself, yet was showing itself in the second century.

James, Peter, Clemens.

Forgetfulness of Christ as the God-man, at the root of the Clementine theory.

The Church then was the witness to the world of a living and righteous King, who is the centre of all society, the bond of the visible and invisible world, the Judge of empires, who will shatter in pieces all powers that are not righteous, who will

Summary

LECT.VIII. raise the nations out of their thraldom and death to a new life. Churchmen were secretly cherishing the thought that it would be glorious to have a great city for their centre, to sit there and use the power which the emperors had used, to have the nations for their subjects and not their masters, and therefore to be able to crush them more than the Cæsars had crushed them.

LECTURE IX.

THE CHURCH AND THE PHILOSOPHERS.

THERE are many periods in history in which a separate notice of the relations of the Church to the teachers of philosophy would be quite unnecessary. When philosophers shut themselves up in schools, to dispute even about the greatest and deepest questions—when Philosophy makes itself a profession, apart from the business of mankind—we may afford to leave it for those who prefer it to some other amusement, and who have not discovered that we live for some other end than to talk.

In the second century, there was the ordinary amount of persons who reduced philosophy into a profession, nay, into a trade—perhaps we might say, more than the ordinary amount. But the excess, if it existed, was caused by the fact that there were many who regarded it quite in a different light; who turned to it, not as an escape from the realities of life, but as a help to face them; who considered it as no school business, but connected it with facts, and history, and experience; who sought by means of it to solve contradictions which tormented them in their daily practice; who hoped by it to rule empires better—

Unimportance of philosophy at certain times.

How the case stood in the second century.

LECT. IX. I must say also, to serve and know God better. For Christians, therefore, to be indifferent about the movements of philosophers in this age was impossible. You have seen in a number of instances how impossible it was. They encountered it in the most various shapes, before and after they had accepted the Gospel; it had already given the form and colour to the minds of many when they first heard of Christ: they must determine afterwards in what relation their old search and their new discoveries stood to each other.

The old sects still existing.

For the reason I have just given you, it is not desirable that you should merely learn from some digest of opinions what schools of philosophy were prevalent at this time. You will be told, and told truly, that there were Epicureans, and Academicians, and Peripatetics, and Stoics now, as there had been for many generations before; that they disputed about some old and some new questions; and that names have been preserved to us of disputers who were more famous than the rest. But this information is not exactly what you want. You should try to find out what were the effective thoughts that were at work in the heart of the Roman empire at this time,—what forms they took,—how they mingled with other influences,—how the Gospel

But they did not contain the philosophy of the time.

came into contact with them. You will not find, I believe, that these thoughts cast themselves exactly into the moulds which the digests present to us; they made moulds for themselves, working up more or less of the old material, preserving some of the old names, but not so that they can be described by them; the most living part of men's convictions was that to which these names did not correspond. I will try, though I doubt of my success, to give you a few hints which may enable you to discriminate the habits and modes of thought which most affected this time, and which have left the greatest impression on after times. You will not then wonder that you have heard Justin, Athenagoras, Clemens—even Irenæus and Tertullian—discoursing so much about philosophy, and its bearing upon Christianity.

I. There was what I shall call, though there may, perhaps, be a much better name for it, the *Historical Philosophy*. A man who lived in the empire—after it had swallowed up all Greece and some of the cultivated regions of the East, after the glory of Rome itself as a free city was departed—would ask himself whence the power had been derived which had raised states to consequence, and by which individual men had achieved greatness. He would be struck with characteristic differences between the conquering and the conquered race:—the Latin and the Greek; with the reverence, subordination, and domestic fidelity, which had been the source of strength to the one; with the subtlety, the power of distinguishing, the acknowledgment of mind as mightier than matter, which had belonged to the other. If he was a Greek himself, he would dwell much on this last quality; he would see that it had availed to give the Greek a triumph even in his fall and slavery,—that it had made him the teacher

The historical philosophy.

Comparison of Greeks and Latins.

of his rulers. He would begin to think that in this secret wisdom, this victory of the man over the animal, lay the real power of both races, the real power of each person who had been illustrious in either. In this sense philosophy, or the love and pursuit of wisdom, would appear to him the explanation both of biography and history. But at the same time he could not fail,—if he were an earnest man, with an historical mind,—to observe in the fall of nations, in the humiliation of those that had so many pledges of dominion and permanence, the signs of a government that was higher than man's. Such an observer would listen much more reverently than the mere speculators were wont to listen, to the popular doctrines respecting the rule of the gods, and their interest in human affairs. He would be quite unable to account for the progress of events, and even for the exaltation and depression of individuals, if he cast aside these doctrines with the contempt which the extravagances and absurdities that accompanied them had begotten in the minds of many thinkers of his own and former ages. The grave testimonies of poets as well as of statesmen to a continual Providence over them and over the world, would strike him as worthy of the most serious consideration; it was unphilosophical as well as impious to disregard them. The belief of a directing Power or Spirit over the human spirit, which had been held so strongly by Socrates, and by many besides him, would seem to our thinker still more reasonable and necessary; perhaps the very condition and principle of philosophy might lie in that belief. Holding it, he would feel as Socrates did, that it was not safe to trifle with popular opinions; that they all pointed to a truth which men could not grasp, but which was essential to their existence. But he would be as sensible as Socrates was—more so, because the progress of centuries and of corruptions had made the effects of superstition more palpable— what perils lay in many of the current and popular notions; how they destroyed the moral strength and freedom of men; how they degraded the nature of the divine Power; how they made evil and not good an object of reverence and fear to man. Such a man as I am giving you a sketch of could not, therefore, attach himself to any school or sect of philosophers. His opinions would seem to those who did, often indefinite, often contradictory; perhaps they would not seldom seem so to himself. But they would be the result of a fair and honest study of history. There might be many mistakes in his conclusions about it, as well as in his judgment of the facts of it; but, on the whole, his observations must be important to himself, and important to after times. They must have taught him of principles which concerned his own being, and the life of the universe. If he could not fully act out his own convictions of what was right, he will have discovered some of the causes of his failure, something of the source whence his help must come. If he could not harmonise all the puzzles of generations, he could at least put them in such order—he could group them so together—that when the light fell upon them from some higher sun; they would no longer appear as mere atoms whirling and striking against each other in a chaos.

Plutarch, the specimen of these historical students.

You must not think that I have been drawing a fancy sketch. If you read Plutarch of Chæronea, and compare the work of his which you have known from childhood with his more learned and elaborate, but not really more instructive and philosophical, works, you will find that I have represented to you an actual man, the most remarkable assuredly of a class, but still one who could not have existed alone,— who shows us what was passing in a number of other minds, though they might not be able to utter it as he did.

The Pythagoreans.

II. The next class of thinking men who were producing a strong impression at this time, I shall denote by what will sound more like the name of a sect than that which I chose under the last head. I must call them the *Pythagoreans*, for it is the name by which they would probably have liked to call themselves. But there had been a Pythagorean school existing for many ages in Greece, and still possessing its regular teachers, with whom they would not have wished to identify themselves at all, to whom, in fact, they had no real resemblance. Their delight was to think of the man whose name this sect had adopted, not of its doctrines and disputations.

Traditions of Pythagoras.

They did not, indeed, know much of Pythagoras. He had left no writings; the traditions respecting him were most of them very uncertain. What is clear about him, is that he felt himself inspired with his wisdom by God; that the divine Unity was the great object of his search; that he gathered about him a band of zealous, loving disciples; that he cultivated in them habits of silence, and reverence for some Being whom they could not see with their eyes, or comprehend with their understandings; that his ends were political; that he desired to reform society more than to propagate a doctrine; that he actually established a community in South Italy, which passed through many struggles, and at last was extinguished, —these were the facts of his history which made the miraculous tales of him credible to the men of this time, and made them think that if they proposed to themselves the same objects as their Samian master, they might, perhaps, receive the divine power on which he appeared to depend. It is clear from the books of Lucian of Samosata, the great wit and scoffer of this age, that these Pythagorean doctors were many of them pretenders and quacks; that they connected themselves with the ordinary enchanters, and perhaps supplied them with a doctrine which they might use for the purposes of their trade. All of them may have been liable to fall into this depravity; few may have been altogether free from it. But it would be a great mistake to suppose that even those who were most chargeable with imposture, or most yielded to the temptation to become impostors, did not start with a higher aim, and did not retain to the last some of the impulses which had prompted them at first. One of them, who belongs to the first century, but whose name

Influence of them on the second century.

Their false-hoods.

LECT. IX.
Apollonius.

became chiefly celebrated in the third, Apollonius of Tyana, must, I think, have been an enthusiastic young man, with a real desire to improve the condition of the world around him, with a conviction that it could only be reformed by Divine Wisdom, and that the influence of that Wisdom must be exerted to deliver men from their slavery to visible and evil powers. If he ultimately cared only to magnify his own name, and to establish his influence over people and kings, the history is a sad and a too common one; we might be sure that his means would then become wicked, because his end was wicked; that being false at heart, he would pretend that the divine power which he had once looked for to maintain him in speaking the truth, was imparted to make his lies effectual.

Wherein the importance of this movement consists.

Under all its conditions of good and evil, this Pythagorean teaching was very strikingly indicative of the direction which men's thoughts were taking in the second century. It showed how little they could acquiesce in the mere formulas of older schools, and yet how little they could separate themselves from the ages that were past; how needful it was that they should establish a connexion with those ages, and should recover, as the most precious part of their inheritance, the truths which the earliest teachers and lawgivers had proclaimed. This necessity came forth very remarkably in a portion of the Pythagoreans, who appear to have been less busy in the affairs of the world, and more busy in their closets and their hearts. One of these, Numenius, discovered

Numenius.

that Moses had anticipated the principles which Attic philosophers had afterwards unfolded. He had an instinctive conviction that the Hebrew lore must in some way illustrate and interpret the Greek lore; and when he began to inquire in *what* way, he seems to have reached this point, that the absolute and eternal Being, the I AM of whom Moses spoke, He who Pythagoras said was only to be thought of in silence, must act upon men and the universe, though a Being like Himself, one with Himself.

<small>LECT. IX.</small>

III. The third most interesting and living form of thought at this time would be ordinarily described as the *Stoical*. If you will qualify that word by calling it the Roman-Stoical, I do not object, though I question whether there would not be a little cheating in the use of such a double adjective, like that which we practise when we talk of a knife as the same, though the blade and handle are both new. At any rate, the Stoicism which I am going to describe to you is unlike, in nearly all particulars, to the notion which we have formed, and not wrongly formed, from some of the intimations we have of it in the times from which it dates its origin. Marcus Aurelius, of whom I have already spoken to you in his imperial character, is the Roman Stoic of this period. To him we refer when we speak of the influence of this form of philosophy on the time. It is manifest from his writings that he was surrounded by many, who, though immeasurably inferior to himself, yet had both communicated impressions to him, and received an impression from him; so that we should be autho-

<small>*The Roman Stoicism.*</small>

<small>*Writings of Marcus Aurelius.*</small>

rized, even if he had not governed a world, in taking him as the representative of a state of mind of which very many were, consciously or unconsciously, partakers.

His character the opposite of that we usually attribute to the Stoics.

You ought, then, to understand that Marcus Aurelius, instead of being, what we are wont to suppose a Stoic must be, a man of a specially hard, unbending nature, was peculiarly tender and considerate of others. His failures were on this side. He had an indifferent wife, and a detestable son. His main error was over-indulgence to both, an unwillingness to believe anything wrong of them. He had a profound affection and reverence for his mother; there was not one of his friends towards whom he did not show an almost overwhelming gratitude. He was willing to learn from all quarters, from the schools which were at the furthest remove from the Stoics,

His modesty and self-suspicion.

as well as from them. He was, so far as we can judge, humble in his opinion of his own doings; certainly, self-suspicious and watchful over his thoughts as well as over his acts. The severity which entitled him to be called a Stoic was directed towards himself; he evidently felt that he knew errors in his own heart which he could not attribute to his fellow-men; and that, therefore, Roman justice obliged him to pass a sentence on himself which he could not pass on them.

His sense of an inward Judge, and of his duty to his people.

He was conscious, at the same time, that he was not competent to sit in judgment upon the transactions of his own life; he was thoroughly convinced that there was a Judge continually near him and with him, to whom his secret intents were exposed. He never for a moment fancied that he could separate himself from the people whom he governed, or make a character or secure a reward for himself whilst he was indifferent to them. He was not to call himself a philosopher, and to despise people who were not philosophers; his philosophy was to make him more conscious of his responsibility as their guardian, or it was worth nothing.

I give you the picture of Marcus Aurelius as I find it in his writings, not being conscious of any motive or inclination to exaggerate his merits, but saying of him what I think is true, and what excellent Christians have said of him before, applying the lesson to their own humiliation. If he was such as I have represented him, we should not take any pains to conceal the fact from ourselves and others, but rather lay it to heart, and ask what it means. I believe the Gospel will tell us what it means; that nothing else can; and that some of the preachers of the Gospel in this century were able both to interpret the fact, and to understand what obligations it imposed upon them; how bound they were to proclaim that which Marcus Aurelius did not believe; how it was confirmed, not refuted, by that which was right and wise in him; how little he could find any substitute for it.; how, if he persecuted it, they must die for it.

IV. I have one more class of influences to mention, which I think I ought not to pass over, because they must have been powerful, though the subject is one that I do not at all understand, and could not speak

Lect. IX.

Explanation of his life in the Gospel.

The physical philosophers of this time.

LECT. IX.
Galen.

much of without exposing my ignorance. Galen, the great physician, belongs to this age; he was intimate with Marcus Aurelius, and was honoured by him. No man, I suppose, in his own sphere better deserves the name of a philosopher; for he seems to have been an honest searcher into the mysteries of nature, as well as an earnest and reverent one. Nor did he in the least confine himself either to the labours of his own profession, or to the studies which immediately bear upon it. He felt how closely it was related to the whole life of man; how impossible it is to separate nature from that which is above nature; how much those who deal with the body of man have need to understand the entire man. Like those I have spoken of hitherto, he was not the follower of any one of the sects, which were as numerous and as strange in medicine as in morals. Neither did he attempt a formal and artificial reconciliation of their opinions, but marched boldly on in the investigation of nature, and so learnt what there was in these theories which answered to facts, and what contradicted them.

All these men ignorant of Christianity, indifferent to it, or opposed to it.

Not one of those courageous and intelligent students whom I have enumerated felt that the Gospel was speaking to them. All, with more or less decision, concluded that either it had nothing to say to the questions with which they were occupied, or that it stifled these questions, or that it gave a false answer to them. What Plutarch thought of it we guess only by his silence. Many of the Pythagoreans even in that century felt that it was an intruding rival into their province. Marcus Aurelius not only endeavoured to put it down as a statesman and religious man, but still more emphatically, and with a kind of personal indignation, because its disciples, being vulgar people, had attained by a kind of spring to that contempt of death, and that power of encountering it in its worst form, which was one of the special and hardly won privileges of the trained philosopher. Galen had seen some Christians, for whose zeal and fidelity he expressed the kind of admiration which a friendly and truthful onlooker might express; yet though he was no sceptic or heathen fanatic, but a devout man, he never seems to have fancied that the Gospel could assist him in his inquiries, or throw any fresh light on the relation of spirit to body. *Feelings of Marcus Aurelius and Galen.*

On the other hand, Justin, as we have heard, embraced Christianity expressly as the true philosophy. That was the form in which it revealed itself to him; he claimed it, and knew it by that title. I hope you have got enough glimpses into his character to have seen that the Gospel was not less dear to his inmost heart—was not embraced less by him with the spirit of a child—because he contemplated it thus. His account of the struggles through which he passed is evidence enough that he yielded to the Son of God as a weak and faint warrior, who knows that he has no strength left in himself, and has found the only Lord he ever ought to have obeyed, not as a servant who is seeking a new master, because he wants greater independence and higher wages. A more genuine conversion than his, one could not easily find or read of in any *Reference to Justin.*

time. We feel at once that it could not have been as true as it is, if he had cast his old life aside, and pretended to think all philosophy contemptible. A comparison of his writings with some who did adopt that language, will show whether he or they bowed most simply and humbly to the Scriptures, and most submitted his wisdom to theirs. Nevertheless it may fairly be questioned—I ventured to throw out the doubt, when I was alluding to his story—whether the words, "Christianity is the true philosophy," were well chosen to express Justin's inmost conviction, and whether the adoption of that formula did not greatly embarrass him in his after thoughts and practice. He certainly did not mean that Christianity was another *sect* of philosophy; he vehemently disclaimed sectarianism, as inconsistent with the idea of philosophy. Nor did he mean that the Gospel was a search after wisdom, which every philosophy is and ought to be. He looked upon it,— his Dialogue with Trypho proves decisively that he did, nay, it is the very burden of the dialogue,—as the announcement of a truth from above, which could not be arrived at by any seeking. This conviction he could not sacrifice. But neither could he sacrifice the belief that the divine Teacher had awakened those thoughts which the revelation met, and that the revelation, instead of making him less a seeker than he was before, led him continually to more earnest and more devoted investigations into the mysteries of the eternal Mind. He was, I think, puzzled to reconcile in words these

Objections to his formula.

Embarrassment which it caused him.

two testimonies of his conscience. He reconciled them, *in fact*, by his strong faith in the living and divine Word—a faith which comes out in all the brightest and noblest passages both of the Dialogue and the Apology, and which formed the radical and substantive belief in Justin's heart. Still that inconvenient phrase, of Christianity being the true philosophy, must have affected, it seems to me, injuriously, his influence on philosophers. *They* could not but regard him as a rival professor,—as a man who had a scheme to produce which was to slay their schemes. If it was this, why not assume some other name? why not declare at once that he was come with authority and commission to settle all controversies? If it was not this, why should not the philosopher's cloak denote in his case that he who bore it was willing to discuss and debate all questions on fair and even ground? Such objections I think would be raised, and Justin could not fairly dispose of them by alleging (though the allegation would have been perfectly true) that nine-tenths of the philosophers were dogmatists and not seekers. His object should have been to bring them out of that false position, to make them earnest questioners, to help all who were so. Here then one discovers, in another instance, the infirmity of good men, which led them to set up the Gospel as a substitute for, or competitor with, that which it found living and powerful, not as the interpreter and regenerator of it.

My reason for admiring Clemens Alexandrinus

LECT. IX.

Effect on the philosophers.

Inferences.

Difference in the case of Clemens Alexandrinus.

His view of history.

is, that I believe he apprehended thoroughly that truth which was in Justin's inmost soul, but which was disguised by some of his forms of speech. Never losing sight of Christ as a Person; never permitting himself for a moment to think of Him only as living and acting when He was revealed in our flesh, though attaching a supreme importance to that revelation; Clemens was able to regard all the events recorded in the history of the world as acts which had received their form and determination from Him, however they might be turned awry by the self-will and unbelief of man. He could look at the great and heroic deeds done in one age or country, or another, not as glorifying the creatures who had performed them, but Him from whom the impulse to them had proceeded, and whom they had, however ignorantly, obeyed. He could take the Bible as, what it seems to be, an exposition of God's acts towards a creature whom He has formed in His image, and whom He is reclaiming from all the sensual idolatries to which he is addicted. He could recognise in that addiction the fullest and saddest evidence of the infection of the nature of man, of his downward tendency, of the power which the outward world acquires over him, of the temptations of the evil spirit. But he could never admit that all these tendencies are so mighty as God's order and grace. He must accept the battle of the Son of God in our nature, and His victory, as the everlasting answer to that assertion of the devil, as the vindication of His own righteous dominion.

THE SECOND CENTURY. 379

Though the force of these statements, which I think are fairly deduced from the books of Clemens, was partly weakened in their effect on the historical school to which I have alluded, by the want of stronger political sympathies in him, yet the more we consider them, the more we must feel how wonderfully they correspond to the anticipations and cravings of that school; the more we must hail them as the divine answer to those affectionate, serious, though often perplexed inquiries, after a thread through the labyrinth of ages and dispensations, of nations and races, of destiny and human freedom, which we hear from Plutarch the biographer, as well as Plutarch the speculator! *LECT. IX. How it met the wants of the historical school.*

To believe again that the divine Word, instead of leaving men to wander on in their darkness and ignorance, had been continually illuminating the consciences of men respecting Himself, and inspiring them to greater efforts for the improvement of their fellows,—what a help was this to the Pythagorean, who read in the scanty traditions of past times, which he helped out with others gathered elsewhere, and with the dreams of his fancy—that there had been somewhere a great heaven-sent Reformer, and that the power which quickened him could not be dead, but might still have its appointed instruments, and produce still mightier renovations in a decayed and perishing society! What a deliverance was it from the vague, fantastical anticipations of some divine help to the sage, not granted to the crowd—from the giddiness of brain and heart that came along with *His witness to the Pythagorean. The Pythagorean's social reformation.*

the sense of having received it, and the final prostitution of gifts to selfish and unworthy ends—to hear of God's interventions in his world as not sudden and irregular, of the Word as the continual and orderly Teacher of the spirits of men! How the meaning of the solemnity and awe which Pythagoras had urged upon his disciples was interpreted, when submission of the spirit to this divine Teacher, that he might rescue it from its restlessness, and bring light out of its darkness, was declared to be the great blessing of all! What a satisfaction was it to the craving for energetic work, that the divine Word had promised to send His Spirit from the Father, that His disciples might testify of the truth which would make men free! And when those of this school listened to these lessons, who had perceived the necessity of a divine Mediator between the absolute Essence which they dared not think of, and the world which they could not contemplate without Him, what clouds might be scattered, which their own thoughts and the speculations of generations had gathered! what joy and rest to dwell, by awful meditation and humble prayer, in the Father, the Word, and the uniting Spirit! And then with what comfort, too, might such an inquirer learn the truth of those notions of Sacrifice which, as they existed in the world, he had felt part of his mission to denounce; to feel that in casting himself at the cross of Christ, and confessing the great Sacrifice, he was not practising those dark rites which had really set the creature above the Creator, but pronouncing the great sentence upon them,—acknowledging that the only acceptable sacrifice is that which is grounded on the words, "Lo, I come to do thy will, O God!"

Of course, it is impossible to say how many of either of these schools were actually brought into the fold of Christ, or brought through the means of Clemens. That the catechetical school was a mighty instrument of good—mightier because silent and often censured—I think there is clear evidence in the next age. But all these secrets are with God. What I want you to see is, that taking this form, the Gospel did not present itself as a rival philosophy to the heathen world, but as a message from God; and yet that it crushed no reed, quenched no smoking flax, but hailed and recognised whatever was earnest and beautiful in the belief and hopes of men, as having their origin and their satisfaction in the well-beloved Son.

And although I can easily conceive that if Clemens and Marcus Aurelius had met, neither might have understood the other, and they might have parted in disappointment; though it is right and safe to set such a result before oneself as probable, and according to experience, that we may not exalt human agents, or fall into silly fancies of what this or that person might have done which was not done; though if a man goes forth with any fancy that he has some special medicine for the diseases of his fellow-men, or some special way of applying it, God will ordinarily confound his vanity, and make his quackery evident to others and to himself; yet I do believe that the

Lect. IX.

Effect of this teaching not to be understood or measured by us.

The doctrine which Marcus Aurelius needed.

doctrine of the divine Word, as the Teacher and Light of men, was the one, and the only one, which could have met that deep sense in the mind of the emperor of an actual Judge and Ruler of His spirit, whom he found it almost impossible to distinguish from the dæmons of his country, or from the speculations of his own mind, or from an overruling destiny. Thanks be to God! if that is His truth, He could convey it to the heart of Marcus Aurelius through the dying prayer of some martyr, or without any instrument at all, as well as through the most learned Alexandrian doctor.

The Divine Word a guide to the natural student.

I fully believe, though this is a subject on which I must not enter, and which I trust wiser men will hereafter consider and illustrate, that Galen's studies in nature might have been stripped of many superstitious accidents, and have been pursued with fresh bravery, and humility, and hope, if he too had conceived of Christians, not as a new sect, with a heap of new and strange opinions, but as the witnesses of One by whom all things had been created, and in whom they subsisted. The illumination of the paths of physical science has surely come to men, and may come in greater brightness still, from the faith that He who awakens and guides the thoughts of His children towards the kingdom of peace and righteousness, is the same who teaches them to explain the secret order of His visible kingdom, that He may be glorified in both.

Reference to Tertullian's contempt and hatred of philosophy.

I am loth to add a word which can look like further disparagement of an eminent doctor of the Church; but as I have quoted the terms in which

Tertullian speaks of Socrates and of philosophy generally, I must now explain why these words drew from me such expressions of indignation. Their harshness and cruelty are painful; but these are only the external signs, as it seems to me, of a much more radical evil. By such language Tertullian was denying *in fact*, what he would have wished to kill any one for denying *in terms*, that Christ lived before all worlds. Nothing, he intimates clearly, could be known of Him, except what it pleased Him to declare by His Church after the incarnation. To say this, was not to insult the memory of Socrates; it was to make an outrageous assault upon St. John; it was to deny his express and most sacred words. And it was the most mischievous of all forms into which this denial could have been put; for it is one which flatters the pride and exclusiveness of Christians, while it robs their Master of His glory. It makes the testimony of the Cross to heathen philosophers of no effect; but it has had the more fatal consequence of leading the professors of the Gospel to trust in that profession, and not in the living God.[1]

[1] It may be thought by some that the miraculous powers claimed by the early Christians must have especially scandalized the philosophical sects generally, and a physical philosopher like Galen particularly. I apprehend that considerable mistake prevails about these claims. The belief that Christ had, by curing the sick and raising the dead, given proofs of His own dominion, and that the same acts performed by the Apostles proved that He was not ruling *less* after He ascended than before, was undoubtedly a fixed and rooted one in their minds. The Apologists brought it forth outwardly, in the shape of arguments and evidences. There was little question that the same powers might be used again,—no broad and formal line was drawn about the age of the Apostles, to confine them within that. But I think the reader of the

documents written in the second century will be rather struck with the rarity of any pretensions of this kind than with their abundance, and that he will find them in general connected with some displays of unrighteous power, attributed to the dæmons by the enchanters, which the Church is said to have overcome in the name of its Lord. Even the story of the Thundering Legion, in the time of Marcus Aurelius, whatever be the foundation of it, is put forth as an illustration of the effect of prayer in the name of Christ, not of some agency exercised by any man or body of men. The philosophers, who were often themselves so much mingled with the magicians,—whose physical science and practice were so much confounded by the people, and often by themselves, with magic,—could certainly at this time draw no inference against the Gospel, from any attempts which its followers made to interfere with the operations of ordinary laws.

LECTURE X.

THE CHURCH AND THE SECTS.

YOU are aware that the word "Heresies" means "Sects." The sects of the Jews, Pharisees, Sadducees, Herodians, Essenes, were the heresies of the Jews. The different Samaritan parties, which were very numerous before and after the time of our Lord, were the heresies of the Samaritans. The Christians were said by the Jews to follow the Nazarene sect or heresy.

We have seen how the Apostles were taught that they did not belong to a sect, but to a Nation, of which Christ was the King; then how they were gradually taught by the Spirit who had imparted to them that lesson, that they were the seed of a universal family, in which those whom Jews had accounted utterly unholy were included. How hard it was to realize this faith, how hard it was to keep this faith, we have proofs enough in the Apostolical history. This is the great attestation of the presence of the Spirit among them, more than all gifts of tongues, and of healing—they *were* able to keep it. They did not sink into a Nazarene sect, though they were always in danger of sinking into it. The heresies or sects which were

margin: LECT. X. *The word Heresies.*

The Spirit's teaching.

How He formed the Church and preserved it.

The Nazarenes.

on all sides of them did not overpower them. They were able to maintain their position as a family which God had called out to be a witness to the world. They were able to draw men out of their sects and heresies into this family. They were able to lay bare the foundations of a Church.

I recal your attention to these facts, which I took some pains to impress upon you in my Introductory Course, because I suspect that we do not in general connect them with those which we hear of in the second century. We fancy that the Christian sects or heresies occupied a position wholly different in reference to the Christian Church from that which the Jewish sects or heresies occupied in reference to the nation out of which they sprung. The difference we suppose to be this. The Sadducees and Pharisees were evidently men of credit and respectability; many of them rich, all of them claiming their place as children of the Covenant. They might denounce each other as bad Jews, as not holding the true tradition of the fathers. But instead of being exiles from the commonwealth of Israel, they were its most honoured guides and champions. The Christians had not power to cast them out. They had power to cast out the Christians. They were able to say, 'Theirs is the intruding heresy, we will put down the professors of it.'

On the other hand, you probably suppose that the Christian heretics must have been always numerically insignificant compared with the body which was able to describe itself as the Church; that they never can have resembled the Pharisees and Sadducees; that they were always an outlying rejected class. Much that you hear from different sides will confirm you in this opinion. Some will try to impress you with the belief that the opinions of the Church were so clear, and definite, and ascertained, that it could at once turn round to any strange teacher, produce its vouchers, denounce his doctrine, procure his expulsion from the fold. Others will represent the heretics as bold and heroical assertors of the freedom of opinion, and the right of private judgment, against a tyrannical majority, or against doctors who had established for themselves an undisputed supremacy. Either statement leads to the same inference as to the difference between the state of things in the Jewish and Christian world; neither, I believe, will bear examination.

When we read the Epistle to the Corinthians, we perceive at once that those who bound themselves to the names of Paul, of Apollos, of Cephas, were not sects lying outside the Church, but were the different parties within it, which had sway over it. The Judaizers in Galatia were the prevalent influence there. Those who are pointed out at Colosse as inculcating the opinions which were the forerunners of Gnosticism, if they are not to be identified with it, had, to all appearance, the ascendency in the Church. Yet all these are censured by St. Paul because they were bringing in divisions,—because they were establishing sects or heresies. In the Epistle to the Hebrews, the party which was dragging the Church

The sects strong in the Apostolical Churches.

towards apostasy, by exaggerating the glories of the old Covenant, and building all their hopes upon its continuance, were, one has every reason to think, superior in authority, numbers,—assuredly in conceit of their orthodoxy—to those who sympathised with the writer of the Epistle. And all the Apostles speak of a time in which there should be an influx of notions and opinions from all directions, which, if the Church had no help but in the resources of its members, or in its machinery, would certainly crush it.

The Ebionites triumphant in Judæa.

I have given you my reasons for thinking that these anticipations were fulfilled in the Apostolical age. And the first spectacle which presented itself to us when we entered upon the new century was that of the Church in Judæa struggling, feebly and ineffectually, against the Ebionitic tendencies of its members. There can be little doubt that the Ebionites, strong in the opinion that they were the true successors of St. James—that Christ had come for the express purpose of reviving the old law and faith of the Jews,—that they had now the primitive religion of the world,— were the predominant party in the Church till they were driven by the war in Hadrian's time, either to enlist in the armies of the false Christ, or to seek an alliance with the Gentile Christians, whose society they had abjured.

The Samaritan heretics powerful.

The few glimpses one can get of the condition of Samaria would certainly lead us to suppose that the Christians there, besides sharing in this Ebionitic tendency, were greatly influenced by Simon and by Menander, who, far from being insignificant men, easily crushed by the decrees of Overseers or Doctors, were probably men of wealth, as well as of talent, using the power which was most reverenced at that time—using it, besides, in a period of commotion, when such persons are most sought after; possessing both a Jewish and Gentile reputation.

Antioch had apparently a more settled polity than most of the Churches. But the character of Ignatius, as it comes forth in all our records of him, would show that it owed its order and harmony far less to his dogmatical precision, to his sagacity in discerning the limits where truth passes into error; to his acquaintance with the Magian lore; than to his apostolical simplicity, to his parental government, to his strong belief in Christ as a Person, in whom he dwelt and who dwelt in him. On that ground he could assert a unity and fellowship with all the Churches, East and West; on that ground he could hold out the most solemn warnings against those who disturbed it. But it was disturbed in Syria as elsewhere, and we have no reason to suppose that men taking so high an ascetical ground as Saturninus and his followers did—seizing so vigorously on some of the points on which Ignatius had dwelt, and giving them forth with plausible additions, appealing to a number of Jewish, and a number of Persian sympathies—may not have established a very strong party in the Church, one which could not be overcome without great conflict. I need scarcely remind

The influence of Ignatius in averting heresies, what?

Saturninus.

you that the Syrian Fathers had no material weapons in their armoury; and that they made so much use of their intellectual weapons, is a proof that the enemy was a formidable one.

Marcionites and Montanists.

How far Marcion's influence may have extended, we have no means of ascertaining; that it must have been strong in his own inhospitable region, and that it must have stretched much beyond that region, Tertullian's vehemence would seem clearly to prove. For the power of Montanism in Phrygia, and its wide diffusion, the same witness, whose feelings in this case were so different, may be safely appealed to. The letter of Clemens Romanus to the Corinthian Church, and the testimonies of Dionysius respecting Athens, would show that Greece retained its old characteristics. In Alexandria the evidence is far more decisive. There we have every reason to conclude that Basilideans, Carpocrateans, Valentinians, and the other numerous sects, held not an undisputed ascendency in the Church—for each would dispute the ascendency of the others, and there would be a continual production of new opinions and modification of the old—and there must have been many souls waiting for the kingdom of heaven who were driven by the strifes about them to seek peace elsewhere than in any opinions—but still held so much influence as to overshadow for a long time every other. It may not be safe to assume that the most earnest men in the Church would not, in a statistical table, have been set down as belonging to one of these schools; just as Simeon, and Anna, and Joseph, would

Alexandrian sects, their ascendency.

all have been described as Pharisees, and the lawyer, who answered our Lord discreetly, as a Sadducee, till a time came which set them loose from their factions, and made them understand the grounds of their union.

Alexandria affords the most striking instance, I think, of a process by which men emerged slowly into the deep and settled belief, that they had a foundation in Christ which was deeper than the foundation of opinions, and that to substitute the one for the other —to make opinions the bond of union, as the sects were doing—was to destroy the Gospel and the Church. We may not look into the long and painful struggles by which they were led to the full apprehension of this truth, and thence to the belief that their lives should be spent in the uprooting of heresies; we may only affirm confidently, that if the Scripture means anything, it was the same Spirit who first brought the Christian Church out of the Jewish sects, that guided their minds into these struggles and through them. To dream that Pantænus and Clemens were enabled, by the force of decrees, or of some formula which was recognised as authoritative in the Church, to secure the submission of the members of the numerous and powerful schools by which they were surrounded, is to trifle with history. I thank God that they did overcome those schools; because I believe that in doing so they asserted the holy and blessed name of God as a haven and a resting-place for the weary and heavy laden, for men of all kindreds, and peoples, and tribes—for men who never could rest in opinions

Lect. X.

The Church rising out of the sects and schools.

No power of putting down schools.

LECT. X.
Secret of the victory of the Church.

and notions, the dullest or the cleverest, whether they were the deposits of ages, or were struck afresh in the mint of some restless brain—but who could be at peace in themselves and with each other when they had laid down their arms and gone to the Father, who had reconciled them in His Son, who embraced them with His Spirit. But I am sure that they overcame by the blood of the Lamb, and the word of His testimony—by holding forth Christ as the true uniting Sacrifice; not by any peremptory decision, or ecclesiastical censure, or any tradition before which their opponents were forced to stoop.

Clemens spoke of an apostolical tradition; why and in what sense.

It is quite true that Clemens appealed to an Apostolical tradition as much as Irenæus did. The nature of the appeal proves how strong his opponents were, and with what arguments they were wont to fight. One traced his opinions to a disciple of Matthias; another said that all which he taught had been learnt from a scribe of St. Peter's. Clemens answered them in their own style: 'This tradition of yours only takes you back to the beginning or middle of our century. We say that the faith in Christ the living Word of God, has come to us directly from the Apostles themselves.' If he had had nothing more to say than this, the schools which had already established their position, and had a compact band of champions, would have smiled, as they probably did, at his presumption. Uniting themselves for once, they would have told him that he was maintaining a ridiculous strife, not with one of them, but with all; they would have asked him how he knew more about the tradition of the Apostles than they did. But he was able not only to talk about it, but to produce it. He trusted in the thing itself, not in the persons from whom it came. The Father, and the Word, and the Holy Spirit, were mightier, unless his whole profession was a lie, than the persons who had been the instruments of making the Name known, and who had received the commission to baptize in it. Clemens could thank God that they had received it; their tradition was unspeakably precious to him : he loved to think that they were still beholding the battle in which he was engaged, and taking part in it. He knew that they would have disclaimed him as an ally if he had set any one of them, or all of them together, in the place of Him of whom they had lived and died to testify.

I do not take the Church of Alexandria as in all respects a specimen of the Churches. Its discipline and its work were peculiar. There was in that city, for reasons which I have explained to you, a tumult of opinions, and at the same time a skill in classifying and constructing opinions, which could be found nowhere else. Alexandria was the native seat and capital of Gnosticism—at least, in all its more refined forms. But the principle which I have laid down is one which I have already illustrated by the case of Irenæus, in Gaul, who was so far removed in temper and in erudition from the Alexandrian catechist. Whatever may have been his reverence for the traditions of Polycarp—though his reverence for him as a man was one of the most affecting traits of his

LECT. X.

What the tradition was.

Irenæus a witness for the Name of God; not for a tradition about the Name.

LECT. X.

character—he was obliged, when he undertook the arduous task which he had assigned himself, to make the Gospel of St. John his standing-point; for he discovered that all the heresies which had grown to such a startling bulk, and had spread into such strange varieties, bore upon the Person of Christ; that they all began and ended with the question, whether He was really the Word of God, and whether, being such, He had been made flesh and dwelt among men. If, therefore, he would resist heresies, he must plant his foot upon this ground. Traditions about Christ might be very interesting and valuable, but Christ Himself was needed to bind men together, and take the place of the opinions which had separated them. Irenæus could confute heresies while he brought Him forth livingly and personally. Him the Syzygies and the Ogdoads knew; when a disciple of His used any other charms to scatter them, they could leap on him and overcome him.

The polity of the Church precious, because it testifies of a Person, not of notions.

You must not suppose, because, I speak thus, that I am retracting any thing which I have said before respecting the importance of the polity of the Church, its prayers and its sacraments. The principle for which I am contending is this, that Christ alone could be the centre of a polity, that He alone could bind its members in one. The heretics could make schools; they could not build men up as members of a family. Opinions were their foundations. The opinions of this man about God, or humanity, or the universe, produced the opposing opinions of that man. There was an endless whirl and interchange of notions, but no rest and no progress. For men to live together and grow together, every one contributing to the life and nourishment of the other,—each kindly action helping to the increase of knowledge, each accession of knowledge making action more free and healthful,—the diversities of gifts, and powers, and modes of thinking making themselves more manifest as the sense of fellowship and unity becomes stronger—there must be a living root, and a living sap continually proceeding from that root. The Church's polity, where all orders and offices betoken under-springs of life, and bear witness of them to the world, is precisely of this character. This was what the truest and holiest men of the Church were trying to realize. The causes that disturbed the working of this polity, which they were sure God had established, were the subjects of all their mourning. But these evils they knew could only be checked, this divine fellowship could only be sustained, by confessions and thanksgivings and litanies for the Church and for the world, by continually recurring to the pledge and sign of their uniting covenant, by continually feeding upon the Sacrifice which had been given for the life of the world—had been given that the self-exaltations and self-glorifications, the strifes and seditions which were its sin and its death, might be taken away.

Prayers and Sacraments.

It should be no matter of surprise to us, that the Church in Rome,—which had a greater experience of the contentions and heresies by which the different Churches were tormented than any other could have had, because the representatives of them all gathered

Church in Rome, its idea of putting an end to heresies.

in the capital, and which had besides by origin, education, habit, a stronger instinct about the importance of government and the necessity of obedience for the sake of work,—should have been eager to check these opinions, and should have hoped, sometimes by acts of exclusion and excommunication, sometimes by conciliation and temporising, to bring about a durable peace. It would be hard to censure these experiments in this early period merely because some of them evidently proved abortive, and some produced positive mischief. They may have been undertaken oftentimes with a good intent, even when they led to disastrous results. They showed a craving for a necessary end, if the means which were chosen to accomplish it were not wise. They at least bore witness to the truth, that opinions are not so precious *Victor's failures.* as peace, though truth may be much more precious than either. Victor of Rome apparently made a grievous mistake in his negotiations with Praxeas and the Montanists. He did not assert the truth of God's unity against the perversion of it in the Monachism of the one; he stimulated rather than checked by his *His good intentions.* vehemence the fanaticism of the other. He incited Tertullian to be its advocate and the Church's adversary. The lesson as to *this* mode of putting down heresy and establishing unity is instructive, and should be laid to heart. Yet I think there is another way of treating it which is more dangerous still.

Carthaginian tendency. To oppose sects and heresies by decrees, because they interfere with good order and efficient work, was the temptation of the Roman Church. It led to a dangerous assumption of authority in the person of its spiritual father, to a hasty suppression of men's thoughts, as if they were to be put down merely because it was convenient to put them down. The temptation of the African Church was to crush heresies by setting up a certain opinion which should be maintained as the right opinion on the ground of tradition or of prescription. According to this view of the case, the heretics were not wrong for exalting opinions into the place of Christ, but only for choosing one opinion about Him instead of another. I believe that to learn the difference between these two principles and methods is to learn the cardinal lesson of ecclesiastical history, the one which all its darkest and its brightest records are intended to impress upon our hearts. I shall only make one more remark on the subject now; it is this. It was a blessed thing for the Christian Church in the second century, that the representatives of Rome and Carthage could not understand one another, but maintained their respective theories against each other. Victor's wish to raise government and order above opinion had a true meaning at the root of it. Tertullian's protest on behalf of an opinion had a true ground in it; for it was a witness that a man cannot surrender his conviction at the pleasure of another man. The real peril was, that these two maxims should ever become united; that the ruler and the politician should become the dogmatist, now bidding men bow down before the true opinion, now before his own judgment-throne, which was to give opinions the force of laws.

Worship of opinions.

Misunderstanding of Rome and Africa a blessing.

Possibility of their union.

LECT. X.

Final lesson.

If that fearful conjunction should be seen in any subsequent part of our history, we shall be taught how impossible it is for the Church to preserve its unity, or to heal the distracted sects and heresies of the earth, unless it confesses that it has its ground in One who is not the stifler of thoughts, but the Quickener and Inspirer of them; who is not the conservator of Opinions, but who for this end was born, and for this end came into the world, that He might bear witness to the Truth; who has been, is, and ever will be, the Way, the Truth, and the Life.

Understand, then, that the distinguishing of the Church from sects and heresies, was not man's work, but God's. Because that distinction is more deep and eternal than the distinction of day and night—because the well-being of mankind is involved in the discovery of it,—therefore we may be sure that it has been brought forth and manifested by every Christian who went forth to conquer the gods, not in the strength of an opinion, but in the strength of the Cross; by every martyr who died, not for his opinion, but for his King and Brother; by every emperor who persecuted the Church, not for its opinions, but for its political Order and Unity; lastly, by those very efforts to suppress heresy, which really assumed its principle, and gave it greater virulence; because their weakness, their inconsistency, and the injury which they have done to the truth, when they are revealed by God's judgments, serve for the vindication and establishment of it.

NOTES.

Note 1.—The question respecting the marriage of Presbyters, to which I have alluded in my remarks on Tertullian, has been handled by the learned and excellent author of "Hippolytus and his Age," and will probably receive much fresh illustration in the new edition of that work, which is promised. I can hardly think that the great and important principles which are involved in that question, can depend on the evidence which Chevalier Bunsen hopes to produce in favour of the early date and authority of some of the Apostolical Constitutions. Both the sound and the mistaken views of the early Church on the primary institution of Humanity, must have been determined, I should fancy, by deeper considerations than any which could express themselves in premature and hasty efforts to legislate. Such efforts, if they were made, must surely be one of the indications that the Church was striving to be like the heathen round about, and was forgetting those truly Apostolical constitutions—so different from mere decrees—so directly grounded on eternal principles — which are contained in the Epistles of St. Paul. But if M. Bunsen should fail, as I almost hope he may, in establishing this point, we shall only feel more deeply our obligations to him for leading us to the Liturgies which expressed the true life and unity of the early Church. Amidst the numerous claims which he has upon the personal gratitude and affection of a number of Englishmen, illustrious and insignificant, this will surely always be felt by us as a claim of a still higher kind. Nationally, we should thank him for teaching us the worth of our greatest national possession ; as members of the Catholic Church, we should thank him for reminding us that there are bonds of faith and love which, even in the judgment of those who honour criticism most, are more precious than that—which, even in the judgment of those who find most fault with portions of our polity and our theology, may yet keep us in the fellowship of past ages and of other lands—of the Fathers of the Church in the second century, of our own Saxon Fathers in Germany.

Note 2.—I have not been able to read, till these Lectures were almost ready for the press, the portion of Dean Milman's new and important work on the Latin Church, which belongs to the period treated of in them. But there is one passage of such evident truth and such great value, that I must beg the reader to connect it with what I have said of the Roman Church, and to receive it as both a correction of, and a supplement to, my imperfect account of its condition in the second century.

"For some considerable (it cannot but be an undefinable) part of the first three centuries, the Church of Rome, and most, if not all, the Churches of the West, were, if we may so speak, Greek religious colonies. Their language was Greek, their organization Greek, their writers Greek, their Scriptures Greek, and many vestiges and traditions show that their ritual, their liturgy, was Greek. Through Greek the communication of the Churches of Rome and of the West was constantly kept up with the East; and through Greek every heresiarch, or his disciples, having found his way to Rome, propagated, with more or less success, his peculiar doctrines. Greek was the commercial language throughout the empire,—by which the Jews, before the destruction of their city, already so widely disseminated through the world, and altogether engaged in commerce, carried on their affairs. The Greek Old Testament was read in the synagogues of the foreign Jews. The Churches, formed sometimes on the foundation, to a certain extent on the model, of the synagogues, would adhere for some time, no doubt, to their language. The Gospels and the apostolic writings, so soon as they became part of the public worship, would be read, as the Septuagint was, in their original tongue. All the Christian extant writings which appeared in Rome and in the West, are Greek, or were originally Greek; the Epistles of Clement, the Shepherd of Hermas, the Clementine Recognitions and Homilies; the works of Justin Martyr, down to Caius and Hippolytus, the author of the Refutation of All Heresies. The Octavius of Minucius Felix, and the treatise of Novatian on the Trinity, are the earliest known works of Latin Christian literature which came from Rome. So was it, too, in Gaul: there the first Christians were settled, chiefly in the Greek cities, which owned Marseilles as their parent, and which retained the use of Greek as their vernacular tongue. Irenæus wrote in Greek; the account of the Martyrs of Lyons and Vienne is in Greek. Vestiges of the old Greek ritual long survived, not only in Rome, but also in some of the Gallic Churches. The *Kyrie eleïson* still lingers in the Latin service. The singular fact related by the historian Sozomen, that, for the first centuries, there was no public preaching in Rome, here finds its explanation. Greek was the ordinary language of the community, but, among the believers and worshippers, may have been Latins who understood not, or understood imperfectly, the Greek. The Gospels, or Sacred Writings, were explained according to the capacities of the persons present. Hippolytus, indeed, composed, probably delivered, homilies in Greek, in imitation of Origen, who, when at Rome, may have preached in Greek: and this is spoken of as something new. Pope Leo I. was the first celebrated Latin preacher, and his brief and emphatic sermons read like the first essays of a rude and untried eloquence, rather than the finished compositions which would imply a long study and cultivation of pulpit oratory. Compare them with Chrysostom.

"Africa, not Rome, gave birth to Latin Christianity."—*Milman's History of Latin Christianity*, vol. i. book i. c. i. p. 27.

THE END.

www.ingramcontent.com/pod-product-compliance
Lightning Source LLC
Chambersburg PA
CBHW070008010526
44117CB00011B/1460